MaliBhagavatam

Divine Story of SriKrishna for Children

About The Cover Design

The cover design of this book is symbolic like its contents. Just like the Srimad Bhagavatam holds deep spiritual and philosophical meanings within its words and stories, so too does the image on the cover of this book.

The overarching colour is blue, pointing to the presence of Sri Krishna in every aspect of our life and work. Sri Krishna is portrayed as a shadow-silhouette since it's impossible to visualise the grandeur, beauty and expanse of the Supreme Truth. To reduce Him to a mere human with defined facial features would, to me, be like trying to compress the ocean into a teacup. His various facets are spread and permeated across the universe and therefore it is best for every devotee to imagine Him in his or her unique way.

The person who is reading out the story actually represents my beloved father, V. Madhavan Nair "Mali", the author of MaliBhagavatam, who used to read out his stories to me and my dear sisters Malini and Madhavi when we were children. We would sit, entranced, at his feet!

Sri Krishna's presence and stories are so very attractive that Nature herself stops in her tracks and trains her attention on His mischief and His magic! Cows, birds, trees … every part of the environment is not only enchanted but also blessed by His stories. His flute and Presence graces everything and everybody!

As you can see, my imagination has run riot!

Reuben Antony, a gifted graphic artist, has harnessed technology including AI, to bring my imagination to life on the cover. He has mined images from the deep recesses of my mind and presented them with consummate artistic skill for all to enjoy.

MaliBhagavatam

Divine Story Of Krishna For Children

V Madhavan Nair "Mali"

Translated from the original in Malayalam by V.K.Madhav Mohan

Malibhagavatam is authored in Malayalam by the legendary V Madhavan Nair "Mali" whose books have enriched generations of Malayalam readers. This book is translated into English by his son V.K.Madhav Mohan. The English translation is entitled "Mali's MaliBhagavatam - Krishna Speaks To Children"

V.K.Madhav Mohan

Vanamali 39/23 Near Krishna Hospital

Kochi 682011, India

madhavmohan55@me.com

Contents

त्वमेव माता च पिता त्वमेव।

त्वमेव बन्धुश्च सखा त्वमेव।

त्वमेव विद्या द्रविणं त्वमेव।

त्वमेव सर्वं मम देव देव॥

Tvameva Mata Cha Pita Tvameva
Tvameva Bandhushcha Sakha Tvameva
Tvameva Vidya Dravinam Tvameva
Tvameva Sarvam Mama Deva Deva

You alone are my Mother and Father,
You alone are my Relative and Friend,
You alone are my Knowledge and Wealth,
You alone are my Everything,
O Lord of Lords.

This prayer is from Pandava Gita and is believed to have been made in total surrender to Lord Krishna by Queen Gandhari

Forgive Me:

क्षमस्व मे

This English translation of my revered father's divine Malayalam Malibhagavatam is my humble tribute to him.

Malibhagavatam has been printed in many, many editions since it was first published more than 50 years ago.

By telling stories of Krishna in the simplest of ways, Mali has not only sparked interest in reading in myriads of children but also lighted the lamp of Krishna Bhakti in their innocent hearts.

May Achan and Krishna in His Infinite Mercy forgive me for the many mistakes that I have made in this work and in my life.

मन्त्रहीनं क्रियाहीनं भक्तिहीनं सुरेश्वर ।

यत् पूजितं मया देव परिपूर्णं तदस्तु मे ॥

अपराधसहस्त्राणि क्रियन्ते हरनिशं मया ।

दासोऽयमिति मां मत्वा क्षमस्व पुरुषोत्तम ॥

Mantraheenam Kriyahinam Bhaktihinam Sureshwara |

Yat Pujitam Maya Deva Paripurnam Tadastu Me ||
Aparadhasahasrani Kriyante Haranisham Maya | Daso'yamiti Mam
Matva Kshamasva Purushottama ||

O Lord of Lords, my worship may have been incomplete, with errors in mantras, rituals, or devotion. Please accept it as complete and perfect.

I commit thousands of offenses day and night. O Purushottama

(Supreme Lord), considering me as Your servant, please forgive me.

This prayer is from the Kṣamāprārthanā Stotram (Prayer for Forgiveness), traditionally recited at the conclusion of rituals like the Durgā Saptashatī Pāṭha (Chandi Path)

About This Book

Countless Malayalees have grown up reading MaliBhagavatam. With simple but powerful storytelling Mali has enabled generations to enjoy, understand and learn from the action filled life of SriKrishna on earth. His language and writing style blazed an endearing trail of writing for children. The vivid imagery he conjured up in his fast-paced stories sparked not just interest and enthusiasm but also Krishna Bhakti in their hearts.

Mali was always aware that his readers included adults too on a large scale. He would often say that stories have a universal appeal. And so, it was no wonder that parents enjoyed his books as much as the children for whom the books were purchased. When they grew up, those children fanned out all over the globe in pursuit of happiness and success. Today, they have children and grandchildren of their own. Though they live far away from their roots, they harbour a deep desire to reconnect with their childhood, their spiritual heritage and ...with Srikrishna. More importantly, they are anxious that their children and grandchildren too grow up on the foundations of their identity and roots.

This book is for all of them.

It is an attempt to bring Mali into the home and hearts of all those who want to belong to the glorious heritage of the motherland. Language is no barrier! Those who have not been able to read the original MaliBhagavatam in Malayalam can now savour Mali's writing in English and in so doing can experience Krishna's blessings in their own lives.

In translating this work, I have assiduously steered clear of making my own interpretations. Word for word I have tried to render Mali's clear and simple writing into English while adhering to his style scrupulously. All mistakes are mine and mine only. All positive impacts are only due to Mali's greatness and Krishna's grace.

What I have done differently is to provide detailed footnotes explaining all the concepts and practices that are mentioned in MaliBhagavatam. In that respect, this book doubles as an introduction to Hinduism.

Hare Krishna!

May SriKrishna bless all beings!

V.K.Madhav Mohan

Who Is This Book For?

Vast numbers of Indians (including me) have grown up without a base in our own mother tongue. English is the language not only of communication but also of thought. So, in many ways, we've been robbed of the grandeur of Indian language, culture, history and heritage. In that respect we are disadvantaged!

This book helps alleviate some of that disadvantage. Parents who have no felicity in their mother tongue can now read out the story of Krishna in English to their children. The footnotes give them an ability to answer the inevitable questions with some degree of comfort!

So, this book is meant for everyone but especially those Indians who are living not just in India but around the world. The Indian diaspora will find it particularly useful in building an Indian identity within their children and connecting them back to their roots. It is my fond hope that this book will generate a renewed interest in learning Indian languages and Sanskrit.

My Journey: Writing This Book

One morning in early January 2025 I was listening to and chanting Vishnusahasranamam, as usual. Suddenly, I received an internal message!

"Translate Achan's MaliBhagavatam", said the message injected deep into my consciousness. That's it! That's my purpose in the immediate future! No ifs, no buts! It was all clear as day. There was no doubt at all!

Here I was, without any formal study or background in Malayalam embarking on this, the most ambitious endeavour of my life. Translating Achan's MaliBhagavatam! I had not dreamt even in my wildest dreams that I would, rather, I could, even visualise such a possibility. Of course, Achan and Amma had imbibed in me a deep love and devotion to Krishna and his exploits. But nothing had prepared me for such a huge leap of faith. And leap of faith it certainly was!

I was simply not equipped for such a big venture.

My Malayalam is rudimentary to say the least. Throughout my life I've been the butt of condescending comments like "how come Mali's son doesn't know Malayalam". My self-confidence was not ever dented by those humouring me only because of the shield protecting me. That shield i s Achan's love and encouragement flowing from his words: "I've been part of the Malayalam world. That doesn't mean you must make it your world too. Go out and give time and space for your talents. Be a citizen of the world while at the same time being grounded in your heritage". Though he was steeped in Malayalam literature and everything Indian he was also such an extraordinarily eclectic genius. Sensitive like no other, he understood my aspirations and stood like a rock, unquestioningly, behind everything I did. While I'm sure he worried, his support, understanding and acceptance were the fuel that powered me in my life and career. My journey has been on a very different trajectory from his. But it has been rooted in the values and character that he built within me. In his eyes I could do no wrong. And that is the ultimate shield that has protected me throughout my life. Gentle but sure, tender but clear, respectful of tradition but ever creative, he is the ultimate role model. He is my guiding light, my Guru, now and forever.

He had told me, "Write, that is your path". Now, at this final stage of my life I'm finally following the path he indicated to me. I guess all that went before in my life has been preparation for this phase.

So, when I received the message, there was no doubt or question in my mind.

I did not know if I was capable. I did not know if I could. But a few hours after I received the message, I just took up MaliBhagavatam and began the ultimate journey of my life! I had jumped in. I had plunged into the deep waters of Srimad Bhagavatam and Malayalam. I had to get to the other shore! There was no other way. There was no turning back! And so, it began.

At first, I was thrashing about in panic. Then, a calm descended on me. Narasimha Stotram came into my consciousness. I began chanting it incessantly. That gave me a strength like I have never experienced before. I could see Achan's sweet smile of encouragement constantly. Amma's blessings enveloped me. In front of me, the photo of Saibaba of Shirdi kept a steady stream of blessings coming my way. But more than anything else, I could feel Krishna's presence flowing through a kind of love I have never experienced before. Every second, every breath was inspired by that love.

I settled into a rhythm and discipline that I did not know I was capable of. I was at my computer at 0630 hrs and just read, understood, referred, wrote, edited, proof checked and repeated the cycle endlessly. I was away from MaliBhagavatam and my MacBook Pro only for the duration of workouts, showers and food. This became my safe place, my life and my work. This was my Tapas.

Pages turned, slowly at first. There was never any frustration or uncertainty or stress. It was pure joy to read Achan's simple, evocative and charming prose. Sometimes the prose bordered on delightful poetry. He had created the enchanting, divine world of Gokula, Vrindavan and Vaikuntha and I'd been welcomed into that world. This was my safe space. There is no question of leaving it ever. Krishna is addictive!

Soon the pace picked up. I became more comfortable with the language and the process. Pages sped past. Day after day, minute after minute, relentless, consistent and joyful, propelled by love. That's how I lived and wrote for 67 days. Finally, Krishna was preparing to leave the world. Kali Yuga was beginning. And I had reached the other shore!

This book is not my effort.

Achan's and Amma's blessing fueled it.

But it is entirely the result of Krishna's grace and His love.

I had made the leap of faith, and Krishna had held me lovingly and deposited me on the far shore.

A2I: Srimad Bhagavatam And AI

Srimad Bhagavatam is nectar. MaliBhagavatam is its sweetest version! Vedavysa wrote it and Suka Maharshi narrated it to Parikshit. But when? No one knows clearly but 5000 years ago is a good guess.

When I began the translation of MaliBhagavatam my knowledge of Malayalam, Sanskrit and indeed the heritage was limited. Krishna showed me the way. The way was to plug into 5,000 years of human evolution. It was a natural symbiosis of Artificial Intelligence and Ancient Intelligence!

Malibhagavatam seamlessly integrated with ChatGPT 4o in my journey. I was able to understand unfamiliar words and usages in Malayalam. Adding a large dose of common sense, I was able to find a way through! While translating Achan's writing I was able to mine the vast storehouses of Ancient Intelligence instantly at the touch of a key. That is how I have been able to provide the backstory and context of various concepts, characters, locations and rituals. These have all been listed as footnotes. All the footnotes have been created using ChatGPT 4o.

Ancient Intelligence (AI) has converged with Artificial Intelligence (AI) in this book to spark Krishna Bhakti in the heart of the reader. The story is addictive. The footnotes and backstory provide not just a panoramic view of the grand Indian heritage but also build a foundational knowledge of its nuts and bolts.

The combination of Ancient Intelligence and Artificial Intelligence is a winning formula for the emergence of a New India that builds on its legacy and takes it forward. I call the combination A2I -Ancient+Artificial Intelligence.

Dearest Children,

You've read MaliRamayanam, haven't you? And MaliBharatam after that?

Now, here is MaliBhagavatam for you!

Dont you remember the story of Parikshit from MaliBharatam?

Suka Maharshi narrated the Bhagavatam to Parkshit.

And how did Suka Maharshi learn the Bhagavatam? From his father, Vyasa Maharshi.

Bhagavatam has so many, many stories! But not just stories do it contain.

Shastras, mantras, Divine Truths, prayers, descriptions and explanations, so many aspects are all parts of the Bhagavatam.

When you grow up you must try to understand all of them.

But for now, stories are sufficient! You know what I've done?

I've written the stories in a shortened form, in a certain order and structure.

This order and structure may differ slightly from the original Bhagavatam.

But I've only done that for you to understand it all easily!

Do you know how grand is the grace and power of the Bhagavatam? There are stories about that too.

We must read those stories first.

Come, let's begin!

Power, Grace, And Glory of Bhagavatam

Suka Maharshi began preparing to narrate the Bhagavatam Story. That's when some Devas arrived. They had urns full of Amrutam.

"Maharshi, please after accept our offering of Amrutam and reveal the Bhagavatam to us. Let Parikshit defeat Death after listening to Bhagavatam. And along with that, let us also enjoy it and be blessed. We can both benefit from this exchange."

The Devas were full of hope.

Amrutam had the power to keep Death at bay.

But the Bhagavatam has even greater power, grace and glory than Amrutam.

Does a mere black rock have the same value as a precious stone? That's the huge difference between Bhagavatam and Amrutam.

Suka Maharshi rejected outright the request of the Devas. Shouldn't we understand the greatness of Bhagavatam?

Brahma set up his weighing scale.

On one tray he loaded the entire Shastras. And on the other he placed Bhagavatam.

The tray with Bhagavatam sat lower, much lower.

Once the Sanaka Maharshis conveyed important insights to Sage Narada.

By reading and listening to Bhagavatam any life-form can attain Moksha (Liberation from birth and death). And, as long as they don't listen to Bhagavatam they'll never receive Moksha.

Any home or house in which Bhagavatam is read or listened to becomes holy and transforms into a place of pilgrimage.

Gaya, Prayag or Kashi are not equivalent to Bhagavatam.

Yogic sacrifices (Yagas or Yagnyas) don't have even one sixteenth the power of Bhagavatam, such is its greatness.

Bhagavatam is another form of Bhagavan, the Supreme Lord!

Great people experience happiness and peace when they help others. But Vyasa Maharshi had an opposite experience!

He categorised the Vedas into four. Wrote and explained many Puranas. And on top of all that, wrote the magnificent Mahabharata. All for the welfare of the entire world.

And yet, he was not happy. Serenity and peace eluded him. He felt restless and uneasy.

What's the reason for this?

The Maharshi thought and meditated deeply on this question. No answer emerged.

He was drowning in distress and desolation. That's when Narada Maharshi arrived.

"You have known everything there is to know. So, why are you distraught?"

"That is true, O Maharshi. All knowledge I have mastered. And yet my soul has not found peace and contentment. I beseech thee, please tell me the reason for this unease."

Clearly, Vyasa Maharshi was desperate. "I will certainly tell you. Please listen. You have done so many wonderful things. Even written and transcribed the Vedas and so much else. And yet, you have not done the one thing you should do. Write the story of Lord

Sree MahaVishnu! That is what will fill your Atma[1] with the ultimate bliss. The power and glory of Sree MahaVishnu is so great and limitless. I have myself directlyexperienced this bliss, the grace of Lord MahaVishnu."

Maharshi Narada spoke with conviction and the deepest compassion. And then he proceeded to share and explain his personal experiences. Maharshi Narada had a previous birth.

He was not a Maharshi but the son of a 'dasi'[2], a female attendant. His childhood was spent in taking care of Yogis[3].

The Yogis would praise of Lord MahaVishnu and His attributes incessantly.

And the child would listen intently.

Vishnu Bhakti bloomed and took deep root in his heart.

The Yogis had great affection for him.

Before they left, they would present him with Gyanopadesam[4], spiritual knowledge.

---

[1] Atman, the immortal, indestructible soul, as described in all the Upanishads and Shastras

[2] Dasi refers to a woman in servitude, derived from the Sanskrit root Dasa, servant or slave.

[3] From the Sanskrit root Yuj, to unite or join, symbolising the union of the individual Self, Atman, with the Universal, Brahman. Yogis embrace not just physical perfection but a total dedication to self-discipline (Tapas), spiritual practice (Sadhana), Meditation (Dhyana), Detachment (Vairagya) all of which lead to the final destination of Liberation (Moksha).

[4] Transmission of spiritual knowledge by a Guru to a disciple. Compound word in Sanskrit, made up of Gyana (knowledge, wisdom or spiritual insight) and Upadesam (instruction, teaching or advice). Gyanopadesam refers to the imparting of knowledge or wisdom aimed at guiding the disciple towards understanding deeper truths, especially within the context of the Srimad Bhagavatam, Bhagavd Gita, Upanishads and Vedanta.

The child's knowledge expanded. Along with it, Vishnubhakti deepened too. Suddenly, one day a tragedy overtook the boy. His mother, the Dasi, stepped out to milk the cow. She was bitten by a serpent and passed away. The boy's circumstances changed completely.

No one to love him or raise him with care. Lord MahaVishnu was his only refuge.

He left home and trudged North.

Travelled for a very long distance and arrived in a forest. He sat in meditation and forgot his pain. Ceased to be aware of everything else.

MahaVishnu appeared but disappeared in the blink of an eye. The boy's heart was wracked in sorrow.

"Just caught a glimpse of Bhagavan. Didn't get enough, want to see Him more, much, much more. Every day, every moment, constantly."

An overwhelming, uncontrolled, deep driving desire to see the Vision. And then the voice of the Lord Himself was heard. "Little boy, because of your devotion I have revealed Myself to you and given you this Darshan[5]. But in this life, you will not be able to see Me again. However, in the next life, you will. You will become the foremost of my devotees. The Bhakti you hold for Me is indestructible."

---

[5]from the Sanskrit root "Drsh", to see. Auspicious sight or vision of a deity, saint or sacred object. Also holds reference to the 6 schools of Indian philosophy, Shad Darshana's, namely: Nyaya (logic and epistemology), Vaishesika (atomism and metaphysics), Samkhya (enumeration and dualism), Yoga (discipline and self-realisation, Purva Mimamsa (rituals and dharma) and Vedanta (end of all knowledge and metaphysics)

Thereafter the boy spent his life in devotion. When that life ended, he was reborn.

He took life again. And that too, as the son of Brahma Narada!

"So, Vyasa Maharshi, don't despair. I'mtravelling far and wide, playing the Veena[6] Harikeerthana. I can go to all the Three Worlds, as and when I feel like. Andsinging whenever I need, Bhagavan graces me with His Darshan."

With that little story about his personal experiences, Maharshi Narada took leave and went on his way.

Didn't I say earlier that you'll attain Moksha by listening to Bhagavatam? There are some stories about that too.

The main character in one of them is none other than Maharshi Narada! The miseries of "Kali Yuga"[7] are visible all over the Earth.

Narada is travelling constantly, carrying a heart full of pain.

---

[6] Veena is a stringed musical instrument with 2 sound boxes (called Tumba or Kudam) with which it produces a deep melodious sound. It is revered because of its association with Goddess Saraswati (Goddess of Wisdom, Learning and Arts). There are 4 types of Veenas: Rudra Veena (long necked, fretted and used in Hindustani Music), Saraswati Veena (large, resonant body with a rich tonal quality, used in Carnatic Music), Vichitra Veena (fretless and producing a gliding, resonant sound) and Chitra Veena (a modernised, fretless version played with a slide, popularised by the genius Chitra Veena Raivkiran)

[7] Kali Yuga (duration: 432,000 years) is the fourth and final Yuga (Cycle of Time) described in ancient Indian scriptures. It is marked by moral decline, materialism, conflict & corruption and spiritual darkness. The other 3 Yugas preceding Kali Yuga are : Satya Yuga, The Age of Truth or Golden Age (duration: 1,728,000 years), Treta Yuga, The Age of Three-Quarters or Silver Age (duration: 1,296,000 years where Dharma stands on 3 legs, a decline in righteousness and virtue, the Age of Advent of Lord Rama), Dvapara Yuga, The Age of Duality or Bronze Age (duration: 864,000 years during which Dharma stands on 2 legs signifying a further deterioration, the Age of Advent of Lord Krishna. These 4 Yugas form a repetitive cycle called Chaturyuga or Mahayuga; the cycle totals 4.32 million years.

Arriving on the banks of the river Kalindi he saw a disturbing sight. Sitting on the ground was a beautiful young woman.

On either side of her were two old men, both lying unconscious.

The young woman is crying in deep sorrow. Several female companions are attending to her. Narada approaches them.

The grief-stricken woman beseeches the sage, pitifully.

"Maharshi, please tarry a while here. Please help me overcome this anguish."

Who are you? And who are these old men and these women?

"What is the reason for this distress?" The Maharshi asked out of concern.

"My name is Bhakti[8]. And these old men are my sons, Gyana[9] and Vairagya[10]. These women are Ganga and other holy rivers. I was born in Dravida. Grew up in Karnataka. Nourished in Maharashtra and other places. While in Gurjara, I suffered many injuries at the hands of people who had no Bhakti at all. Eventually, I reached Vrindavan. That's when I regained my youth. My sons had already become old by then. Why is it like this?"

Narada tapped into his divine insight. That's when he understood the true state of affairs.

"Bhakti,this is the time of Kali. Adharma[11] is holding sway now, everywhere. No human beings are paying any attention, they're not even looking twice at you. Your sons have some faults in them.

---

[8] Devotion

[9] Knowledge

[10] Detachment

[11] Non righteousness, injustice and moral disorder; opposite of Dharma. Adharma represents the forces of darkness, selfishness, ignorance, corruption and leads to downfall of individuals and societies.

That's why they've grown old. Now aren't you in the holy land of Vrindavan? That's why you have regained your youth and your sons have attained some peace, temporarily. And so, they're sleeping now."

"Maharshi, please awaken them," Bhakti entreated the sage.

Narada caressed the old men. Then he pressed his lips against their ears and called their names loudly. Following that he revealed the Vedas. Read the Gita. The old men started to awaken. They let out yawns and tried to standup but couldn't. They didn't open their eyes and were about to fall asleep again.

Narada's efforts bore fruit only partially.

"Why?" He thought deeply but he couldn't arrive at an answer.

With intense hurt in his heart, he called out to Bhagavan. A disembodied, divine voice began to be heard. "Narada, to dispel the sleep and old age of these people a good deed has to be performed. The most evolved Maharshis will tell you what it is."

What is this good deed?

Who are these most evolved Maharshis? There's no sign of them!

Narada was deeply troubled. He left the place.

He met many Maharshis and asked them. Some said they didn't know.

And others were sure that the answers could never be found.

Many were surprised. Narada is after all, the foremost of the Yogis. There seems to be something even he doesn't know!

I must know that which I don't know by performing Tapas[12]. To do just that he came to Badaryashram[13].

Soon the Sanaka Munis[14] also arrived.

"O Mahatmas, Your arrival is my great good fortune. What is the good deed indicated by the celestial voice? How is it to be performed? How can Bhakti, Gyana and Vairagya be helped? Please shower your mercy on me and tell me." Narada's plea was answered by the Sanaka Munis.

"Reading Bhagavatam is the good deed. If you do this Gyana and Vairagya will get rejuvenated. Along with their mother Bhakti, they will then rejoice and be present in every home."

Then, along with Narada, the Sanaka Munis went to Haridwar.

---

[12] Tapas, austerities, meditation and prayer

[13] Sacred hermitage in Badrinath, Himalayas. on the banks of the river Alaknanda. Where Lord Vishnu in his form as Badarinarayan, is believed to have meditated. Goddess Lakshmi is believed to have taken the form of a Badari tree (jujube tree) to provide shade for Him. Badarsyashram holds great spiritual significance and power. Adi Shankaracharya established the Badrinath Math (monastery) here as one of the 4 (Chaturdham) monastic centres.The 4 Chaturdham monastic centres are: 1. Badrinath (North): Jyotirmath 2. Dwarka (West): Sharada Math 3. Puri (East): Govardhan Math and 4. Sringeri (South): Sringeri Sharada Peetham. This is not to be confused with Char Dham, the 4 shrines popularised by Adi Shankaracharya to attain Moksha. These shrines are Badrinath (Vishnu), Kedarnath (Siva), Gangotri (Origin of river Ganga) and Yamunotri (Origin of river Yamuna).

[14] Sanaka Munis also known as Kumaras. The 4 Sanaka Munis are: Sanaka, Sanatana, Sanandana and

Sanatkumara. They are believed to be created out of the mind (Manas) of Brahma and not physically; hence they are considered Manasaputras. They are believed to be the greatest, purest, most evolved and eternally youthful Sages. Representing the purest thought, devotion, detachment and innocence, they are the ultimate source of spiritual wisdom for Maharshis, devotees and even Gods and Goddesses.

There, they commenced reading Bhagavatam in front of a massive audience.

Suddenly, into the venue strode three people: a beautiful young woman and her two young sons. They certainly were Bhakti, Gyana and Vairagya! All their troubles had vanished just because of their desire to listen to Bhagavatam!

"From now where should I live?" Bhakti wanted to know from the Maharshis.

"In the hearts of people who have devotion to Vishnu[15]," answered the Maharshis.

And what happened after Bhagavatam reading was completed? Bhakti and her children became so well nourished! Even if a devotee is poor, he is fortunate.

Bhakti resides in his heart, so he's blessed because Bhagavan has a special affection for Bhakti.

Whenever Bhakti calls, He comes running from Vaikunta and begins to live within the devotee!

Even ghosts and demons have attained salvation after listening to Bhagavatam!

Once there lived a Brahmin named Atmadevan.

Though he was learned and lived according to the rules of Dharma, his mind was not at all at peace because he had no son.

Atmadevan's wife was named Dhunadhuli. She simply wouldn't listen to anyone. Would talk needlessly, and be ready to fight with anyone! Strange woman!

---

[15] Vishnubhakti, devotion to Vishnu

Atmadevan performed pious deeds, donated alms and undertook various religious penances.

Still, he had no children. He became so dejected that he was tired of life. He left home and went into the forest.

Afternoon came and he felt very thirsty. He found a lake, drank from it, quenched his thirst and sat upon the banks. A Sanyasi[16] appeared.

"You seem to be so very dejected. Why are you so sad? Please tell me."

"I don't have any children. That is like death. The cow that I have cannot have calves. The tree that I plant doesn't flower. Flowers and fruits dry up when they reach my home. That's how unfortunate I am."

Atmadevan burst out crying.

Using his spiritual prowess the Sanyasi fathomed the reasons for Atmadevan's plight.

"You are experiencing the effects of your past Karmas[17]. You're not going to have children, not just in this life but for seven lives. That is your destiny. So, crying is pointless".

The Sanyasi's words were of no solace.

---

[16] An ascetic who has renounced his family, wealth and worldly life to focus on self-realisation to attain liberation (Moksha)

[17] Action or deed in Sanskrit. The Principle of Karma is that every action (including thoughts & emotions, not just physical action) produces a corresponding result (fruit) either in the present life or in a future life

"Please don't say that. You have Yogic powers[18]. Please I beg you, use them to grant me a child. Otherwise, I'll end my life this very moment." Atmadevan had made up his mind.

The compassionate Sanyasi then gave Atmadevan a mango. "Please give this mango to your wife and a child will be born," he said. Atmadevan went back home.

However, Dhunadhuli's thoughts were quite different! "Won't pregnancy cause me great inconvenience? I'll have to live a subdued life. Won't be able to eat whatever I want, whenever I want. Bringing up a child is so full of effort! No, I don't want a child at all!"

She did not eat the mango. But told Atmadevan that she had eaten it and he believed her. Dhunadhuli's sister came to stay with her and help in housework. "Dhunadhuli, I'll have a baby soon. But I'll give that baby to you and lie to everyone that my baby has died. Don't worry, I'll live in your home to raise the child. You just need to pretend to be pregnant."

What a plan!

Dhunadhuli was relieved and happy. But she was very curious. Will eating the mango create a baby? Will the cow have a calf if she eats the mango? She fed the mango to the cow.

Let's see what happens!

Atmadevan returned home after months of travel. He saw a little baby boy!

----

[18] Referred to as Sidhis, extraordinary powers attained through deep spiritual practices including meditation, Pranayama (breath control) and mastery over mind and body. These powers are described in Patanjali's Yoga Sutras and other scriptures.

Dhunadhuli said, "I had a baby," and he believed her, blindly. What a big sin indeed!

The boy was named Dhunadhukari.

And what about the cow which ate the mango?

She too gave birth but not to a calf. A human baby! A beautiful, divinely radiant boy!

With just one defect! His ears were like those of a cow

So, he was named Gokarna[19].

The boys grew up together in Atmadevan's household. And yet how different they were from each other!

Dhunadhukari was cruel while Gokarna was just the opposite; kind and full of wisdom.

Dhunadhukari ate with his left hand, used to thrash wandering ascetics and push children into the well; he stole and set fires. Gambling and extravagance were part of his character. And finally, what else did he do?

Beat up his own parents, Atmadevan and Dhunadhuli and rendered them helpless. Then, he took all their money and went away.

Atmadevan was beside himself with grief. "Isn't it better to die," he thought.

That's when the wise Gokarna gave his father some sage counsel. "Please go to the forest and perform Tapas. Only then will you find peace."

---

[19] Literally," Cow's Ear" in Sanskrit

Atmadevan left home, went to the forest and through sincere Tapas, attained Moksha.

Dhunadhukari lived as a rogue. He used to shout at his mother and hit her too. Dhunadhuli couldn't take it anymore. She jumped into the well and ended her life.

Meanwhile, Gokarna set out on a pilgrimage.

Dhunadhukari had five wives. Every one of them had evil intentions! They wanted the costliest silk clothes and gold ornaments. And together, they nagged Dhunadhukari constantly.

But how would he have any money left to buy all this? Hadn't he spent it all without a care?

The wives wouldn't stop nagging him. He was forced to give them whatever they wanted.

Where did he find the money? By robbing others, of course! The wives understood. They knew about his robberies.

And they started to worry, not about the wrongdoing. They talked amongst themselves.

"Surely, someone would lodge a complaint against Dhunadhukari. The King's soldiers would surely investigate and certainly detect Dhunadhukari's crimes. He would be sent to the dungeons or worse, be sent to the gallows."

"But why should we care about what happens to him? We only want all the stolen property to remain with us. Let's keep all the ornaments and money for ourselves. It's better to kill and bury him as soon as we can. So that he can't be found. We can always tell everyone that he has gone away from home. We'll be safe then and so will all the money and ornaments."

The greedy wives made a wicked plan. That night the dreadful incident unfolded.

Dhunadhukari was fast asleep, snoring loudly. The women crept stealthily into his room.

They carefully tied a strong rope around his neck. And all of them, together, pulled on it with all their strength. The rope tightened and suffocated Dhunadhukari.

His eyes became bloodshot, his arms and legs started flailing and he began sweating profusely in the throes of a final struggle. And then, mercilessly, they covered his face with burning coals. Only then did he die.

Quickly, without remorse, they buried the dead body, without anyone noticing.

Many days passed. Dhunadhukari wasn't seen anywhere at all.

"Where is he?" Neighbours started asking about him.

"He's travelling to a very distant place," the wives answered. They shared the ornaments amongst themselves and left the house. Each went her own way.

Since he died unnaturally and suddenly and his last rites weren't done, Dhunadhukari transformed into a ghostly spirit, trapped between realms.

He became a whirlwind and spun round and around. Suffering unbearable thirst and hunger with no way to drink or eat. And no one to help!

In the depths of limitless misery, the ghost cried out in desperation often. "Oh God, how strongly has this distress caught hold of me."

Gokarna was in the middle of his pilgrimage. Somehow, he got to know about Dhunadhukari's death.

There wasn't anyone to perform his last rights. And what happens if last rights are not performed?

The dead person's Atma is completely lost with no destination at all. In a way isn't Gokarna the dead Dhunadhukari's brother?

So, Gokarna went to Gaya and performed Shraadham[20] and then returned home. The house was empty, night fell, he was sleepy. Gokarna lay down. It was midnight.

There, a terrible being!

It became an elephant, then a goat, an ox, a human being. Changing forms and prancing about.

Anyone else would have been terrified but not Gokarna. Since he was a Maha Yogi, there was no question of fear. He realised that this was a Pretatma, a spirit without a resting place, neither here nor there, not on earth or anywhere else.

He asked, "Who are you? Pisacha[21], Preta[22] or Rakshasa[23]? Why have you come? And that too, at this time, the dead of night?"

---

[20] Sharaadham is a ritual performed to honour and offer gratitude to ancestors (Pitrs) for creating and nourishing

the family lineage; it is believed to enable Pitrs attain Moksha (Liberation) and thereby remain at peace so that they can bless descendants with peace and prosperity. The term Shraadham derives from the Sanskrit root Shraddha, faith, devotion and sincerity

[21] Malevolent, grotesque terrifying beings from the Sanskrit root "Pis", to devour and "aacha"," one who eats or devours", Pisacha beings that devour impure substances including human flesh and are part of the dark and malevolent aspects of existence

[22] Restless, wandering spirits in a state of suffering because last rites were not done properly; from the Sanskrit roots "pra" (forth, forward) and "ita" (gone) ...Preta means "gone forward", departed from the mortal world.

[23] Powerful, supernatural, murderous demons mostly evil, but some can be noble too. Rakshasas are believed to be descendants of Pulastya, one of the Seven Sages (Sapta Rishis) from the Sanskrit root "Raks", to guard or protect...and "Sa", related to or pertaining to. Given their wicked reputation, this may seem contradictory but the term originated from beings fiercely guarding or protecting

The being burst into tears! Unable to pronounce words, too weak even to speak.

Gokarna said a prayer and sprinkled holy water around him. The prayer bore fruit instantly.

The being obtained the power of speech!

"Gokarna, I'm none other than your brother, Dhunadhukari. I've committed countless sins. My wives connived and killed me. That's how I became a Preta. Now, you're my only hope. Please help and save me!"

"Performing Shraadham at Gaya is the way to make Pretas attain Mukti [24] (freedom) and I've already done that." Gokarna was reassuring.

"It's no use even if you do 100 Shraadhams at Gaya, I won't obtain Mukti. Because I've done so many horrible things and accumulated such a huge amount of sin. I'm the worst sinner. You have to find some other way," the Preta begged Gokarna.

"What! You haven't attained Mukti even after Gaya Shraaddham was performed? Astonishing indeed! Then let me think of some other way," said Gokarna. By morning word had spread, Gokarna has returned! Many scholars began arriving to meet him.

---

sacred places. Over a period of time, they began to be seen negatively, as opposing divine forces.

[24] Mukti is a profound concept from Hinduism, Buddhism and Jainism; it means liberation from the cycle of birth, death and rebirth (known as Samsara). From the Sanskrit root "Muchya", to release, let go, to free.

Gokarna enquired about the ways to attain Mukti. The scholars began to examine all the Shastras[25]. Though they couldn't find a proper answer, one thing became clear, Suryadeva[26] knows! He can show the way to Mukti!

Gokarna stopped Suryadeva in his path.

"Bhagavan, I have to release Dhunadhukari's Preta somehow. Can you please show me the way?"

Suryadeva's direction was clear. "Read Bhagavatam aloud and complete it in 7 days".

Gokarna began preparations for the Bhagavatam reading. To listen to the reading, many, many people arrived.

From the cities, blind, mentally and emotionally disturbed people. Old. All kinds.

Those who are aware of sins, and those who wanted to rid themselves of sin.

They came in multitudes. A vast assembly of people gathered to listen to Bhagavatam.

Dhunadhukari's Preta saw a clear path toMoksha; listening to Bhagavatam, every line of it.

Where should it sit and listen? Searched for many places, finally found a bamboo with 7 branches. With an opening at the bottom.

---

[25] Authoritative scriptures. From the Sanskrit root "Shaas", to instruct, teach, govern or discipline, and

"Tra" instrument or means. So, Shastra means "an instrument of instruction".

[26] Sun God, giver of life, light and energy. Often depicted as a radiant deity riding a chariot drawn by seven horses representing the seven days of the week or the seven colours of the rainbow. Symbolises the light (knowledge or consciousness) which dispels darkness (ignorance).

The Preta entered and sat down to listen intently. The reading began in the morning and ended in the evening.

When the day's reading concluded, a strange thing happened. The first branch of the bamboo broke and fell to the ground.

The same thing happened the next day.

When the day's reading ended, the second branch of the bamboo broke off.

What happened after seven days? Bhagavatam reading was completed.

The seventh and final branch of the bamboo also fell off. And the Preta obtained Moksha, and a beautiful body too.

A blue tinged divine body!

The blessed Dhunadhukari fell in gratitude at Gokarna's feet.

"O dear brother, because of your grace I have obtained Moksha. Such is the greatness of Bhagavatam!"

An aircraft from Vishnuloka[27] arrived and landed.

Radiant messengers and emissaries of Lord Vishnu, Vishnudoota, many of them were in the aircraft and they escorted Dhunadhukari to Vishnuloka.

But before they left Gokarna wanted to clear a doubt. "So many people who listened to Bhagavatam. But only Dhunadhukari attained Vishnuloka. Why is that?"

---

[27] Vishnuloka or Vaikuntha, the Divine Abode of Lord Vishnu, the final destination of souls which have attained Moksha and been liberated from the cycle of birth and death. Vishnuloka signifies the ultimate state of union with the Supreme Lord in bliss and splendour beyond time and space.

"It is true that many people listened to Bhagavatam. They did not concentrate their minds on it as much as needed. But Dhnunadhikari was just the opposite. Gokarna, please read Bhagavatam once again. Let them all listen with a lot more Shradha[28]. Then, they too will attain Vaikuntham. And the Lord will bless you too," replied the Vishnudootas.

Gokarna read Bhagavatam aloud again. This time, when the reading was concluded, Lord Vishnu Himself, appeared and granted Vishnuroopa[29] and Vishnuloka, not just to Gokarna but to all the listeners too.

When does Lord Vishnu manifest on earth? Whenever Adharma spreads everywhere.

When Dharma begins to vanish! Adharma[30] has to be destroyed and Dharma has to be established. That is Bhagavan's objective.

---

[28] Faith and devotion

[29] Divine Form or Manifestation of Lord Vishnu, the Supreme Lord. Granting a vision of Vishnuroopa symbolizes Moksha and a permanent connection and access to Lord Vishnu.

[30] The very opposite of Dharma. Adharma symbolises all thoughts and actions that violate harmony, justice and ethics

Matsya Avatara

Now, let me first tell you the story of Matsya Avatara[31].

Brahma was fast asleep. That was just the opportunity that the Asura[32] seeking.

He stole all the Vedas and ran away with them. If the Vedas are lost, isn't that the end of everything? Shouldn't they be retrieved? Only Lord MahaVishnu can retrieve them!

Once there lived a Rajarishi[33] named Satyavrata.

He was performing Tarpanam[34] in the river Kritamala. Cupping his hands together, he gathered up some water.

A small fish was in the water he scooped up. Satyavrata put the fish back into the river.

"O King, there are big creatures in the river. They will eat me. Please, show mercy. Don't abandon me to them," the fish pleaded.

---

[31] From Sanskri, "Avatar", meaning descent or manifestation of the Supreme Lord, Vishnu to right the wrongs and destroy Adharma. As explained by Lord Krishna in Bhagavad Gita Chapter 4, Verses 7-8, whenever righteousness declines and unrighteousness prevails, I manifest myself to protect the virtuous, destroy the wicked, and reestablish Dharma."

[32] From the Sanskrit "A" which is a prefix or negation. "Sura", divine or luminous being, meaning not Divine, beings full of life but driven by excessive desires, ego and evil intentions.

[33] Rajarishi a unique king who balances spiritual wisdom with the practicalities of governing, for example, King Janaka, father of Sita.

[34] A sacred Vedic ritual to honour and pay respects to ancestors; it is the offering of water with sacred substances and sesame seeds. Derived from the Sanskrit root "Trp", to satisfy or satiate.

Satyavrata took the fish into his Kamandala[35] and carried it home. What did he see the next day?

The fish had grown very big in just one night! It couldn't fit into the Kamandala anymore.

"It's very difficult for me to live inside this vessel. Can you please find a bigger place for me?" the fish requested.

Satyavrata then placed the fish in a pot full of water. The fish soon outgrew the pot.

Satyavrata transferred it to a pond. But the fish quickly became too big for the pond. Satyavrata then released the fish into a large reservoir. That too became too small for the fish!

Now, it's only the sea that's fit for the fish. And Satyvrata took the fish and let it out into the sea. The Rajarishi realised that this was no ordinary fish.

"You've taken the form of a fish but who are you? Aren't you really Lord MahaVishnu? What are you intending, O Lord?" Satyavrata asked with devotion.

Bhagavan explained his intentions clearly. "Satyavrata, the seventh day from today is when Pralaya[36] will occur. The entire world will sink in the deluge. The sea will heave with huge waves. Complete darkness will set in. You must immediately collect all medicines, seeds and saplings and keep them safely with you. A

---

[35] Traditional vessel used to carry water by sages and ascetics

[36] Catastrophic flood, the Great Deluge, causing destruction and dissolution preparatory to a new cycle of creation. MahaVishnu takes the form of a fish to save knowledge from destruction.

ship will arrive with the Saptarishis[37] and the great serpent Vasuki[38]. Get into this ship. Use Vasuki as a rope and tie the ship to my horn. I will travel in the ocean till the deluge subsides."

Days went past, one after the other.

On the seventh day, Pralaya engulfed the world.

Dense, black rainclouds crowded the sky. The heaviest rainfall battered the world. Cyclones and strong winds wreaked havoc. The ocean roared across shores. The ship with Saptarishis arrived and so did Vasuki.

And not just that.

A golden, one horned Great Fish, Maha Matsya[39] also appeared. MahaVishnu in the Matsya Avatara[40].

Satyavrata boarded the ship, carrying all the medicines, seeds and saplings with him. Then he used Vasuki as a rope and tied the ship to the horn of the fish.

Bhagavan saved Satyavrata from the Pralaya, and gave him the Divine Knowledge, Tattvopadesam[41].

Then, Bhagavan sought out Hayagriva, killed him, retrieved all the stolen Vedas and entrusted them back with Brahma.

---

[37] The Seven Sages, highly enlightened beings, considered Manasaputras, mind-born sons of Brahma the Creator.

[38] King of Serpents, known for his devotion and loyalty to Lord Vishnu and Lord Siva.

[39] Fish

[40] the First incarnation of Lord Vishnu in the series of 10 incarnations, Dasavatara.

[41] From the Sanskrit Tattva, principle or reality, and Upadesa, teaching, guidance or instruction. Tattvopadesa means the divine teaching relating to Atman, Brahman and Paramatma. Sat (The Ultimate Truth of Existence), Chit (Consciousness) and Ananda (Bliss)

Kurma Avatara

Let me now tell you the story of Kurma Avatara.

The Devas[42] were beautiful and eternally young. And when they were cursed by Sage Durvasa[43]? Instantly they became deformed, ugly, and old!

Along with Brahma they rushed to seek Lord MahaVishnu's help. Drinking Amrutam will remove deformities and restore youth.

However, Amrutam is at the bottom of the Palazhi[44], the Ocean of Milk Only if Palazhi is churned will the divine drink rise to the surface.

This cannot happen if only the Devas churn the sea. They will need help from the Asuras too.

But the Devas and Asuras are sworn enemies!

Lord MahaVishnu described a way out of the difficulty, "Time now favours the Asuras. So, for the time being you have to make peace with them and obtain their help. Then, using the Mandara Mountain[45] as the churning rod and Vasuki as the rope you have to churn the Ocean of Milk. I will also assist in this."

The Asuras also desired Amrutam. So, they extended the help that the Devas requested. Enemies united for common cause!

---

[42] Deva, God or Divine Being, symbolises light, goodness and positive energy.

[43] Story of this curse is detailed in MaliBharatam

[44] Ocean of Milk, Ksheera Sagara in Sanskrit, symbolizes purity, abundance and higher spiritual knowledge.

[45] Mandara Mountain, symbolises perseverance and cooperation to achieve a higher purpose.

Together, they uprooted the Mandara Mountain and carried it towards Palazhi.

After quite a distance, fatigue overtook them.

The mountain slipped from their hands and fell to the ground. A lot of them were trapped under the mountain and died.

Since they didn't have the strength to carry the mountain, the survivors were dejected.

That's when Lord MahaVishnu appeared.

With one arm, He lifted the mountain effortlessly and placed it on Garuda[46]. Then, He too mounted Garuda.

Garuda flew to Palazhi and set the mountain down. Devas and Asuras followed on foot.

There was an agreement to give Amrutam to Vasuki as well.

The great serpent wrapped itself around Mandara. His head was extended to one side and the tail to the other.

Lord MahaVishnu caught hold of the head and along with Him, the Devas too.

The Asuras were left with the tail.

When the Devas are holding the head, we're holding the tail? The Asuras didn't like that at all!

Won't it become a big problem if the Asuras refused to hold the tail? Lord MahaVishnu quickly went to the other side and

---

[46] Garuda is revered as the vehicle of Lord MahaVishnu and is known for strength, speed and loyalty, and also for power, protection and freedom. He is the son of Maharishi Kashyapa and Vinata which makes him the King of Birds and half-brother of snakes (Nagas) who were born of Kashyapa's other wife Kadru. Garuda is the sworn enemy of snakes.

took hold of the tail. So did the Devas. The Asuras were able to grab the head, they were happy!

Both the groups started vigorously churning the Ocean together.

Then, another disaster!

The spinning mountain began to sink into the Ocean. Those who were churning all became dejected.

The entire effort has been pointless. What's to be done next?

Lord MahaVishnu came to the rescue again! He took the form of a tortoise.

A tortoise with a body spread across 100,000 Yojanas[47]. The tortoise lifted the mountain on to its back.

Devas and Asuras resumed the churning.

The mountain began to spin like a top, and the tortoise enjoyed the sensation, like scratching an itchy back!

Churning continued for a long time. Those who were churning were exhausted, yet there was no sign of Amrutam.

Now, Lord MahaVishnu began to churn and then the entire situation changed.

The deep and wide Ocean began to froth and heave. And from its depths rose the most potent venom, Kalakudam[48]. Thevenom begantospread up and down, everywhere, in all directions.

Won't the entire world be destroyed by this dangerous toxin?

Everyone was terrified and they all prayed desperately to Lord Siva for help.

---

[47] A measure of distance. 1 Yojana = 15 km approximately
[48] A poison so toxic that it could destroy all of creation

And do you know what Lord Siva, the embodiment of compassion, did? He took the Kalakudam in his cupped hands and swallowed it!

The venom accumulated and remained in his throat like an ornament, coloured blue.

A few drops of the venom fell on the ground and were consumed by snakes, scorpions, and similar animals. Even today these creatures carry a lot of venom!

Many divine beings and objects rose to the surface of the Ocean of Milk. They were all accepted by various beings.

The holy cow, Kamadhenu, was taken by the Maharshis.

The silver coloured, four-tusked elephant, Airavata by Devendra. The divine tree, Parijata by the Devas.

The great gem, Kaustubh, went to Lord MahaVishnu.

And similarly, many things to many beings.

Lakshmi Devi too ascended to the surface of the Ocean. She was so very beautiful!

Those who saw her were overwhelmed. So great were Her purity and grace that they are indescribable. Several offerings were made to Her.

Varuna offered yellow silk and the necklace, Vyjayanthi. Saraswathi Devi offered an exquisite pearl necklace. Vishwakarma, priceless ornaments. Brahma, the extraordinary Lotus flower. Serpents, beautiful earrings. So, so many gifts!

Laksmi Devi graciously accepted all the offerings. And then, took Lord MahaVishnu as her husband.

Another Devi, Varunidevi, the Devi of intoxicants, also came to the surface.

And the Asuras accepted her. Do you know who came next?

The Deva of Ayurveda, Dhanvantari, holding a sacred vessel in his hands. The vessel contained Amrutam!

The Asuras spotted this, grabbed the vessel and ran away with Amrutam. The Devas were caught in a strange predicament.

They didn't get Amrutam. On top of that, their enemies had made off with it.

All their hard work to obtain Amrutam had come to nought. Lord MahaVishnu prepared to help the Devas.

He took the form of beautiful Mohini and proceeded towards the Asuras. "I want Amrutam first," every Asura staked his claim.

Arguments broke out amongst the Asuras, then fights, and finally pushing and shoving and fisticuffs.

That's when the enchanting Mohini arrived on the scene.

Her grace, beauty, and aura were such that the Asuras trusted her totally. They requested to her, "Please distribute Amrutam amongst us. This will ensure that everyone gets it and that each will have an equal share."

"Whatever I do may be right or wrong. But you will have to accept what I do. Only then can I serve Amrutam," she said.

The Asuras agreed to Mohini's conditions.

She made them sit in orderly lines and took charge of the vessel containing Amrutam.

But she served Amrutam to the Devas who had arrived quietly and were sitting on the other side!

Amongst the Devas were Surya[49], and Chandra[50], and the Asura, Rahu, disguised as a Deva.

They pointed out Rahu to Bhagavan. By this time Rahu had already put Amrutam into his mouth. Bhagavan used Sudarsana Chakra[51] to cut Rahu's head off. Because Amrutam had not reached Rahu's stomach, his body fell to the ground.

But his head had life[52]! So, Bhagavan made him a planet.

Rahu developed great anger and hatred towards Surya and Chandra. After all, weren't they the ones who had revealed Rahu's disguise to Bhagavan?

Even today, Rahu opposes Surya and Chandra through eclipses!

Vishnubhagavan did not give Amrutam to the Asuras because they were not his devotees.

But he gave it to the Devas who were devoted to Him. He mounted Garuda and departed.

Imagine the anger of the Asuras! Not only did they not receive Amrutam but their enemies, the Devas, got it! So now, the Asuras were bent upon destroying the Devas.

The immensely strong Mahabali was the leader of the Asuras and the infinitely courageous Devendra was the leader of the Devas.

Both sides had innumerable warriors. The war was extremely violent.

---

[49] Sun

[50] Moon

[51] Lord MahaVishnu's divine weapon, a spinning, sharp edged disk with serrated edges. Symbolises the ability to enforce truth and justice and destroy evil. From Sanskrit root "Su", auspicious or good, and "Darsana", vision or sight.

[52] Amrutam makes immortal anyone who drinks it

The Asuras suffered more losses and devastation.

Devendra killed many powerful enemies and also wounded the mighty Mahabali.

And if the war continued? The entire Asura race would be wiped out.

So, Brahma sent Sage Narada to pacify Devendra and make him stop the war.

Mahabali suffered defeat and wounds. But that doesn't mean that he was weak. In reality he was a great King. His greatness will be understood and appreciated when we come to the story of Vamana Avatara.

But before that, I have to tell you another story. The story of Varaha Avatara.

Varaha Avatara

Sanaka Munis[53] are 4 in number. They eternally appear to be 5 years old and can travel anywhere, anytime. No one will ever dare stop them.

Once, they went to Vaikuntha to see Lord MahaVishnu. Vaikuntha is protected by 7 surrounding walls.

Sanaka Munis went past 6 walls and reached the 7th wall. Guards, Jaya and Vijaya, stood in the doorway.

The Munis attempted to enter without permission. Jaya and Vijaya got angry and stopped them. And in turn, the Munis became furious. They cursed the guards.

"You deserve Papaloka[54]. Go there immediately."

The curse brought Jaya and Vijaya back to their senses. They were terrified.

But what's the use of being terrified? The curse is bound to prevail.

Both of them begged the Munis for "Sapamokhsa's"[55] release from the curse.

---

[53] Muni, from the Sanskrit root "Man", to think or meditate. Munis focus on self-control, silence, meditation, deep thought and solitude. Rishis, derived from Sanskrity root "Rs", one who perceives after achieving spiritual knowledge through divine revelations or study of Vedas. Rishis are known for composing hymns. Rishis focus on knowledge, teaching and contributing to spiritual texts.

[54] Papaloka, from Sanskrit,"papa", sin and "loka", world. World of Sin, a hellish realm where sinners face the consequences of their actions.

[55] Sapamoksha, from Sanskrit "Sapa", curse and "Moksha", release or redemption from the curse by obtain Divine blessings or performing virtuous acts.

Lord MahaVishnu, of course, knows everything that happens anywhere! Coming out to the doorway he spoke to the Munis, "Jaya and Vijaya insulted you. That is equivalent to insulting me. For that I am seeking your forgiveness. The bad consequences of the mistakes of the servants affect the master like leprosy affecting the entire body. Your curse is justified, no doubt, but still, I have a desire. Let them return to Vaikuntha after they suffer the consequences of the curse."

The Munis were full of devotion, "O Bhagavan, may your desire be fulfilled".

Lord MahaVishnu then gave His divine instruction, "Let Jaya and Vijaya be born as Asuras and be filled with hatred towards Me."

The cursed guards fell from Vaikuntha.

What a fall!

The Devas who were all watching, gasped with sympathy and sorrow!

Kashayapa Maharshi had thirteen wives, all of them sisters. Twelve of them had children. Only Diti was childless. She shared her sorrow with her husband.

Kashyapa possessed divine powers.

He could see the future and told Diti what was to come. "You will beget two children. Both will be terribly wicked and cruel and will finally be killed by Lord MahaVishnu. But one of them will have a son who will be Lord MahaVishnu's greatest devotee."

Jaya and Vijaya are going to be born as Asuras.

Diti was pregnant, not for ten months, not for ten years, but for a hundred years!

During those hundred years the entire world was plunged into pitch darkness. And then both babies were born.

At that very moment, powerful tempests began to rage. Lightning struck everywhere continuously.

Trees fell. Oceans and rivers became turbulent. The cries of owls and foxes rent the air. Cows started bleeding. Idols of deities began to shed tears. All kinds of bad omens appeared!

Hiranyakashipu was the older of the two boys and Hiranyaksha, the younger.

And when they grew up?

Both were extremely tyrannical and mighty.

The story of the younger brother must be told first and the older one's after that.

Hiranyaksha became so powerful that no one could oppose him. And he wanted to wage war, always.

To do battle with the Devas, he invaded Devaloka. The Devas fled in sheer terror.

"Oh, I can't fight with the Devas, so now I'm going to take on Varuna.[56]" Hiranyaksha plunged into the ocean.

Varuna's army too ran away in fear. Hiranyaksha challenged Varuna.

But Varuna declined the challenge. "Hiranyaksha, I'm not going to fight you. Why don't you go and do battle with Lord MahaVishnu. With that all your arrogance will be destroyed," said Varuna.

"Oh, does this Vishnu have that much power? Well then, I'm going to subdue him," Hiranyaksha decided.

---

[56] Lord of the Oceans, Rivers and Water, keeper of the cosmic and moral order.

He began to look for Lord MahaVishnu everywhere. But couldn't find Him anywhere.

Eventually, from Sage Narada he learnt that Lord MahaVishnu is at Rasatala.

Hiranyaksha reached Rasatala.

Do you know that there are 14 worlds? Rasatala is one of them.

Lord MahaVishnu had gone there, for a reason.

Swayambhu Manu is the son of Brahma. Brahma had asked Swayambhu Manu to rule the earth. But he just couldn't do it because the earth was lying submerged in water.

It could only be ruled if it's lifted out of the water! How can it be raised up?

Brahma just couldn't think of way to do it. He prayed to Lord MahaVishnu to find a solution.

Suddenly, from inside Brahma's nose a tiny boar jumped out, a boar only as big as a thumb. Within a few moments the boar grew to be as big as an elephant. And soon it was the size of a mountain!

Its tail was held aloft. Entire body covered with stiff hair. Big, bloodshot eyes. Long, white tusks protruding from its nose. The boar was none other than Lord MahaVishnu!

The boar dived into the ocean and quickly reached the bottom. Placed the earth on its tusks and rose to the surface.

That's when he arrived, Hiranyaksha!

Wasn't he roaming in search of Lord MahaVishnu? Well, now he'd found Him!

"Oho, disguised as a boar? No matter what disguise you wear, I'm not going to spare you. You have killed so many Asuras. I'm going to take revenge for all that. Because of you so many of my relatives are deep in sorrow. After killing you, I'll wipe their tears," Hiranyaksha roared in fury.

"Alright, kill me and wipe their tears. You must certainly do that. Or else you won't keep your promise and that will bring you shame," Bhagavan replied with sarcasm.

The duel was most horrifying!

Hiranyaksha was very strong and courageous.

No matter how strong or brave, how can anyone stand up to Lord MahaVishnu?

Bhagavan killed him forthwith.

The He placed the earth properly in its place and returned to Vaikuntha. That's the end of the Hiranyaksha story!

Narasimha Avatara

And now, for the story of Hiranyakashipu but connected to that story is the story of Narasimha Avatara.

Hiranyakashipu is ruling haughtily after conquering all the worlds. Countless Asuras are ever ready to obey every command.

Do you know what atrocities they inflicted?

Flattened villages. Set fire to homes. Thrashing saints and devotees. Robbing, stealing and murdering as they please. It was all a glorification of Adharma!

Didn't Lord MahaVishnu kill Hiranyaksha?

Hiranyakashipu trembled with rage and swore a terrible oath. "I will cut MahaVishnu's throat and with his blood I will perform Tarpanam[57] for my younger brother."

Hiranyaksha's death caused immense grief to many, his mother, wife, children, relatives, friends.

Hiranyakashipu tried to console them. But no matter how much the grief, the one who is dead is never going to come back to life.

So, the reality is that it is pointless to grieve, as shown by Suyajna's story.

Hiranyakashipu narrated the story of Suyajna. King Suyajna died in battle.

His wives rushed in panic to the battlefield.

---

[57] A sacred Vedic ritual to honour and pay respects to ancestors; it is the offering of water with sacred substances and sesame seeds. Derived from the Sanskrit root "Trp", to satisfy or satiate.

The body was drenched in blood and covered with injuries. Shattered ornaments scattered on the ground.

Face shrouded in dust, caked in mud. The sight was unbearable for the wives. They collapsed, beating their chests and wailing in grief. A young boy arrived on the scene.

Actually, it wasn't a boy. It was Kalan, Death in disguise. He spoke to the King's wives, "People come from somewhere and then return to where they came from. So, what is there to grieve over? Everything is Bhagvan's pastime! And if He desires? What was lost in the street will be returned to its rightful owner; clothes kept safely within the house will disappear; a child

abandoned in the forest by its parents will live while a child being brought up with love at home will die. Look at your husband lying here. Can he hear your wails? Can he say anything to you? No! So let me tell you a story.

Once upon a time there lived a hunter. He used to trap birds in a net. Then, he would kill and eat them to satisfy his hunger. Once a female bird fell into the net. The male bird, her husband, was overcome with grief. In their nest, baby birds were waiting anxiously for their mother. But she was not going to come. The male bird is crying inconsolably, remembering aloud many things. But does the hunter show any mercy? He shoots down that bird too with an arrow. All of you are crying just like the male bird. No matter how much you cry, you are not going to get your husband back."

And with that Kalan vanished.

Why did Hiranykashipy narrate this story?

To douse the grief of sorrowing relatives of the dead king. But in his heart hatred for Lord MahaVishnu was smouldering.

"I must extract revenge from the killer of my younger brother. For that I have to build up my strength. To become strong, I have to perform Tapas. That has to be done in the forest."

With all these thoughts driving him, Hiranyakashipu went into the thick jungle.

He balanced his entire body on just one big toe which he planted firmly on the ground.

Raised his hands, lifted his gaze to the sky, thus began his Tapas. A Tapas of tremendous concentration and intensity. Time sped past. Tapas continued.

The heat from it spread across the universe. Rivers and oceans became polluted. The earth began to quake. Stars fell from the sky.

The Devas were very worried and sought help from Brahma.

Brahma went to Hiranyakashipu, His body was covered with grass. Skin, flesh, and blood were all being eaten by ants and insects. He is not aware of anything. So immersed is he in Tapas.

Brahma addressed him, "Hiranyakashipu, end this Tapas. Ask for your boon. I haven't seen this kind of Tapas being performed even by divine Maharshis. No one is going to perform such a penance in future either. With this Tapas, you have won me over."

Brahma then sprinkled holy water from his Kamandala on Hiranyakashipu.

In the next instant Hiranyakashipu regained his health and vigour. He became strong and his body seemed golden!

And then he asked Brahma to grant the boon. "None of your creations can kill me. I cannot die during daytime or at night. Nor can I die within a building or outside it, on earth or in the sky." Brahma was shaken.

What a powerful boon!

But there was no way Brahma could reject it. Hiranyakashipu obtained the strength he desired. He subjugated all classes.

Shook up every aspect of all the worlds. Destroyed Dharma.

Made Swarga [58] his home. How beautiful was Swarga! Stairways made of pearls, crushed emerald floors, walls built with diamonds, pillars plastered with rubies.

Magnificent Swarga was now under the control of Hiranyakashipu!

Lord MahaVishnu, Siva, and Brahma were the only three that had not been subjugated by Hiranyakashipu. Everyone else obeyed his wishes, unquestioningly. Maharshis sang his praises.

The earth provided harvests without even being tilled, oceans and rivers offered up precious gems, trees presented fruit.

Hiranyakashipu had suppressed everyone and everything and bent them to his will!

He discarded the Shaastras[59]. He stopped thinking about what is right and wrong and imposed a new law. All Yagas[60] would now be to worship him!

Yet, Hiranyakashipy suffered one major defeat.

---

[58] Celestial paradise. It is depicted as a paradise with beautiful palaces, gardens, rivers of nectar (Amrita), and endless pleasures.

[59] Scriptures

[60] Yaga refers to a sacred ritual or sacrifice performed in accordance with Vedic scriptures. It involves offerings made to deities, accompanied by precise chanting of mantras and adherence to specific ceremonial procedures. The primary purpose of a Yaga is to maintain cosmic order, seek divine blessings, express gratitude, or fulfil religious obligations

And that too, strangely, at the hands of his own son! Toys hold the attention of children.

But not for Prahlada.

His attention and Shradha[61] were totally on Lord MahaVishnu. The boy was often immersed in meditation. He would be motionless, like a statue. Sometimes he would cry and laugh at other times. Singing sometimes, dancing at other times.

Vishnubhakti[62] can make you do all these things! Education commenced for Prahlada.

He had two gurus. They were the sons of Shukracharya, the guru of the Asuras.

One day, Hiranyakashipu was lovingly caressing Prahlada in his lap. "Son, what is the greatest thing that you have learned," he asked with fatherly affection.

Pat came the answer from Prahlada, "Vishnubhakti." Hiranyakashipu was shaken.

"What is this? Vishnu is the enemy of our race, the Asuras. And yet, my own son has developed faith and devotion to Vishnu?" Hiranyakashipu's mind was agitated.

The gurus were disturbed too. Secretly, quietly, they asked Prahlada,

"Tell us the truth. This Vishnubhakti of yours, did someone else teach it to you or did you feel it from within yourself?"

Prahlada replied, "I just need to think of Lord MahaVishnu and my mind gets attracted to Him like iron filings to a magnet."

---

[61] Faith and devotion
[62] Devotion and surrender to Lord MahaVishnu

The gurus were very worried. "Won't Hiranyakashipy be furious with us? We have to get Prahlada to change his mind."

They scolded the pupil, tried to scare him even beat him. That's how Prahlada's education continued.

Some time went past.

One day the gurus took Prahlada to the palace. He bowed in greeting and reverence to his father.

Hiranyakashipu embraced his son, placed him on his lap and kissed his forehead. Then he asked a question, the same old question. "Son, what is the greatest thing that you have learned?"

"Vishnubhakti." the same old answer!

Hiranyakashipu confronted the guru in rage.

"You, apology for a Brahmin[63], did you teach this to my son? Are you a traitor, having joined my enemy to harm me?" Prahlada's guru shuddered in terror.

"O Lord, we did not teach him any of this and no one else did either. He learnt it on his own. Please don't blame us. And please don't be furious with us."

Hiranyakashipu turned towards Prahlada. "You, betrayer of your family and lineage!

The gurus didn't teach you this so from where did you learn it?" Prahlada replied calmly, "Dirty minds can never attain Lord MahaVishnu."

Hiranyakashipu's anger exploded. He threw his son to the floor from his lap and commanded the soldiers, "MahaVishnu is the killer of my younger brother. My son is a devotee of that Vishnu. His

---

[63] Priests and scholars

loyalty is not to his father but to his father's enemy. And he is only five years old!

A diseased part must be cut off. Only then can the rest of the body be saved. Take him away and kill him."

The soldiers surrounded Prahlada. And began beating him mercilessly.

What can we say other than astonishing! Prahlada was completely unhurt!

What did Hiranyakashipu do then?

Trained killer elephants were made to trample Prahlada. There was no effect!

Serpents were made to bite him. The poison did not affect him.

He was flung into a raging fire. Abandoned in thick fog. Buried alive. Bound hand and foot and thrown into a well. They did their very best to kill him. But Prahlada did not die.

Hiranyakashipu was plunged into deep thought. "There is no doubt that my son has some great power. Will he be the cause of my death? In any case, let him study for some more time. Maybe he will correct his erroneous ways and improve."

Prahlada continued his education once he got a break. The Guru had to attend to some domestic matters. The children called Prahlada to play with them.

Instead, Prahlada invited them all to his home. They sat around him. All of them were very fond of him.

Prahlada talked with them for a long time. The subjects of his talk were Gyana and Bhakti. "I learnt all this from Sage Narada," he said.

The children were surprised. All of them were being taught by the same Gurus and no one else and yet Prahlada said he was taught by Sage Narada!

Prahlada told them the story of how it all happened.

It was many years ago. It was a time when Hiranyakashipu had gone to perform Tapas. The Asuras were left without a leader. Devendra attacked and defeated them.

The Asuras ran for their lives.

Devendra then destroyed everything he laid eyes on. Not just that, he also kidnapped Hiranyakashipu's wife. The Asura Queen was pregnant!

The baby she was carrying was Prahlada. The Queen protested and cried out loudly. Devendra ignored her pleas and dragged her away.On the way, he came upon Sage Narada. The Sage told him that his actions were wrong. He did not dare disrespect Sage Narada.

So, he released Hiranyakashipu's wife.

Sage Narada took the Asura Queen to his Ashram[64]. She was protected and cared for until her husband came for her. Sage Narada imparted teachings about Dharma and Gyana.

The Asura Queen promptly forgot all of that later. But everything was imprinted in the mind of the baby in her womb! And Prahlada remembered it all after his birth.

HavingheardallthisfromPrahlada,alltheotherchildrenalso understood Lord MahaVishnu's greatness.

Bhakti towards Lord MahaVishnu took root in their minds and hearts too.

---

[64] Hermitage, places for spiritual learning, meditation and communal living.

The Gurus informed Hiranyakashipu about this. "You, traitor to the family. If I get even mildly annoyed, all the Three Worlds t r e m b l e in fear and yet you disrespect me? On what basis are you so disrespectful? Whose support makes you dare to do this?" Hiranyaksha demanded to know.

But Prahlada was not afraid at all.

Isn't he standing on the strong foundation of Vishnubhakti? Why should those who have Vishnubhakti be afraid?

"Father, Vishnu Bhagavan's strength is my foundation. He is my Protector. Father, you are travelling on the wrong road. Your mind is your enemy. You are arrogant about your victory over the ten directions. Please conquer your mind first," replied Prahlada.

"Oh, so there is another Bhagavan other than me? And that Ishvara[65] is everywhere, right? So, why is he not in this pillar, here?" asked Hiranyakashipu.

Prahlada looked at the pillar and folded his hands in obeisance. "He is, Father. Even in this pillar, He is present." Hiranyakashipy let out a fearsome roar, leaped forward, landed a powerful blow on the pillar. There, a noise from within the pillar! Not an ordinary noise.

A noise that sent shivers through all the worlds.

A creature emerges from the pillar! Not an ordinary creature. A creature that is both a human being and a lion at the same time! A thick mane around his face.

Eyes like hot, molten gold. Tongue like a flashing sword. Terrible, long fangs. A body touching the sky. Avatara of Lord MahaVishnu. Narasimha!!

---

[65] Supreme God, creator, maintainer, destroyer of everything.

How right was Prahlada. Ishvara is present everywhere, even in a pillar!

Hiranyakashipu jumped to confront Narasimha. Raised his mace and swung violently, but it had no effect.

Narasimha caught hold of Hiranyakashipu. He slipped out, rushed forward, and thrust his sword. Narasimha grabbed him again and flung him across the knees, Hiranyakashipu was now pinned down on Narasimha's lap. Narashimha then extended his claws, ripped open Hiranyakashipu's stomach, pulled out intestines, and wore them around His huge neck.

And then sat on Hiranyakashipu's throne.

Hiranyakashipu couldn't be killed by any of Brahma's creations. That is part of the boon he had received.

So, he died at the hands of Vishnu Bhagavan. Because Vishnu Bhagavan is not Brahma's creation!

Hiranyakashipu's boon also prevented him from being killed either in the sky or on the ground.

That is why Vishnu Bhagavan laid him on His lap and killed him. Neither could Hiranyakashipu be killed during the day or at night.

That is why Vishnu Bhagavan killed him at dusk which is not day nor is it night.

He could not die either inside or outside a building.

That is why Vishnu Bhagavan killed him in the Sabha, which is a large assembly hall, which is neither a room nor outside.

Brahma, Siva, Devendra, Devas, and Maharshis all arrived on the scene. All of them stood in reverence, chanting praises of Lord MahaVishnu.

None had the courage to approach the fearsome Narasimha still quivering with rage.

Even Lakshmi Devi was afraid to go near her Lord. What is the way to quieten the fury of the Lord?

Brahma sent Prahlada.

Prahlada went up to the Lord and prostrated at His feet.

Bhagavan calmed down immediately and gently raised up his little devotee. And blessed him by placing His divine hands-on Prahlada's head. "What boon can I grant you," asked the Lord.

He would be pleased to grant him anything. That's how much affection He held for Prahlada. "Prabhu, I am always praying to you but not for anything in return. People who pray for something in return are not devotees. They are people who transacts business. My devotion should be immortal. That is all I need," said Prahlada.

"Prahlada, I am pleased with you. You will become the Asura Emperor and rule with grace and glory for a long time. After that you will unite with Me," Bhagavan's divine words bathed him in blessings.

"My father has insulted you. That is a great sin. Can he please be released from that great sin?" Prahlada beseeched the Lord.

"Because of you, your father and indeed your entire race has now been purified."

Lord MahaVishnu showered his blessings on Prahlada and disappeared. That is how the first life of Jaya and Vijaya ended.

After a long time had passed, they were born into their second life.

When Lord MahaVishnu incarnated as Sri Rama, Jaya, and Vijaya were born as Ravana and Kumbhakarna.

Then they took their third life.

When Lord MahaVishnu incarnated as Sri Krishna, the brothers were born as Shishupala and Dantavaktra[66].

I will tell that story later.

Now, let me narrate the story of Vamana Avatara.

---

[66] Also known as Dantavakra

Vamana Avatara

You will remember that Devendra had wounded Mahabali.

Mahabali endeavoured to avenge not just that but also to conquer and rule Swargaloka.

He conducted the great Yaga or Sacrifice called Vishwajit[67]. Chariots, bows and arrows, quivers, shields, horses, flag masts all emerged from within the sacrificial fire.

With double the strength Mahabali attacked Swarga. This time it was certain that opposing him was futile. So, Devendra ran away along with all the Devas.

Mahabali entered Swarga triumphantly and took over Indra's[68] position.

To strengthen his position Mahabali conducted a hundred Ashwamedha Yajnas[69].

---

[67] Yaga or Sacrifice to attain powers to "To conquer The World".

[68] Indra, another name for Devendra.

[69] The Ashwamedha Yajna (अश्वमेध यज्ञ) is one of the most significant and grand sacrifices mentioned in ancient Hindu scriptures, especially in the Vedas, Mahabharata, Ramayana, and Puranas. The term "Ashwamedha" is derived from two Sanskrit words:

Ashwa" meaning "horse." Medha" meaning "sacrifice."

Thus, Ashwamedha refers to a horse sacrifice ritual performed by ancient kings to assert their supremacy and ensure prosperity for their kingdom.

Purpose of the Ashwamedha Yajna:

1.Royal Supremacy: The primary objective of the Ashwamedha was to declare the king's sovereignty over surrounding regions. The horse symbolized the king's power, and by allowing it to roam freely, the king challenged others to accept his supremacy or engage in battle.

Aditi, mother of the Devas is the sister of Diti, mother of the Asuras. Both of them are among the thirteen sisters married to Kashyapa.

I have mentioned this earlier, if you remember! Devas have run away.

The Asura King has conquered Devaloka. Aditi was thus, deeply saddened.

That's when Kashyapa arrived.

Aditi shared her sorrow with her husband.

There is a vow named Payovrata[70].

2.Prosperity and Strength: The yajna was believed to bring prosperity, fertility, and strength to the kingdom. It was also a way to invoke blessings from the gods for the welfare of the people.

Process of the Ashwamedha Yajna:

Release of the Horse: A consecrated horse was set free to roam across neighbouring territories. The king's army followed it, and any ruler who stopped or captured the horse had to fight the king performing the yajna

[70] Payovrata:

After the Devas were defeated and expelled from heaven by Bali, Aditi, their mother and the wife of sage Kashyapa, became distressed. She sought a way to help her sons regain their rightful place.

Sage Kashyapa advised her to perform the Payovrata, a ritual dedicated to Lord Vishnu, to seek His intervention.

The Payovrata Ritual:

1.Duration:The Payovrata was to be observed for twelve days, starting from the twelfth day (Dvadashi) of the bright fortnight of the lunar month.

2.Diet: Aditi was required to consume only milk (payo) during these twelve days, hence the name Payovrata (vow involving milk).

3.Worship of Lord Vishnu: Aditi performed daily worship of Lord Vishnu with great devotion. She prepared an altar, offered milk, fruits, flowers, and sacred water, and chanted mantras glorifying Vishnu.

4.Mantra Recited: Aditi chanted a specific Vishnu mantra during the ritual: "Om Namo Bhagavate Vasudevaya"

This mantra is a powerful invocation of Lord Vishnu, symbolizing surrender and devotion.

Aditi must embark on this vow and pray to Lord MahaVishnu. That was the direction given by Kashyapa. Aditi undertook the vow with utmost devotion and discipline. Lord MahaVishnu was pleased.

He manifested and promised her, "Aditi, this is a good time for the Asuras. It is not possible to defeat them now. But your penance must bear fruit. So, I will be born as your son to save the Devas."

Lord MahaVishnu incarnated with all the attendant signs and indications. However, He hid all of that and took the form of a short, celibate boy.

This was Bhagavan's Vamana Avatara.

Mahabali is camped on the Northern bank of the river Narmada where he is conducting the Yagna.

Vamana arrived there.

People within the Yagna enclosure came saw a beautiful sight. A boy Sanyasi is walking in, an umbrella and Kamandala in his hands, a yellow rope around his waist.

Wearing the sacred thread across his body[71], matted hair on his head.

What a wonderful aura he radiates!

Is this Agni (Lord of Fire) or Surya (Sun God) in the form of a young boy?

Mahabali, Sukracharya and all the assembled Maharshis welcomed the boy Sanyasi with respect.

Mahabali addressed the boy, "I think you are the human form of the Tapas of the Brahma Rishis. Your arrival has purified me, not just me but also my entire lineage. I am certain that you need

---

[71] Sacred three Yajnopavita worn by Brahmins

something. What is it? Cows? Gold? A house? Whatever it is, please don't hesitate to ask!"

Vamana replied, "O King, no cowards have ever taken birth in your lineage and neither have those who break promises. Isn't this the lineage of the great devotee Prahlada and the brave Hiranyaksha and Hiranyankashipu? What I need is something very small, very negligible, just enough land to cover three of my footsteps."

Mahabali is foremost amongst the generous of the generous. No matter how much he has given, he is never satisfied!

After all, the boy Sanyasi needs only three steps worth of land.

"I am the Master of all the worlds. I'm happy to give you even entire islands. So, please ask for whatever you want," Mahabali requested the boy.

"O King, one who is not satisfied with three steps worth of land will not be satisfied with an island. He will then desire the entire earth comprising seven islands. And after he obtains the entire earth? He will then want all the three worlds. And after that? He will still not be satisfied. Therefore, I need only three footsteps worth of land," said Vamana.

What could Mahabali do other than provide just the three footsteps worth of land?

He began preparations for the ritual of giving. Sukracharya[72] warned his disciple. "What you are doing is not at all correct. This is not an ordinary Brahmachari[73]. He is none other than

---

[72] Guru of the Asuras, son of Sage Bhrigu and his wife Khyati
[73] Celibate practising austerities for spiritual upliftment

Lord Mahvishnu. If you go ahead with this land donation you will be ruined."

But Mahabali was clear and firm in his reply. "O Guru, I am the grandson of Prahlada. I have to prove that I spoke the truth when I made the promise. Is there a greater Adharma than speaking an untruth and not fulfilling my promise? I will adhere to the truth even at the cost of my life."

Sukracharya was taken aback and angered by Mahabali's disobedience. He cursed his disciple, "May all your wellbeing, abundance, and success be destroyed." Mahabali was not affected by the curse.

He was sure that his fate was sealed but he still fulfilled his promise.

Vamana grew rapidly in size. An indescribably large size! His first step covered the entire Earth.

The second step covered Swarga and other areas. There was no place for the third step!

Bhagavan reduced his size and became the small Vamana again.

Lord MahaVishnu seems to have deceived Mahabali with Maya[74], the force of illusion.

Therefore, He has to be killed forthwith. The Asuras raced towards Bhagavan.

Bhagavan's soldiers arrived immediately to confront the Asuras, a pitched battle followed.

---

[74] From the Sanskrit root "Mru" meaning to measure or to form; conveys the idea of creation, transformation and illusion, the cosmic illusion that covers the true nature of the Supreme Reality, namely, Lord MahaVishnu or Bhagavan.

Mahabali ordered the Asuras to stop fighting and move aside. Meanwhile do you know what Garuda did?

He tied up Mahabali with the Varunapasha[75], the divine noose of Varuna. "Give me the land for my third step. If you don't fulfil your promise, Naraka[76] is your fate," Vamana reminded Mahabali.

"O Bhagavan, falling into Naraka, losing my position, dying at your Hands, I'm not afraid of any of that. But I am terrified of the bad reputation that will follow me if I lead a life of untruth. Here, I offer my head. Please place your third footstep on my head." Mahabali replied.

Prahlada arrived on the scene. Mahabali couldn't rise and offer his obeisances.

Wasn't he on lying on the floor, tied up with Varunapasha?

All he could do was to look at his grandfather with tearful eyes and lower his head in reverence.

Prahlada addressed Lord MahaVishnu, "O Bhagavan, you provided Mahabali with Indra's position and then took it away. That was a great blessing for him. For those who have abundance

---

[75] Noose used by Lord Varuna, God of Oceans, to uphold truth and justice and maintain discipline

[76] The term "Naraka" is derived from the Sanskrit root "नर" (nara), meaning "man" or "human," and the suffix "क" (ka), which denotes a place. Thus, "Naraka" can be interpreted as "the place of humans" or "the abode of souls." Primary Meanings: Hell or Underworld: A realm where souls undergo punishment for their sins and misdeeds committed during their earthly lives. Purification Realm: Beyond mere punishment, Naraka serves as a space for the purification of the soul, allowing it to atone and eventually attain Moksha (liberation)

of wealth and power do not have Knowledge of the Divine Self."

"Please, Lord, free Mahabali," Brahma beseeched Lord MahaVishnu.

And then Lord MahaVishnu spoke these divine words, "Once I have decided to bless someone, I will first erase the abundance created by their wealth, position, and power. Mahabali is great. Wealth, power, and titles have all deserted him. Yet, he has not deviated from the truth."

Bhagavan then looked straight at Mahabali and spoke directly to him. "Go to Sutala[77], built by Vishwakarma[78]. Neither Devendra nor anyone else will dare misbehave with you. You can see me there at all times and I will always protect you."

The great Mahabali obeyed the Lord's instructions in total surrender and left for Sutala.

---

[77] The term "Sutala" is derived from Sanskrit, where "Su" (सु) means "good" or "auspicious," and "Tala" (तल) means "under" or "below." Therefore, "Sutala" can be interpreted as "the good or auspicious lower realm." Primary Meaning: Sutala refers to one of the seven lower realms (Patala Lokas) in Hindu cosmology. It is considered a heavenly subterranean world, distinct from the other Patala lokas, which are often associated with demonic or treacherous beings

[78] Vishwakarma is multifaceted, serving various functions that underscore his importance in the Hindu pantheon:
Divine Architect and Craftsman
Construction of Divine Realms:
•Amaravati: The capital city of Indra, king of the Devas, was crafted by Vishwakarma.
•Mount Meru: The central axis of the universe, surrounded by celestial gardens and palaces, owes its grandeur to his design.
Creation of Divine Weapons and Tools:
•Sudarshana Chakra: The discus weapon of Lord Vishnu.
•Vajra: The thunderbolt weapon of Lord Indra.
•Nandaka: The sword of Lord Vishnu.

So too did Prahlada, as per the Lord's wish.

And now, I will tell you the story of Lord MahaVishnu's incarnation as Parasurama.

Parasurama Avatara

Rama[79] is the younger son of a Maharshi named Jamadagni. Parasu, meaning axe, is the weapon used by Rama. That's how he came to be known as Parasurama.

ThereisakingdomnamedHehayamwithaking named Kaarthaveeryarjuna.

He is not an ordinary king. He is wealthier and more famous than anyone else.

Similarly, he possessed more strength and courage than anyone else. In addition, he has a thousand arms.

No one dared oppose him. Even the mighty Ravana was defeated by Kaarthaveeryarjuna.

Not only defeated but also bound and thrown into the dungeons[80]. Isn't this sufficient to prove Kaarthaveeryarjuna's strength and prowess? There was just one person he couldn't defeat.

And that was none other than Parasurama.

Not just defeat. Kaarthaveeryarjuna died at Parasurama's hands.

No matter who, no one can come anywhere near Parasurama in skill and valour.

After all, isn't he Lord MahaVishnu's Avatara?!

What is the reason for their fight?

---

[79] Not to be confused with Lord Sri Rama
[80] This story is told in Mali Ramanyanam

Kaarthaveeryarjuna came to the forest on a hunting expedition. Ministers, army commanders, families, and soldiers were all with him. Maharshi Jamadagni was residing in the forest to perform Tapas.

He welcomed Kaarthaveeryarjuna and his entourage.

How could he extend hospitality, in the forest, to this large multitude of guests?

That is extraordinary!

Kamadhenu [81] the cow, is part of Maharshi Jamadagni's Ashram. The cow is divine and has the ability to provide whatever is asked of her. No matter how many guests, whatever they want, nothing is difficult.

Kamadhenu could give it all!

"How wonderful it would be if I can possess Kamadhenu." That was the desire of Kaarthaveeryarjuna.

"Maharshi Jamadagni is a Tapasvi[82]. I am his guest. Attacking him and stealing from him is not permissible".

The King forgot all righteousness and ordered his soldiers to take away Kamadhenu and her calf.

Parasurama was not present in the Ashram at that time. When he returned, he found out all that had happened in his absence. His anger boiled over uncontrollably.

---

[81] According to legends, Kamadhenu has the ability to grant any wish, making her a symbol of wealth and well- being.She is believed to be the source of all prosperity and is often depicted as a white cow with a gentle and serene appearance. Kamadhenu is considered a symbol of abundance, purity, and sacredness, as cows hold a special place in Indian culture and traditions.
[82] One who performs Tapas

Hurriedly he took Parasu and rushed to Kaarthaveeryarjuna's capital. The King's army stopped him.

Parasurama killed his opponents.

Then, Kaarthaveeryarjuna arrived to do battle.

He had five hundred bows in five hundred hands and five hundred arrows in the other five hundred hands. But Parasurama was neither nervous nor afraid.

He sliced off the one thousand hands of his enemy and also cut off the head.

Kaarthaveeryarjuna had ten thousand sons. Every one of them was petrified with fear.

Parasurama took Kamadhenu and her calf back to the Ashram. The wrongdoer had been punished.

The divine cow was returned to her rightful place. But Maharshi Jamadagni was not happy.

He said to his son, "Rama, we are Brahmins. Forgiveness is our wealth. Even Brahma's greatness is because of forgiveness. Ishvara's grace falls only upon those who forgive and forbear everything. Your lack of forgiveness has crossed all boundaries. There is only one way to atone for this. You must embark on pilgrimage."

Father is equivalent to Ishvara. The son must obey his father. Parasurama knew that.

He departed for the pilgrimage.

Maharshi Jamadagni's wife is Renuka. Once she made a mistake.

She went to the river Ganga to draw water. There she saw an enticing sight.

A handsome Gandharva[83] was in the river. His beautiful wives were with him.

They were frolicking in the water, playing and swimming. Renuka stood watching them.

She was overcome with a desire if only the Gandharva could become her husband!

It was late when she returned to the Ashram. And Maharshi Jamadagni had known about her desire. Isn't he a Maharshi with divine powers?

In anger he ordered his sons, "Kill your mother right now".

What?

Kill the mother who gave birth to us! What an unthinkable, terrible command. The sons did not obey the order.

Maharshi Jamadagni now ordered Parasurama to kill the sons who had not obeyed him and to kill Renuka too.

It is the ultimate sin to kill elder brothers and Mother but so is disobeying Father.

He had to choose between two heinous sins. Parasurama carried out the killings.

---

[83] In Hindu mythology, Gandharvas are celestial beings known as skilled musicians and singers in the heavenly realms. They are often associated with art, beauty, nature, and divine music, playing an essential role in the cultural and spiritual aspects of ancient texts. Gandharvas frequently appear in the epics like the Mahabharata and Ramayana, as well as in Puranic literature. They are described as expert musicians and singers who entertain the gods, especially in the court of Lord Indra, the king of gods. They are often linked to forests, rivers, and mountains, and are said to inhabit regions rich in natural beauty. Celestial Beings: Gandharvas are considered semi-divine, existing between the realms of gods and humans. They possess supernatural abilities and are known for their charm and elegance.

Satisfied and happy, Maharshi Jamadagni asked his son, "Son, what boon do you want?"

"Father, please bring Mother and brothers back to life without them ever remembering their deaths," replied Parasurama.

Maharshi Jamadagni granted his son's boon.

All those who had died came alive and stood up.

None of them even knew that they had died a short while earlier. Do you remember the sons of Kaarthaveeryarjuna?

The ones who had been terrified of Parasurama. They were waiting for an opportunity to wreak vengeance.

One day, Parasurama and his elder brothers were not in the Ashram. They had gone into the forest.

Maharshi Jamadagni and Renuka were alone in the Ashram. Maharshi was immersed in meditation, that's when the princes entered the Ashram.

Renuka realised that their intention was to kill Maharshi Jamadagni. The Maharshi's wife pleaded with them in vain.

They ignored her, beheaded the Maharshi and carried his head away with them.

Overcome with grief Renuka cried loudly, "O my son Rama, please come, come". Parasurama came immediately.

Mother sobbing uncontrollably, father lying dead, his head missing.

Can you imagine the son's sorrow?

Suddenly the sorrow boiled over into fury, fury towards the killers of his father, fury towards the entire Kshatriya dynasty to which the killers belonged.

Parasurama took Parasu in his hands.

Reached the capital of the enemies and massacred everyone. Made a mountain of their heads, created a river of blood, built five ponds in Syamanta Panchaka[84], retrieved his father's head and returned to the Ashram. Re-attached the head and cremated the body with all necessary rites. Roamed the earth destroying the Kshatriya dynasty, not once, but twenty-one times!

[84] According to the legend, after Parashurama completed his mission of destroying the Kshatriyas (warrior class) twenty-one times as a form of retribution for his father's murder, he sought purification from the sin of killing so many warriors. He created five sacred ponds at Kurukshetra by striking the ground with his axe. These ponds were filled with the blood of the slain Kshatriyas, but after his intense penance and prayers, they turned into holy water bodies.

SriRama Avatara

Yet another Avatara of Lord MahaVishnu is SriRama[85].

After SriRama Avatara is when Krishna Avatara occurs. The main story of Bhagavatam is the story of SriKrishna. Before that divine and beautiful story is narrated, certain other stories need to be told.

The stories of Devas, Asuras, Maharshis, Kings, a variety of stories. Kardama, the Maha Yogi, performed Tapas, concentrating on Lord MahaVishnu.

It stretched for a long, long time. Eventually, Lord MahaVishnu appeared. He spoke to the Tapasvi, "Kardama, on the third day from today, the First King, Swaayambhu Manu[86] will come here. Devahuti is his daughter. Swaayambhu Manu will request you to marry her. You must accept that request. I will be born out of this wedlock between you and Devahuti."

Lord MahaVishnu as my son!

What greater good fortune can there be? Kardama waited.

---

[85] Mali Ramayanam is the complete story of SriRama

[86] Swayambhu Manu – The Adi Raja (First King)

In Hindu tradition, Swayambhu Manu is regarded as the first human being and the progenitor of mankind, often called the Adi Raja or the first king. The word "Manu" is derived from the Sanskrit root "man", meaning "to think," symbolizing him as the archetypal man and lawgiver.

Meaning of Swayambhu: Swayambhu means "self-born" or "self-manifested," indicating that Manu was created directly by Brahma, the creator god. He is believed to be the first of the fourteen Manus who appear in each cycle of creation, known as a Kalpa (a day of Brahma, approximately 4.32 billion years).

Swayambhu Manu and his wife, Shatarupa, are considered the ancestors of the entire human race.

The third day dawned.

Swaayambhu Manu arrived along with his wife and daughter.

Kardama married Devahuti. They had nine daughters. Kardama prepared to leave for performing Tapas.

"It is true that we have nine children but all of them are daughters. We don't have a single son," Devahuti lamented to her husband.

Kardama consoled his wife, "Soon, a son will be born. And that son will be none other than Lord MahaVishnu Himself."

Bhagavan was born soon thereafter to Devahuti. And what was he named?

Kapila.

There is a Shaastra named Sankhya - a Maha Shaastra that provides human beings with Knowledge of the Self. It was available in ancient times. But over a long period of time, gradually, it vanished. It has to be revived and recreated. That was Kapila's purpose.

Kapila first imparted Sankhya to his mother. Then he left home and travelled far and wide to teach it to everyone.

Devahuti followed her son's teachings, lived her life, and attained Mukti[87].

Prasooti and Aahuti were the two sisters of Devahuti and Uttanapada and Priyavrita were the two brothers. Daksha Prajapati was Prasooti's husband, known by the shortened name, Daksha. He is the son of Brahma.

----

[87] Moksha, liberation from birth and death, merging with Lord MahaVishnu

From practising Tapasya he obtained great spiritual power, Tapashakti. Daksha had many daughters, Sati is one of them.

And, who is Sati's husband? None other than Siva himself!

Daksha and Siva began to dislike each other. Munis[88] and Devas jointly conducted a Maha Yaga. The proud Daksha strode into the venue of the Yaga. Everyone had respect for Daksha.

The entire gathering rose and welcomed him ceremonially. Only two of those present did not rise - Brahma and Siva. Brahma is of course Daksha's father, the father does not stand up when he sees his son. But Siva's situation is not the same.

He is the husband of Daksha's daughter. So, he ought to rise to his feet.

However, Siva continued to remain seated. Daksha felt tremendous anger towards him. So, what did Daksha do?

He criticised Siva loudly so everyone could hear. "Look at his impudence.

Isn't he my daughter's husband?

When he sees me, he must rise and greet me with reverence. That is the proper way to behave towards elders. What insolence he has!

I have given my daughter to him. What a mistake that is! He is despicable.

Bhootas[89] and Pretas[90] are his companions.

---

[88] In Sanskrit, "Muni" (मुनि) refers to a sage or ascetic who has taken a vow of silence or is deeply immersed in meditation and spiritual practices. These individuals are revered for their wisdom and self-discipline.
[89] Ghosts
[90] Explained earlier

Ash from the crematorium is what he smears on his body and he wears a necklace of bones.

He claims to be Siva the embodiment of grace and auspiciousness but in reality, he is Ashiva, the very opposite.

I hereby curse him.

May he not receive his share of the benefits of this Yaga!" And then Daksha stormed out.

As time went past, the mutual dislike increased between Daksha and Siva.

And now it was about to explode! Daksha is conducting a Maha Yaga.

He has invited everyone, the Devas, Maharshis, guests are arriving in hordes.

The only two who have not received invitations are Siva and Sati. Daksha has deliberately not invited them because of his dislike for Siva.

True, Sati is his daughter but isn't she also Siva's wife? Neither Siva nor his wife need come!

Sati saw many Devis going for the Yaga along with their husbands. There was excitement in the air!

Am I the only one not going? Sati spoke to her husband, "Look how many people are going to participate in Father's Yaga. Do you know how much I want to go too? All my sisters would have arrived by now. How I want to see them! Father did not invite us. That is true. But we can still go without an invitation for he is Father after all. Please permit me to go."

Siva smiled at her. "Sati, there are some who see faults in others. They cannot see their own faults. You must not consider the homes of such people as your own and go to them. Injuries inflicted by arrows are nothing. But the pain caused by the harsh words of your own people is much, much worse. Daksha's love is for his other children. If you go, he will insult you because you are my wife. He is the one who has humiliated me. From now you have nothing to do with him. Do not go. And if you do go? Inauspicious things will happen."

Satidevi found herself in a very difficult situation, gripped by various emotions.

A strong desire to see and participate in Father's Yaga. Anger towards the husband who is preventing her from going. Immeasurable respect for her husband and so, deep discomfort in not acceding to his wishes.

Eventually, she left for Father's home.

Some of Siva's attendants accompanied her. And when she reached Father's house?

Satidevi realised that her husband was right. That she had made a monumental mistake. The father did not welcome his daughter.

Siva had also not been allocated his share of the Yaga. Satidevi was sad and angry.

"Father, does anyone other than you criticise and insult Bhagavan? Merely pronouncing the two words, Siva, is sufficient to cleanse all the sin of those who say it. Even Brahma's eyes cannot see the faults of Siva, only your eyes can. I am unfortunate to be born as your daughter. Because I am Daksha's daughter, I have now become Daakshayani. What if from now Bhagavan calls me Daakshayani? I will not be able to bear it. I do not want life any more. I hereby discard my body."

Satidevi sat down on the floor, embraced the path of Yoga and reduced her body to ash in the fire of Yoga.

After witnessing Satidevi discarding her body, Siva's attendants became furious. They attempted to disrupt DakshaYaga.

Daksha's Head Priest, Bhrigu Muni chanted holy mantras and lit the sacrificial fire.

From the fire rose Devas named Ribhus. They used glowing embers to chase away Siva's attendants. Daksha was saved but only temporarily.

Siva learnt of all that had happened from Narada. Enraged, he leapt up from his seat.

Laughed in a terrifying manner, threw down his matted hair, and instantly, there arose a frightening creature. A form that pushed against the sky. Hair like raging fire, three eyes like the burning sun. A garland of skulls, fangs jutting out of his mouth, many arms wielding weapons.

"Veerabhadra, you are a part of me. Go to the venue of Daksha's Yaga. Destroy Daksha and his Yaga," Siva ordered the creature.

Soon, Daksha and his entourage saw a sight to the North. A pillar of dust is coming close to them.

Strange!

No strong wind is blowing and neither are herds of cattle on the move. How can such a lot of dust be kicked up?

All doubts were cleared soon. Veerabhadra and his group had arrived! What mayhem unfolded after that!

Veerabahdra and his companions bounded forward, broke apart the venue of the Yaga, smashed the vessels used for the Yaga, extinguished the sacred fire of the Yaga, made the entire venue impure, tied up all the priests. Didn't Daksha insult Siva?

When Siva was being humiliated, three people had made big mistakes. Stroking his beard, Bhrigu Muni had shaken with mirth.

Bhaga Muni had gazed upon the scene with intense enjoyment and Pooshav had bared his teeth in hearty laughter.

Now, they were about to be punished for the mistake they made on that day.

Veerabhadra plucked out Bhrigu Muni's beard, gouged out Bhaga Muni's eyes and broke all of Pooshav's teeth.

From now, they dare not make fun of Siva! Other Maharshis fled in terror.

Veerabhadra pounced on Daksha. Strangled him and then, ripped his head from the body and flung it into the fire.

Set fire to the entire venue of the Yaga. And then returned to Kailas[91], the abode of Siva.

The Maharshis who had escaped went to Brahma with their tale of woe. Brahma said to them, "You too are wrongdoers. Why didn't you give Lord Siva his share of the Yaga? Go and seek forgiveness from Him. Bhagavan helps those who fall at his feet. Will He not show compassion?"

Thereafter, Siva showered his grace and said, "Daksha will live if a goat's head is attached to his body. Bhrigu will grow back his beard and moustache. Let the toothless Pooshav eat mashed food."

---

[91] Mount Kailash, standing at 6,638 meters (21,778 feet) in the Transhimalaya of Western Tibet, is revered in Hinduism as the earthly abode of Lord Siva. According to Hindu beliefs, Siva resides here with his consort Parvati and their children, Ganesha and Kartikeya. This sacred peak is often depicted as the centre of the world.

When the Devas attached a goat's head his body Daksha came alive. Daksha's mind was clear like a wound that has healed completely.

He tried to sing praises of Siva but just couldn't speak the words. His eyes were gushing tears.

Finally, with much difficulty he was able to say, "Bhagavan, I committed a terrible wrong. You meted out appropriate punishment to me. I only need your blessings from now."

After receiving Siva's grace, Daksha returned to his home and completed the Yaga.

That is when Lord MahaVishnu manifested and said, "There are people who see Me, Brahma, and Siva as different. They are ignorant. I create, maintain, and destroy the world. I take a different form for each of these roles. That is all. In reality, all three are The One."

After discarding her body, Sati was born a second time as Parvati, the daughter of Himavan,

Siva was her husband in her second life too.

And now, the story of Dhruva!

You will remember that Uttanapada and Priyavrata are Swaayambhu Manu's sons.

Uttanapada has two Queens, Suruchi and Suneeti. Uttama is the son of Suruchi and Dhruva is the son of Suneeti. Suruchi is Uttanapada's favourite.

One day, the true colours of that Queen became clear. Uttanapada was coddling Uttama in his lap, Suruchi was standing by his side.

The five-year-old Dhruva came into the room, he too wanted to climb up on to his father's lap. He ran up to the King.

Suruchi did not like that at all, she scolded the little boy. "Move aside. Do not climb up on his lap. Only my son has that right. You are not my son. Go and perform Tapas. Then be born as my son. Only then can you sit on Father's lap."

Cruellest of words!

Uttanapada was listening. He ought to have disciplined his Queen but didn't. Poor, poor Dhruva!

So very young, mind as tender as a flower. That mind was mortally wounded and the innocent heart, shattered. He ran away, sobbing. Went to his mother, his life giver and shared the hurt with her. Suneeti held him close to her bosom and sat him down in her lap. The son is wracked by sobs and so is the mother.

"O, my son, I am most ill-fated. Your father is ashamed that I'm his wife. This is the fruit of my Karma, what else can I say? You were born as my son, grew up drinking my breastmilk, that is the reason for your sorrow. What Suruchi said is true in a way. You must perform Tapas. Because only Lord MahaVishnu can end your sorrow," said Suneeti. Dhruva left the palace to perform Tapas.

Such a little child, what does he know? On the way, he met Narada Maharshi.

"Little child, you are going to perform Tapas by concentrating on Lord MahaVishnu, aren't you? That is not as easy as you think. It is difficult even for Maharshis. Return home. That is best," Narada said to the boy.

However, Dhruva did not turn back. He was resolute.

Narada Maharshi was pleased. "Alright, be that as it may. Go to the forest named Madhuvan on the banks of the river Kalindi. Sit there and perform Tapas," he said.

There are rules and methods for Tapas, Dhruva knew none of that. After all, isn't he such a little child?

Narada Maharshi imparted the appropriate guidance to Dhruva and then the Maharshi went to Uttanapada's capital city.

After Dhruva's departure Uttanapada was overcome with remorse. Where is my son now? Has something bad happened to him? No news at all about him!

The king is sad and worried.

"O King, why is your face dull? What has happened?" asked Narada Maharshi.

"Maharshi, I am without mercy. Dhruva went away because of me. I'm so worried, has he been eaten by wild animals?" Uttanapada answered sorrowfully.

Narada Maharshi reassured him. "Do not worry or be sad. Dhruva is under the protection of Ishvara. He will return before long and his fame and reputation will spread everywhere."

Meanwhile, Dhruva began his Tapas.

Every three days he would eat fruits, this would continue for a month. Then, every six days he would eat dry leaves and grass, that would continue for a month. Then, every twelve days his food would be just air for a month. Then, holding his breath he would perform Tapas standing on one leg for a month.

And for one more month, forgetting everything else, he was immersed in meditation.

Then, Lord MahaVishnu manifested and ordered him, "Dhruva, I am pleased with you. I will place you in a high position up there in a world of stars called Dhruvapada. But that will be later. For now, return home. Reign over your kingdom for many years. Always hold Me in your consciousness."

Uttanapada got the news that Dhruva is on his way back home. He left to welcome his son along with wives and relatives.

He found Dhruva without travelling too far. Father and Mother hugged him, kissed him on the head, turn by turn! And drenched him in their tears of joy. Did they not get back their little son?

Time passed, Uttanapada became old.

He made Dhruva the King and retired to the forest to perform Tapas. Uttama once went on a hunting trip; a Yaksha killed him.

Suruchi could not bear the sorrow, the Queen died of grief.

Dhruva, the great devotee was also a great warrior with infinite valour.

Brother has been murdered by a Yaksha[92]. Revenge has to be exacted from the entire Yaksha clan.

Dhruva marched his army to Yakshapuri[93], the abode of the Yakshas. The Yaksha army clashed against Dhruva's army.

---

[92] Yakshas are ancient nature-spirits or demi-gods in Indian mythology, primarily associated with wealth,

prosperity, and the natural world. They appear in Hindu, Buddhist, and Jain traditions, often depicted as either benevolent guardians or mischievous beings, depending on the context.

Key Characteristics:

1.Guardians of Nature: Yakshas are believed to be the protectors of forests, rivers, lakes, and treasures hidden in the earth.

2.Wealth & Prosperity: In Hindu mythology, they are closely associated with Kubera, the god of wealth. Yakshas are his attendants and guardians of his immense treasures.

3.Physical Appearance: They are often depicted as strong, stout beings, sometimes with supernatural or otherworldly features. While generally benevolent, some Yakshas are portrayed as fierce or mischievous spirits.

[93] Yakshapuri refers to the mythical or celestial abode of the Yakshas, the nature-spirits or guardians of wealth in Indian mythology. In various ancient texts,

What was the result of that clash?

The battlefield was covered by the dead bodies of Yakshas. Surviving Yakshas simply ran away.

Dhruva wisely did not enter Yakshapuri.

He knew that the Yakshas were masters of deception and illusion.

Suddenly a sound like the roar of the ocean could be heard. Swirling dust masked the sky. Blood and gore fell like rain. Snakes, elephants, lions, tigers, and all types of fierce animals appeared. Dhruva was unperturbed.

The great warrior unleashed the Narayana Astra[94].

Yakshapuri is often described as a mystical place rich in natural beauty, treasures, and supernatural charm.

Association with Kubera: Yakshapuri is sometimes equated with Alakapuri, the opulent city ruled by Kubera, the king of Yakshas and the God of wealth. Alakapuri is described in texts like the Mahabharata and Kalidasa's Meghaduta as a place filled with celestial gardens, golden palaces, and treasures beyond imagination.

[94] The Narayana Astra is a legendary and powerful celestial weapon in Hindu mythology, associated with Lord Vishnu (Narayana). It is described in the epic Mahabharata as one of the most formidable astras (weapons) ever created, capable of unleashing immense destruction.

Features and Power of Narayana Astra:

1.Unstoppable Force: Once invoked, the Narayana Astra releases countless fiery weapons and missiles, which target the enemy relentlessly.

2.Divine Protection: The Astra cannot be countered by any other weapon or power. The only way to survive its wrath is by surrendering to it completely, symbolizing surrender to Lord Vishnu.In the Mahabharata, Ashwatthama, the son of Dronacharya, invokes the Narayana Astra during the Kurukshetra war. It wreaks havoc on the Pandava army, but Lord Krishna advises the Pandavas to surrender and drop their weapons, thus saving them

The divine weapon destroyed the deception of the Yakshas, like Gyana (Knowledge of the Supreme Truth) dispels sorrow. The outcome?

Yakshas were being slaughtered again. Swaayambhu Manu descended from Swarga.

He asked Dhruva not to erase the lineage of the Yakshas. Acceding to Grandfather's wishes, Dhruva ceased the battle. "I am extremely pleased, O Dhruva. What boon can I grant you? Please tell me," The Yaksha King, Kubera, requested Dhruva.

"I want to be immersed in unshakeable Vishnu Bhakti forever." That was the boon Dhruva sought.

Kubera[95] granted it.

Dhruva came back to his capital. Dhruva's rule was filled with Dharma, compassion, and virtue. His reign extended - not for a hundred or thousand years but for thirty- six thousand years!

After that, the Vishnu devotee (Vishnu Bhakta) entrusted the kingdom to his son and embraced the forest to perform Tapas.

---

[95] Kubera – The God of Wealth In Indian mythology, Kubera (കുബേരൻ) is the god of wealth and the king of Yakshas, often depicted as the guardian of treasures and riches hidden within the earth and mountains. He is revered across Hinduism, Buddhism, and Jainism as a deity who brings prosperity and abundance.
Attributes of Kubera:
1.Lord of Wealth: Kubera is the custodian of all material wealth in the universe. Though he rules over wealth, he is not considered its creator—that role belongs to Lakshmi, the goddess of fortune.
2.King of Yakshas: Yakshas, the mystical beings of nature and wealth, serve Kubera as his attendants. He resides in Alakapuri, a splendid city said to be located near Mount Kailash.
3.Appearance: Kubera is traditionally depicted as a stout, short man with a potbelly, symbolizing abundance. He often carries a money bag or a pot of gold and rides a Pushpaka Vimana, a flying chariot

One day, an aircraft shining like the reflection of the moon landed near him.

Two Vishnudootas were in the aircraft, they had come to take him.

Dhruva's body was bathed in an aura like the radiance of gold. The great Vishnu Bhakta prepared to board the aircraft but then he realised that it is not right to leave without his mother. Mother will be heartbroken!

The Vishnudoota's pointed out another aircraft. Suneeti was already on board that aircraft!

The aircraft rose up into the sky with Dhruva aboard. It sped past the Moon and the Sun and the stars and headed towards Dhruva Loka.

Generations rolled on, one by one.

It was the time of the RajaRishi[96] Anga. Anga initiated the Ashwamedha Yaga. This Yaga has to be graced by the Devas. So, the priests invoked them.

Devas did not come. Haviss[97] is not defective.

Nothing is wrong with the chanting of Mantras. The austerities and vows have been perfect.

Devas have not been humiliated. Why then are they aloof?

---

[96] Raja Rishi – The Royal Sage. The term Raja Rishi is a combination of two Sanskrit words: Raja meaning king, and Rishi meaning sage or seer. Raja Rishi is a person who embodies the qualities of both a ruler and a sage—someone who possesses worldly authority and power while also living a life of wisdom, virtue, and spiritual discipline.

King Janaka, father of Sita Devi is a great example of a Raja Rishi. .V.K.Madhav Mohan

[xcvii] Offerings

[97] Offerings

Anga was perplexed and concerned.

"There is some problem with me. What is it?" He asked the leaders of his court.

"O King, there is nothing wrong with you in this birth. But in a previous birth there had been a problem because of that you have no son. Only if a son is present will the Devas too be present. Please surrender to Lord MahaVishnu and serve Him. You will then obtain the right results," the leader of the court answered.

Following that suggestion, Anga conducted a Homam[98].

From the Homa fire pit a divine being appeared and handed over a divine Payasam[99] to Anga.

The King gave it to his wife.

The Queen gave birth to a baby boy, he was named Vena.

Later, the King was forced to think that it would have been better had Vena not been born.

That's how cruel and mean Vena turned out to be.

Right from childhood he embraced the path of Adharma. He used to go into the forest and wantonly kill animals.

Deriving a special pleasure from killing.

---

[98] The word "Homam" refers to a Vedic ritual performed by offering various materials into a sacred fire while chanting mantras. It is believed to invoke divine blessings, purify the environment, and bring prosperity and well- being to participants.

[99] Payasam is a traditional South Indian dessert made with rice, vermicelli, or lentils cooked in milk or coconut milk, sweetened with jaggery or sugar, and flavored with cardamom, saffron, and garnished with fried cashews and raisins. It is an essential part of festive meals, temple offerings, and special occasions in South India.

As if that was not bad enough, he would beat up and kill his playmates and indulge in many other types of cruelty.

Children would run away in fear as soon as they spotted Vena.

Anga was extremely sad.

How much he had wanted a child, but the child he got was such a menace. The King tried to discipline Vena, but it was no use at all.

There was no reduction in the cruelty of the wicked boy. The King's despair worsened with time.

His thoughts raced in many directions.

In reality, aren't childless people virtuous?

Only if you have a child will you suffer this unbearable sorrow. Perhaps in a way it is good to have a wicked son.

The father will then be very dejected in life. He will find solace in Ishvara and will search for the path to Mukti. Anga made a decision.

At night when everyone was fast asleep, he acted on that decision. He rose slowly from his bed.

Quietly, he stepped outside.

No one ever saw him again!

There was no king to rule, the kingdom was orphaned.

Ministers, Maharshis, and relatives all met and held discussions. Vena is wicked but isn't he still a Prince?

It's better to have a wicked king than no king at all! They made him the King.

What happened to Vena who was cruel from birth when he was crowned as King?

It was a like a frenzied elephant breaking his chains. He went around committing Adharma at will.Inflicted violence on sages.

Visited countless cruelties on eminent people and implemented a new law banning Yagas, donations, and Homas! How much worse can it get?

The suffering of the subjects can well be imagined. On one side, robbers and dacoits and on the other, the wickedest possible King. Imagine a log of wood burning at both ends, that was the condition of the people.

The Maharshis were troubled. All of them together had made Vena the King.

Wasn't it like nurturing a snake by feeding it with milk? Can he be brought to the right path?

An attempt has to be made. If it works, good.

And if it doesn't, well, another way has to be found. So decided the Maharshis.

They imparted the right advice to Vena but then, he said, "You are all fools. You are prohibited from praying to Ishvara or paying tribute to him. You must now worship me. I am your Ishvara."

Is there a greater sin than this?

Not only are Maharshis being abused, Vena is insulting Ishvara! Vena could not be tolerated any more.

Maharshis destroyed him in the fire of their fury.

The wicked one got his punishment. But there was a problem.

The royal lineage suffered a break. That problem has to be solved.

The Maharshis rubbed the dead Vena's thighs. A creature emerged.

A dark creature with short limbs, prominent jaw, flat nose, bloodshot eyes and brown hair. Maharshis called him Nishada.

His lineage continues.

Maharshis rubbed and massaged both hands of Vena. From one hand a divine man emerged and from the other, a divine lady. The man's name was Prithu, the lady's name was Archiss.

Prithu is a part of Lord MahaVishnu and Archiss is a part of Lakshmi Devi[100].

They became husband and wife, as they should. Prithu's greatness became evident quickly.

Royal palaces employ people to sing the King's praises[101]. They were known as Stutipathakas.

Their job is to extol the King's virtues.

Prithu's palace also employed such Stutipathakas. When they sang his praises do you know what he said? "I am not worthy of praise. I'm just a simple, ordinary person. I'm ashamed and embarrassed when my praises are sung. What you are uttering is mere flattery."

---

[100] Lakshmi Devi is the Hindu goddess of wealth, prosperity (both material and spiritual), fertility, and fortune. She is the consort of Lord Vishnu, and together they symbolize abundance and preservation. Lakshmi is often depicted sitting or standing on a lotus flower, with gold coins flowing from her hand, symbolizing generosity and prosperity.

[101] Stutipathaka.. people employed by kings to sing praises were known by various names in ancient Indian culture, depending on the region and context (Stutipathaka, Charana, Magadha, Suta and Bhata). These individuals were tasked with reciting or singing eulogies (stutis) extolling the king's virtues, victories, and lineage. They often accompanied the king during important events, ceremonies, and battles.

Prithu was blessed with humility that is why he felt that praises were flattery.

Actually, they were not flattery. The Stutipathakas were speaking the truth.

Prithu was a King endowed with every great quality. Yet, a huge difficulty arose.

People were desperately searching for something to eat, the earth was not yielding food.

A fire in the hollow of the trunk burns down the entire tree.

In the same way, the fire of hunger was consuming the entire population. They begged the King, "We are starving. Please help us. Give us food."

What is the reason for this unfortunate state of affairs? Prithu understood.

Bhoomi Devi[102], food!

He was furious.

The Goddess of Earth, was deliberately withholding. He bent his bow and fixed an arrow.

---

[102] Bhoomi Devi – The Goddess of Earth, Bhoomi Devi (also spelled Bhudevi or Bhu Devi) is revered in Hinduism as the personification of the Earth and is considered a mother goddess. She symbolizes fertility, abundance, and sustenance, as the earth provides all living beings with food, shelter, and life. Bhoomi Devi represents the divine balance between preservation and nature. Bhoomi Devi is one of Lord Vishnu's consorts, alongside Lakshmi Devi. While Lakshmi represents wealth and prosperity, Bhoomi Devi represents the earth's fertility and nourishment. In some depictions, she is portrayed seated beside Vishnu or at his feet, edited by V.K.Madhav Mohan

Bhoomi Devi was overcome with fear. She took the form of a cow and ran away. Prithu chased after her. Bhoomi Devi fled for her life in all four directions, to Swarga, into the sky.

Prithu followed her everywhere, relentlessly.

Eventually, Bhoomi Devi was exhausted and stopped running. She pleaded with Prithu,

"O King, protect me! I'm a woman. Killing women is not Dharma. In addition, all creatures live in me. If I die, every creature will also vanish."

But the King was unmoved. In anger he said, "I will certainly kill you. You are not providing any food to my subjects. You're hoarding everything within you, aren't you? I will shatter your pride and kill you now. And, with my Yogic power I will protect my subjects."

Bhoomi Devi replied, "The land is overrun with robbers and dacoits. They are ruining everything. But I have kept food, medicines and all necessities safely in my custody. I have been waiting for a great King. I will gladly provide you with everything that you need. As they say, to drink you need a pot and also the person who can lift it. I will pour out everything needed willingly."

After saying this, Bhoomi Devi, the cow, got ready to be milked.

Every category selected its most eminent member to take what is needed.

Human beings selected Manu and took grains. The Rishis sent Brihaspati and took the Shruti[103]. Creatures with venom nominated

---

[103] "Shruti" refers to the sacred texts or scriptures of Hinduism that were heard or revealed by sages, such as the Vedas and Upanishads. These are

Takshaka[104] to receive all the venom. Mountains chose Himavan to accept minerals and metals.

Many categories were enriched by many things.

Prithu was then overcome with fatherly affection for Bhoomi. That is how she came to be known as Prithvi, daughter of Prithu. Prithu thereafter levelled many mountains, built many villages and towns, cultivated many farmlands. He did many useful deeds. He created abundance, wealth, and happiness everywhere!

The great King prepared to conduct Ashwamedha Yagas, not one but a hundred Ashwamedhas!

Even one is difficult so how about a hundred Ashwamedha Yagas? However, many came forward to help.

Bhoomi Devi provided all the necessary materials. Rivers made curds, milk, and ghee flow in abundance. Trees produced juicy fruits; oceans presented gems. Rulers and chieftains delivered valuable commodities. Everyone had so much affection and respect for Prithu!

The Yagas were conducted auspiciously, smoothly, and according to the proper procedures.

Ninety-nine Yagas were completed.

It was when the one hundredth Yaga commenced that the jealousy of one person was exposed.

Not just jealousy but fear too.

---

considered divinely inspired and transmitted orally for generations before being written down.

[104] Takshaka is a famous Naga king mentioned in various ancient texts like the Mahabharata and the Puranas. He is known as the serpent who bit King Parikshit, leading to his death and triggering the narrative of the Bhagavata Purana.

What happens if Prithu completes ahundred Ashwamedhas successfully?

He will become greater than me, realised Devendra! So, the hundredth Yaga had to be disrupted at all costs. So, what did Devendra do?

Disguised himself as a Sanyasi, went to the venue of the Yaga and stole the Yaga horse. And on the sly, disappeared into the sky. Devendra assumed no one had seen him but Atri Maharshi had spotted him.

He informed Prithu's son about what had happened.

The Prince raced after the thief and caught hold of him, that's when he saw that the thief is a Sanyasi. Killing a Sanyasi is a sin.

So, the Prince returned home.

It was only then that Atri Maharshi told him that the Sanyasi is fake, that he was Devendra in disguise.

Then too the Prince was able to retrieve the Yaga horse after Devendra vanished again.

Since he was able to bring back the horse, the Prince became known as Vijitashwa, One Who Won The Horse.

Devendra attempted to steal the Yaga horse yet again. Then too, Vijitashwa won the horse back.

But this time Atri Maharshi insisted that Devendra had to be killed. Vijitashwa readied his bow, yet again Devendra vanished!

Prithu decided that it was high time to kill Devendra. He took up his bow and arrows but the priests stopped him.

A King who has initiated the Yaga cannot go to war. He must invoke the power of mantras.

To bring Devendra by force and offer him into the sacrificial fire, the priests commenced the Homa for this.

Brahma manifested. "It is not possible to kill Devendra. Prithu has completed ninety-nine Ashwamedha Yagas. That is sufficient. It is true that if a hundred are completed he will obtain Indrapada[105]. But even without that Prithu will attain Moksha," Brahma let it be known.

Lord MahaVishnu also manifested. Devendra accompanied Him.

"Devendra has come to seek forgiveness. Pardon him for his wrongdoing," Lord MahaVishnu said. It was Bhagavan's order!

Prithu dropped his animosity towards Devendra and embraced him. Lord MahaVishnu had arrived to grant boons to Prithu.

Bhagavan stood with his arms around Garuda.

Prithu couldn't get enough of this vision of the Lord Himself. He was lost in the wondrous sight.

Bhakti filled his eyes with hot tears. With deep emotion he said, "O Lord, I do not need any boon. I only want Bhakti."

"You have conquered my Maya, the illusions that I create. May your Bhakti for me increase every single day," Lord MahaVishnu showered blessings.

---

[105] Indrapada" can be interpreted as:

1.The position or status of Indra – Symbolizing a state of supreme power, authority, or leadership among the gods.

2.Heavenly abode – Since Indra resides in Swarga (heaven), "Indrapada" is sometimes used to denote a state of bliss or heaven itself.

Prithu is like Bhoomi Devi as far as patience and forgiveness are concerned.

Like the mountain Maha Meru[106] in his constancy and resolve. Like Kubera in wealth.

Like Yama in his ability to teach.

Like the Veda Guru in his knowledge.

The Mahatma, the great soul, Prithu, was endowed with so many qualities.

In reality, only Prithu could equal Prithu! Prithu's rule extended for a long time.

When old age arrived, he went into the forest for Tapas. What was his diet?

Fruits and roots during the first stage. Then, dried leaves in the next stage.

Just water after that. Finally, only air.

In the midst of Homa fires during summer, in pouring rain during the rainy season, neck deep in water during winter, he performed Tapas standing in this manner. Queen Archiss was constantly at his side.

---

[106] "Maha Meru Mountain" refers to Mount Meru, a prominent and sacred mountain in Hindu, Jain, and Buddhist cosmology. Known as "Sumeru" in some traditions, Mount Meru holds immense spiritual, mythological, and symbolic significance across various Indian cultures, including those in Kerala where Malayalam is spoken. Considered the axis mundi (the centre of the universe) in Hindu, Jain, and Buddhist cosmologies, Mount Meru is envisioned as the spiritual and physical centre of all cosmic realms, edited by V.K.Madhav Mohan

She had taken the vow to care for and look after her husband. One day the Queen saw that life had left Prithu.

He had attained Moksha.

The Queen was the ultimate Pativrata[107]. She arranged the ceremonial pyre, placed her husband's body in it, went to the river and bathed.

Bowed to the Devas with Bhakti, touched her husband's feet with reverence, jumped into the fire of cremation and attained Moksha.

Many generations passed thereafter. It was the time of the King named Prachinabarhis.

---

[107] Pativrata is a Sanskrit-derived term widely used in Malayalam and other Indian languages. It is a compound
word formed by:
•"Pati" meaning "husband"
•"Vrata" meaning "vow", "pledge", or "austerity."Pativrata translates to "a woman who is devoted to her husband". The term embodies the ideals of marital fidelity, loyalty, and unwavering commitment that a wife maintains towards her husband within the cultural and social frameworks of Hindu society. While the traditional concept of Pativrata emphasizes a woman's devotion and sacrifice for her husband, modern interpretations have evolved to balance these virtues with individual autonomy and equality. In contemporary society:
•Mutual Respect: The emphasis is on mutual respect, support, and partnership between spouses rather than one-sided devotion.
•Empowerment: Women are encouraged to maintain their individuality, pursue personal goals, and contribute equally to the relationship.
•Shared Responsibilities: The roles within the marriage are viewed as shared responsibilities, promoting equality and collaboration.
"Pativrata" is a multifaceted concept that has evolved over time. While it traditionally signifies a woman's unwavering devotion and loyalty to her husband, contemporary interpretations seek a balanced and equitable approach to marital relationships. Understanding Pativrata involves appreciating its historical roots, literary representations, and its dynamic role in shaping and reflecting societal values in Malayalam and broader Indian culture, edited by V.K.Madhav Mohan

Narada Maharshi imparted Gyanopadesa[108] to the King.

It was in the form of a story.

The story contained many truths and principles.

Once upon a time there was a King named Puranjana. He had a friend.

What was the friend's name and what were his activities? No one knew!

I need a good town to live in comfortably and permanently. Puranjana looked far and wide for such a town.

He didn't like any town he came across. Finally, he selected a town.

It was on the southern slopes of the Himalayas and had nine gates.

Surrounding walls, festive decorations, palatial houses, gardens - the town had it all.

What a beautiful town!

A most beautiful young lady was the owner. She had many female companions and attendants, and also a huge five-headed serpent.

The serpent's job was to guard the town. Puranjana married the beautiful lady.

He settled down to live in the town.

---

[108] When combined, "Gyanopadesa" translates to "Instruction on Knowledge," "Teachings of Wisdom," or "Guidance in Understanding." It embodies the concept of imparting wisdom, offering insightful advice, and providing educational directives aimed at enhancing one's knowledge and spiritual growth.

Comfort was his first aim right from the beginning!

When he found comfort, he was intoxicated with it and forgot everything else. But comfort is bound to end and sorrow will take its place, that is the human condition.

Puranjana became old, that is when he experienced this. An enemy attacked the kingdom.

That enemy was not a man but a woman – Durbhaga, Daughter of Kaala (Yama).

She was leading the army of a Yavana[109] King named Bhaya. Do you know what that army did?

They entered the town from all the nine gates.

Then, they plundered and murdered their way around the town. Puranjana was sad and helpless, he had no strength left.

Couldn't resist the enemy and there was no one to help. What could he do?

There! Yet another danger!

Bhaya's brother Prajvara, set fire to the town!

The five-headed serpent guarding the town prepared to leave like a snake in a tree trunk thinks of running away when the tree is on fire, thought Puranjana.

Then his thoughts turned towards his wife and children. What will be their condition without him?

---

[109] The term "Yavana" is an ancient Sanskrit word that originally referred to Greeks and later came to denote various foreigners, particularly those from the West, such as Romans and other Mediterranean peoples.

When a ship breaks apart, the passengers will jump into the sea, swim until exhaustion and then drown; thinking in this manner Puranjana's mind was deeply wounded

Suddenly, the Yavanas pounced on him, tied him up, and took him away like a cow tied with a rope and led away.

Remember the nameless friend?

He was still with Puranjana, but Puranjana had forgotten him.

His thoughts had only been about his own wife and children. Puranjana died heartbroken.

The King was born again, not as a man but as a woman.

As the daughter of the King of Vidarbha, she became the wife of Malayadhwaja, the King of the Pandya region. And also became the mother of eight children.

When Malayadhwaja become old, he partitioned the Kingdom amongst his children and thereafter went into the forest to perform Tapas.

The wife followed her husband. Tapas continued for a long time. And then what happened one day?

Malayadhwaja was not shaking or moving, like a log of wood.

The wife rubbed her husband's feet, the feet were cold.

Her husband was lifeless!

She prepared the cremation pyre and placed the body on it. Lit the fire.

Was about to jump into the fire when a Tapasvi appeared. "You don't remember me, isn't it? Let me help you remember. In the past you were Puranjana. You had a nameless friend then. I am that friend. At that time, you had forgotten me. All you wanted was comfort and enjoyment. You committed many sins. This sorrow you feel now is the result of all that you did in that life. Actually, you and I are not separate, we are one," said the Tapasvi.

And then he went on to impart Tatvopedasa[110].

Gyana dawned in her consciousness, all grief was erased.

This was the story that Narada narrated to Prachinabarhis.

"Maharshi, there are many hidden meanings in this story. Please explain them clearly to me," Prachinabarhis requested. Yes, there are concealed meanings in the story.

What are they?

Narada revealed them all. "Puranjana is actually Jiva or Soul. And the nameless friend? None other than Ishvara, Himself! The five-headed serpent is the life force, Prana. The town with nine gates is the human body. The daughter of Kaala (Yama), Durbhaga is old age. The Yavana King is death. His soldiers are the various ailments and diseases, mental and physical. Results are based on Karma. The one who gathers more virtue will live in the heavens and the one who commits more sin will become a bird or animal. One whose virtue and sin are equal is born as a human being. Sins are destroyed by Bhakti, that is worship of Ishvara. Therefore, worship Lord MahaVishnu[111]!" Prachinabarhis followed this advice.

---

[110] Tatvopadesa refers to teaching or instruction about fundamental truths or principles. It often denotes
philosophical or spiritual teachings that guide individuals toward understanding the deeper essence of life, reality, or existence.

[111] Tatvopadesa refers to teaching or instruction about fundamental truths or principles. It often denotes
philosophical or spiritual teachings that guide individuals toward understanding the deeper essence of life, reality, or existence.

Handed over his Kingdom to his sons, went to Kapila Ashrama performed Tapas and earned Moksha. Prachinabarhis had ten children.

They were collectively known as Prachetas[112]. All were devout and steeped in Bhakti. They embarked on a journey to perform Tapas.

On the way, they came upon a large, beautiful lake. Music wafted in from the lake, a divine form with a golden radiance rose from it. Lord Siva Himself!

Bhagavan taught Vishnu Stotram[113] to the Prachetas.

While chanting this Stotram the Prachetas commenced their Tapas in water.

The Tapas lasted ten thousand years! Then, Lord MahaVishnu manifested. "Prachetas, there is young lady named Maarisha. Her father is a Maharshi and mother is a Devi. Her mother abandoned her. The little child was brought up by the trees. The King of Trees, Chandra, pressed his index finger to her mouth. Amruta

---

[112] Prachetas refers to a group of ten legendary sages who were sons of King Prachinabarhis. They are significant figures in ancient Indian scriptures, particularly in the Bhagavata Purana. The ten Prachetas meditated under the ocean for 10,000 years to please Lord Vishnu and were eventually blessed by him. The term can be interpreted as "one who is conscious, wise, or enlightened", derived from the root "Chetas" meaning consciousness or awareness, edited by V.K.Madhav Mohan

[113] The Vishnu Stotram taught by Lord Siva to the Prachetas is known as the Rudra Geeta or Siva-taught Vishnu Stuti, which appears in the Srimad Bhagavatam (Canto 4, Chapter 24). This stotram is a powerful hymn in praise of Lord Vishnu, taught by Lord Siva to the ten Prachetas (sons of King Prachinabarhis) to help them achieve success in their penance and devotion. The stotram emphasizes devotion, the glory of Lord Vishnu, and the ultimate unity of Lord Siva and Lord Vishnu. This stotram highlights that even Lord Siva, who is considered one of the highest deities, worships Lord Vishnu and considers Him the supreme being. Reciting this stotram is believed to bring spiritual advancement, peace, and liberation, edited by V.K.Madhav Mohan

flowed down the finger. Maarisha grew up drinking that Amruta. You must marry her. She will give birth to a son who is equivalent to Brahma. You must live for a long time on earth. Afterthatyouwill unitewithme,"sosayingLordMahaVishnu disappeared.

Prachetas came out of the water. They looked at the trees in anger. Fire leapt out of that look and engulfed the trees.

The entire tree species seemed to be in danger of destruction. Brahma manifested, calmed the Prachetas down.

The trees gave up Maarisha to them.

They married her and a radiant son was born! Prachetas lived for a long time on earth.

Afterwards, they earned Moksha, as blessed by Lord MahaVishnu. These stories are all part of Uttanapada's lineage.

It is now time to tell the story of Priyavrata's lineage. Let us go back in time to Priyavrata's youth.

Have to perform Tapas and achieve Moksha that was Priyavrata's desire. However, he was nominated to rule the earth by his father Swaayambhu Manu.

But Priyavrata had no interest in accepting the responsibilities of a King. What happens if I become a King?

I'll have plenty of fame and wealth, will wallow in comfort and luxury. I'll forget Bhagavan.

Oh, I must not do that!

"Priyavrata, first you will have to reign. Tapas can come after that," was the direction given by Brahma.

How can he not obey Brahma?

Priyavrata took over the reins of the Kingdom. Married, had sons and one daughter.

That was Urjaswati, wife of Shukra Maharshi and mother of Devayani[114]. Three of the sons were interested in Tapas right from their childhood. They became Sanyasis and left home and country.

Priyavrata lived with the remaining seven sons.

He suppressed Adharma.

Establishing Dharma everywhere, he ruled with righteousness. Mounted on his chariot, he travelled around the earth seven times.

Since his heavy chariot rolled on the earth, it created seven deep craters. These craters became the seven seas.

Seven islands were also created.

Priyavrata made each of his seven sons the ruler of these seven seas.

After that he gave up his country, family, and a life of comfort and entered the forest to perform Tapas.

Naabhi was one of Priyavrata's grandsons. Merudevi was Naabhi's wife. They had no children.

Do you know how desperately they wanted children?

Of course, everyone knows that Lord MahaVishnu fulfils all desires. So, husband and wife prayed to Bhagavan.

We want a son like Lord MahaVishnu! That was the aim of their prayer. And it was achieved.

A son named Rishabha was born.

---

[114] The story of Devayani is told in MaliBharatam.

He was a partial manifestation of Lord MahaVishnu. Naabhi made Rishabha the King and departed for Tapas. Along with him went Merudevi too.

Rishabha, the great Gyani[115] conducted one hundred Yagas. His reign was filled with virtue.

Dharma was everywhere in the Kingdom. The subjects loved each other.

No one troubled anyone else. Everyone was happy and contented! Rishabha had a hundred sons.

He imparted Dharmopadesa[116] to them and that too, in front of a very large audience. It was a great boon for everyone.

They all learnt so many things!

Rishabha was an Avadhuta[117] and so he left the country.

Ignorant people will only think of an Avadhuta as a madman. Hair is disheveled and unkempt.

Entire body is dirty and dusty.

Will be silent if anyone enquires of him or speaks to him. Sometimes eats or drinks anything.

---

[115] Gyani refers to a learned person, wise individual, or someone who possesses extensive knowledge. The term is derived from the Sanskrit word "ज्ञानी" (Jñānī), which carries a similar meaning. which also includes spirit Knowledge, edited by V.K.Madhav Mohan

[116] Dharmopadesa refers to teachings or instructions that guide individuals on how to live a morally upright and ethically sound life.

[117] An Avadhuta is regarded as a siddha (one who has attained perfection) and a jivanmukta (liberated while still living). They have achieved a state of self-realization and union with the divine.

At other times he will not eat or drink anything. Some hurled abuse and improprieties at him, some beat him.

Some threw stones, some spat in his face.

No matter what they did Rishabha had no anger. The trouble was only for the body, but what is the importance of the body? His Atma[118] was united with Ishvara.

How could anyone else realise the bliss of that state? Rishabha wandered all over the land.

Eventually he came upon a bamboo forest.

The dry bamboos rubbed against each other and caught fire.

The fire grew into a raging forest fire. He gave up his body in that forest fire. Rishabha's eldest son was Bharata.

He ruled the Kingdom for ten thousand years. After that, he arrived in the forest for Tapas.

This is the beginning of that story.

Bharata was doing his evening prayers in the river near his Ashrama. A pregnant doe came to drink water.

Suddenly, the roar of a lion shattered the stillness.

The doe jumped into the river in panic and swam away. In the middle of the river, she began to give birth.

Somehow, she reached the far bank.

The poor doe died of fear and exhaustion and the helpless newborn fawn was being swept away by river. Watching the entire scene, Bharata's heart melted with compassion. He rescued the infant and brought it ashore.

---

[118] Soul…V.K.Madhav Mohan

For some unknown reason Bharata developed an intense affection for the fawn.

He just couldn't be away from it for a moment.

He'd take it along to the garden to pluck flowers and Darbha[119] grass. The fawn would prance about without a care.

Sometimes he would carry it across his shoulders and sometimes he would fondle it on his chest or lap.

If he didn't see it for a short while Bharata would become very fearful. Isn't this a baby without a mother?

Did a wolf or leopard kill and eat it?

He would search everywhere frantically.

Only when he found the fawn would he be relieved.

Even while doing Puja[120] he would not forget it.

He would pause the Puja to check on it.

Occasionally he would sit with his eyes closed and pretend to be in prayer.

The fawn would nudge him with its antlers.

When he scolded it, the fawn would stop playing and sit still.

Bharata's thoughts were only about it. He was obsessed with the fawn!

---

[119] Darbha" (दरभ) in Sanskrit refers to "grass," particularly the sacred grass used in various Hindu rituals and ceremonies, edited by V.K.Madhav Mohan

[120] It refers to the act of worship, offering, or ritualistic reverence performed to honour deities, seek blessings, and express devotion, edited by V.K.Madhav Mohan

What was the result of that? Tapas was interrupted, focus on Ishvara reduced. Strange indeed!

Doesn't a snake catch a rat?

In the same way, death catches human beings. Bharata's death also arrived.

Even at the moment of death his thoughts were on the fawn. He died with his eyes fixed on it.

He was born again, as a deer.

The previous life was fresh in his memory. That was because of his prayers to Ishvara.

The deer that was Bharata or Bharata that was the deer, kept thinking about the previous birth and was deeply saddened.

He had been in the forest for Tapas.

Instead of uniting with Ishvara, his mind had united with the fawn.

What a tragedy!

He felt a terrible sense of remorse. What did he do?

Left the doe, his mother, and took refuge in a temple. There he spent all his time in prayer to Bhagavan.

Eventually, he drowned in a body of water and gave up his animal body. There lived a Brahmin scholar.

He had two wives. The first wife had nine sons. The second wife had one son and one daughter. Bharata had been reborn as that son.

He pretended to be hard of hearing and poor of intellect!

At the same time, within himself, he was always performing Puja to Bhagavan.

The Brahmin decided to teach his son the Vedas. Seeing that the boy could not learn, he was dejected. Actually, that was not the case.

In his previous birth, Bharata had worshipped Ishvara so very much.

As a result of that he knew everything and it was all in his memory and consciousness.

He just did not exhibit it, that's all. The Brahmin attained heaven.

His second wife, Bharata's mother, also ended her life.

The first wife's children mistreated him and treated him like a sluggish fool.

Bharata did menial work but would not ask for wages.

If he received wages he would accept and if he didn't, would go hungry. Some would force him to work.

Whatever the circumstance, it was all the same to Bharata. Neither was he satisfied nor unsatisfied.

Heat and cold, wind and rain, all were the same to him. Sometimes he would not bathe and would wear torn, old clothes. His heart was full of Ishvara.

Every moment he experienced supreme bliss. But no one else ever knew!

His brothers made him guard their farmlands.

There was a prominent member of the Sudra[121] community. He had no children.

He believed that by pleasing Goddess Bhadrakali[122] he would get a son and that Bhadrakali would be pleased by a human sacrifice.

His servants caught hold of a man and led him into the enclosure for the sacrifice.

Suddenly, the man broke his bonds and fled.

The servants went in search of the one who escaped. They stumbled through a pitch-dark night.

By chance they saw Bharata, a tall well-built man!

Much better for the sacrifice than the one who escaped!

They tied Bharata with a rope and took him to the venue of the sacrifice. The master's priest was satisfied.

He bathed Bharata, dressed him up in new clothes, applied sandalwood paste and Kumkum[123] on him. Fed him sweets.

---

[121] The term Shudra refers to one of the four varnas (social classes) in the traditional Varna system of ancient India, as described in Hindu scriptures like the Manusmriti and the Vedas. The Shudras were traditionally designated as the working class, primarily involved in serving the other varnas (Brahmins, Kshatriyas, and Vaishyas) through manual labour and service-oriented professions. They were considered the backbone of society, performing essential tasks such as agriculture, craftsmanship, trade support, and other forms of labour, as edited by V.K.Madhav Mohan

[122] Bhadrakali is a revered Hindu goddess, particularly prominent in the southern Indian state of Kerala. She is considered a fierce and protective form of the Divine Mother, embodying both the nurturing and destructive aspects of the feminine divine. Bhadrakali holds significant cultural, religious, and mythological importance in Kerala and other parts of South India.

[123] A vermillion /red-colored powder made primarily from turmeric and slaked lime. In modern times, synthetic dyes are also used to produce kumkum.

Made him stand in front of the idol of the Goddess. Chanted the Kali mantras.

Took the sword and swung.

Only a moment was needed for Bharata's head to be severed! Just in a moment, the entire atmosphere changed.

Goddess Bhadrakali leapt out of the idol. Bared her terrible fangs, blood red eyes bulged out, revealed her terrifying nature.

She jumped at the priest and grabbed the swinging sword. Severed his head and those of his henchmen.

Tossed and played with them like balls.

Scooped up the blood and drank it!

When facing the danger Bharat wasn't scared. And when the danger passed, he wasn't happy. The Maha Yogi was neither depressed nor elated. Rahugana was a King.

He was once on the way to Kapila Ashrama, travelling in a palanquin[124]. In his path stood a tall, well-built man, Bharata.

The King's attendants thought he was ideally suited to be a palanquin bearer.

They caught hold of him and gave him the job.

Bharata shouldered the pole and commenced walking but he walked very slowly and carefully.

Kumkum is commonly applied on the forehead as a tilak during prayers, temple visits, and religious ceremonies. It symbolizes auspiciousness and is believed to protect against negative energies, as edited by V.K.Madhav Mohan

[124] Called a Palki or Pallak…It is a covered litter, typically designed for one passenger, and carried by porters on their shoulders using pole.. Historically used by royalty, nobility, and religious figures for travel or ceremonial purposes, as edited by V.K.Madhav Mohan

There was a reason for that.

There were ants, worms and many other living creatures on the path. Will they not be crushed underfoot?

That was Bharata's concern.

No living being should be killed!

"Why has the Pallak slowed down" Rahugana wanted to know.

"Lord, we are walking fast. But this huge fellow is very slow. He is strong but is deliberately walking slowly," the Pallak bearers complained.

The King looked closely at Bharata. He has a lot of height and heft, and matching strength.

Not only that, he is young too.

"Your situation is sad. Your body has become thin. You don't have any strength. On top of that you are old. For so long you've been carrying this Pallak alone. I feel pity for you," the King taunted him with sarcasm.

Bharata did not utter a word neither did he speed up.

The King became angry. "Oh, you're trying to ignore and insult me, are you? Alright. I will give you the right treatment."

Bharata spoke up, "O King, you said sarcastically that I am big and strong. Fat and thin applies only to the body. Not for the Atma. You are a King and I'm a servant. But that difference is only the way of the world. Your treatment will not work on me."

The Maha Yogi continued to speak without interruption for a long time about so very many great truths and principles! Rahugana was astonished.

It dawned on him that this was not a porter. "He is a Mahatma! Did I not unknowingly scorn him?"

The King stepped down from the Pallak, fell at Bharata's feet and sought forgiveness.

Bharata imparted Gyanopadesa to Rahugana.

That teaching benefited not just Rahugana but the entire world.

Even today it is studied by those who desire to increase their knowledge. Bhakti has the Shakti (power) to provide Mukti even to sinners.

There are many stories that illustrate the Shakti of Bhakti.

One of them is the story of Ajamila. He used to live in Kanyakubja, was born as a Brahmin[125]. Married a Dasi[126], had ten sons.

Brahmins ought to do Japa[127], Tapa and other pious things.

Ajamila had the tendencies of a Brahmin within him but did not do any Japa or Tapa.

But he did things which he ought not to do - lying, cheating, gambling, and many similar things.

A life filled with sin.

He continued living in this way for a long time. For eighty-eight years.

Narayana was his youngest son.

---

[125] Priest…V.K.Madhav Mohan

[126] In Sanskrit and several Indian languages, Dasi translates to "servant" or "maid." It was often used to refer to women who served in households, temples, or royal courts, as edited by V.K.Madhav Mohan

[127] Japa (Sanskrit: जप) refers to the continuous repetition of a mantra, divine name, or spiritual phrase. It can be performed silently or audibly, as edited by V.K.Madhav Mohan

How much affection did the father have for Narayana? He needed Narayana always around him.

The old man would eat only after feeding Narayana. He found happiness in tenderly holding him.

Finally, that day arrived - the day he was to die.

Three servants of Kaala arrived with a rope in their hands. Ajamila's entire strength was drained away by terror!

Kaala's servants will capture me, tie me up with the rope and drag me away.

Even at that moment, Ajamila's thoughts were fixed on his youngest son. With deep pain he called out long and loud, "Narayanaaa!!"

The call had hardly left his throat when Vishnu Dootas appeared. They prevented Kaala's servants from dragging Ajamila away. "This fellow has been committing many sins for a long time. He must be awarded punishment for those sins. We must take him away with us. Preventing us from doing this is not right," said Kaala's servants.

"It is true that Ajamila has committed sins. However, he has cried out 'Narayana', at the time of his death. That is Lord MahaVishnu's holy name. That call has erased all his sins," said the Vishnu Dootas while untying him.

Gratitude expanded in Ajamila's heart.

He bowed his in reverence to the Vishnu Dootas then he tried to say something.

Before he could say it, he vanished. How hot is the fire of remorse!

His consciousness was singed by the heat. How wicked he had been!

He ought to plunge headlong into hell, Naraka[128].

But four syllables rescued him, Na Ra Ya Na, Lord MahaVishnu's Holy Name!

Just see the power of the Holy Name! Even Death is held at bay by it.

"Never again will I forget Bhagavan. He alone is my refuge," Ajamila decided. He cast aside his wife and children, left home, arrived in Haridwar.

Spent his time meditating on Bhagavan and then, he saw Vishnu Dotaas again. Gave up his body in the River Ganges[129], accepted the form of a Vishnu Dotaa.

Boarded the golden aircraft and reached Vaikuntha.

By now you must have understood the greatness of Vishnu Bhakti! As further proof, let me tell you another story.

An elephant is one of the characters in that story.

Trikoodam is a mountain situated in an island in the

Palazhi[130] Sea.

---

[128] In Hinduism, Naraka is ruled by Yama, the god of death and justice, who judges souls and determines their fate. There are various descriptions of different levels or types of Naraka, each designed to punish specific sins.

[129] The Ganges is a trans-boundary river of Asia which flows through India and Bangladesh

[130] Refers to the "Ocean of Milk" in Hindu mythology. It is a significant concept in the Samudra Manthana (Churning of the Ocean) episode from Indian scriptures such as the Bhagavata Purana, Vishnu Purana, and the Mahabharata, as edited by VK Madhav Mohan

It has three peaks.One peak is pure gold, another is silver, and the third is iron.

A garden spans the valley of Trikoodam, within it lies a vast lake. Countless lotuses are in bloom in the lake. It is home to many aquatic creatures. A dense foliage of trees and creepers surround it.Swans, Chakravakam[131] (Brahminy Ducks) and numberless other birds abound.

What an enchanting place!

One day a herd of elephants came to the lake to drink water. The herd had a leader, he was the strongest of the strong. He was so mighty that lions and tigers would flee in terror when they saw him. That was how powerful, huge, and courageous he was.

How much the lead elephant and his friends enjoyed themselves! They lowered their trunks and drank deeply from the clear water. Then they splashed each other and frolicked in the water.

Blissfully unaware of the impeding danger!

---

[131] Chakravakam (Malayalam refers to the Brahminy duck (scientific name: Tadorna ferruginea), a bird

mentioned in Indian literature and often symbolized in art and poetry. It holds cultural and poetic significance, especially in Sanskrit and regional Indian literary traditions. The Brahminy Duck has a striking orange-brown plumage with lighter underparts and black-tipped wings. Commonly found near lakes, rivers, and wetlands in India. Known for its migratory behavior, traveling to warmer regions during winter. It is medium-sized and often seen in pairs. In classical Indian literature, Chakravakam birds are often depicted as a symbol of love and devotion because they are believed to form lifelong pairs. Poets frequently use them to represent longing and separation, as it is a common belief that the male and female birds cry when separated at night. In Sanskrit and Malayalam poetry, the term "Chakravakam" is associated with love, fidelity, and the pain of separation (viraha). In Indian Carnatic music, Chakravakam is also the name of a raga, which evokes feelings of deep emotion and devotion, as edited by VK Madhav Mohan

Under the water lurked a terrifying crocodile. He caught hold of the elephant leader's leg.

The elephant leader pulled his leg with all his strength.

So did the crocodile apply all his strength to bite and drag the elephant. Other elephants rushed to help their leader.

All of them pulled together to no effect. The crocodile was just too strong!

After a while, the elephants were exhausted and had to withdraw. The leader found himself alone.

His entire effort was to somehow escape with his life but the crocodile simply would not let go.

Neither the elephant nor the crocodile could move an inch. The stalemate continued for ten years.

Then, for a hundred years and then for a thousand years. The elephant's strength drained away, it became certain that he faced death. Now, Lord MahaVishnu is the sole refuge.

The elephant leader immersed himself in praying to Lord MahaVishnu and extolling His greatness.

Oh, what fortune! What great fortune! There, the manifestation of Lord MahaVishnu! A thrill went through the elephant's body and in his heart, boundless Bhakti.

He stretched out his trunk, plucked a lotus and offered it to the Lord. Isn't that all he could do in that situation?

Bhagavan pulled him out of the water and onto the shore.

Along with that, Bhagavan also pulled out the crocodile who would not let go. Then, Bhagavan killed the crocodile with the holy Trichakra[132].

It can only be described as astonishing!

The crocodile's form changed and so did the elephant's!

The crocodile transformed into a Gandharva named Huhu. It was a curse that had made him into a crocodile.

Once, Huhu was bathing in a lake along with some Gandharva women, a Maharshi named Devala also entered the lake to bathe. Playfully, Huhu dived underwater and grabbed Devala's legs.

The Maharshi was furious and cursed him to become a crocodile. Thereafter, he bestowed Huhu with a redemption from the curse.

"When Lord MahaVishnu manifests you will once again attain your previous form," said the Maharshi.

That redemption is what Huhu received now!

The Gandharva sang praises of Bhagavan. Prostrated full length at His feet, took the first step forward with his right leg and departed for Gandharva Loka.

And how about the elephant leader?

He was formerly the King of the Pandya Kingdom, Indradyumna. Indradyumna was a noble and pious man.

---

[132] The Trichakra of Mahavishnu refers to the symbolic representation of the three chakras or divine wheels associated with Lord Vishnu. These are connected to the Sudarshana Chakra, Vishnu's powerful disc-like weapon, as well as his cosmic role as the preserver and sustainer of the universe, as edited by VK Madhav Mohan

Once, he made a mistake unknowingly. He was in meditation, oblivious to everything. Agastya Maharshi and his disciples arrived.

Indradyumna was unaware of their arrival. So, he did not welcome the Maharshi with the appropriate ceremonies. The Maharshi felt that this was deliberate.

He cursed Indradyumna to become an elephant.

Instantly, the King shed his human form and changed into an elephant. Lived for a long time in that form.

Suffered many difficulties and hardships. Yet, he did not abandon the Vishnu Bhakti of his previous life. As a result, Bhagavan saved him.

Not just that, he was made into a Vishnu Doota and taken to Vaikuntha too.

Ajamila and Indradyumna were mere mortals. Devas are much greater than human beings. Devendra was the greatest of them all.

Even for him, Lord MahaVishnu was the source of all strength. There is a story that demonstrates this.

A grand, resplendent umbrella spread out above. Ceremonial fans and whisks made of peacock feathers, silk and gold on either side.

Devas and Maharshis extolling his virtues all around him. Devendra is lounging luxuriously on his throne!

He feels he is more accomplished than anyone else.

This is clearly reflected in his looks, attitude, and disposition.

Into the royal assembly strode Brihaspati, the Guru of the Devas. All the devas hold limitless reverence for Brihaspati.

Everyone stood up and behaved with great respect except Devendra who continued to sit unmoved on his throne. Arrogance had distanced him from his Dharma.

Doesn't arrogance need to be finished? So, what did Brihaspati do?

He turned around and walked away.

After a while, Devendra regained awareness of his duty. The Guru ought to have been respected and honoured, but he wasn't.

It was a big mistake. Forgiveness has to be sought. Otherwise, danger looms.

Devendra went in search of Brihaspati but he was not to be found anywhere. He had vanished.

The Asuras had, for a long time, been looking for an opportunity to attack Swarga but they feared Brihaspati.

It was not easy at all to defeat the Devas in Brihaspati's presence but now that he has forsaken them, this is the right opportunity!

They launched an all-out attack. Devendra and the Devas fled in defeat.

Only Brahma could protect them now. "Devendra, you have insulted the Guru. That is sad and very wrong. You are now experiencing the fruit of that. There is only one way left to you. You have to depend on Visvarupa. He will find a solution," said Brahma. Viswarupa had three heads.

Tvashtava was his father, an Asura lady was his mother.

Depending on someone with Asura blood? But that was the only way out.

Devendra and the Devas went to Visvarupa. "You are our teacher from now on. Please rid us of our enemies," Devendra requested with utmost humility. I don't like this much but I cannot reject your request outright. I will help you as much as I can," replied Visvarupa.

Naryana Kavacham[133] is a very powerful mantra. Viswarupa taught this mantra to Devendra.

Then, as a priest, he commenced a Yaga.

When it was time to offer the Yagabhagam[134] he played a trick. One part of the Yagabhagam he offered to the Devas.

---

[133] The Narayana Kavacham is a powerful prayer dedicated to Lord Vishnu, invoking his divine protection. It's a part of the Varaha Purana, and is considered to be a protective armor, offering spiritual and material benefits. Here is the mantra:
Narayana Kavacham:
ॐ नारायणाय विद्महे वासुदेवाय धीमिह। तन्नो विष्णुः प्रचोदयात्॥
Narayana Kavacham Mantra (Full)
1.ॐ
ओम् श्री नारायणाय विद्महे वासुदेवाय धीमिह
तन्नो विष्णुः प्रचोदयात्।
2.ध्यानम:
नारायणं नमस्कृ त्य नरं चैव नरोत्तमम्। देवीं सरस्वतीं व्यासं ततो जयमुदीरयेत्।
3.कवचम:
नारायणस्य महाकवचं प्रिसद्धं परं मिणम्। यः पठेच्छृद्धया श्रद्धया सदा।
सुरक्षा देिह मायामायो भगवान्।
The mantra is often repeated for divine protection and to invoke the grace of Lord Vishnu. It helps bring peace, prosperity, and spiritual growth to the devotee, as edited by VK Madhav Mohan
[134] The term "Yagabhagam" (यज्ञभागम्) is derived from Sanskrit, where:
Yajna (यज्ञ) means sacrifice, ritual, or offering. Bhaga (भाग) means share, portion, or allotment.
Meaning: "Yagabhagam" refers to the rightful share of offerings in a Yajna (sacrificial ritual). In Vedic traditions, different deities receive specific portions of the offerings made in a yajna. For example: Agni (the fire god) is the primary carrier of offerings to the gods. Indra, Varuna, and other deities receive designated shares. Pitrs (ancestors) also receive a portion in certain rituals. Context in

But another part he secretly gave to the Asuras. However, Devendra saw through that trick.

The Yaga was aimed at overcoming the Asuras.

So how could the Asuras, of all people, be offered the Yagabhagam? In anger, Devendra severed all three heads of Visvarupa.

The three heads became three types of birds, even though Visvarupa died then and there.

Remember, Tvashatavu is Visvrupa's father.

He prepared to wreak vengeance on Devendra, for that he performed a Homa, chanted mantras.

The power of the Homa and the mantras were visible instantly. From the fire rose a terrifying creature, as big as a great mountain.

Hair, beard, and moustache the colour of red-hot copper. Eyes burning as bright as the sun, a three-pointed spear in his hand.

Mouth as big as a cave, agape, swallowing the sky! Tongue, darting out from his mouth, licking the stars.

The terrible creature is Vrtrasura!

Shaking the spear Vrtrasura sped towards the Devas.

They rained various divine weapons, Divayastras [135], on Vrtrasura.

Scriptures: In the Ramayana, Ravana disrupts yajnas and seizes the "Yagabhagam" meant for the gods.In the Bhagavad Gita (3.10-16) and Vedas, yajna is emphasized as a means of cosmic balance, where offerings nourish the gods, who in turn sustain the world, as edited by VK Madhav Mohan

[135] Divyastra (िॱदव्यास्त) - The Celestial Weapons in Hindu Mythology. The term Divyastra (िॱदव्यास्त) is a Sanskrit

compound of: Divya (दिव्य) – Divine, celestial, or supernatural. Astra (अस्त्र) – A weapon, usually one that is

invoked using a mantra or divine energy. Meaning: A Divyastra is a powerful celestial weapon bestowed by gods, sages, or supernatural beings upon deserving warriors in Hindu epics like the Ramayana and Mahabharata. These weapons were not just physical but carried immense mystical powers. Types of Divyastras and Their Powers:

1.Brahmastra (ब्रह्मास्त्र) – Created by Lord Brahma, it is the most powerful astra, capable of

destroying entire worlds. Only the most disciplined warriors like Arjuna, Karna, and Rama could wield it.

2.Narayana Astra (नारायणास्त्र) – Granted by Lord Vishnu, this astra released countless arrows that

targeted enemies based on their hostility. It could only be countered by surrendering.

3.Pashupatastra (पाशुपतास्त्र) – A fearsome weapon of Lord Siva, capable of total destruction.

Only a select few, like Arjuna, received it.

4.Varunastra (वरुणास्त्र) – A water-based weapon given by Lord Varuna, used to counter fire-based

attacks.

5.Vayavastra (वायवास्त्र) – A wind-based astra that could cause hurricanes.

6.Agneyastra (अग्नेयास्त्र) – A fire-based weapon invoked to unleash massive flames.

7.Vajra (वज्र) – The thunderbolt weapon of Lord Indra, symbolizing unstoppable force.

8.Brahmashirsha Astra (ब्रह्मशिरास्त्र) – More powerful than Brahmastra, this could annihilate

entire civilizations.

9.Sharanga (शारंग) – Lord Vishnu's celestial bow, used by Rama and Krishna.

10.Sudarsana Chakra (सुदर्शन चक्र) – Lord Vishnu's divine discus, capable of destroying evil forces

instantly.

Significance in Epics: In the Mahabharata, Arjuna, Karna, and Drona wielded Divyastras during the Kurukshetra war. In the Ramayana, Lord Rama used the Brahmastra to kill Ravana. Divyastras were not just weapons but also tests of character—those who misused them faced dire consequence, as edited by VK Madhav Mohan

Not only did the Divyastras have no effect, he simply captured them all in his mouth!

Devas realised that annihilation is almost certain.

For safety and protection, they prayed and chanted mantras to invoke Lord MahaVishnu.

Bhagavan manifested.

"Prabhu, Vrtra is going to destroy us. Please kill him and save us," the Devas pleaded piteously.

"Go and see Dadhichi Muni. Seek his body. From the bones of his body let Vishwakarma[136] build the Vajrayudha. You will be able to kill Vrtra with Vajrayudha[137]," said Lord MahaVishnu.

---

[136] Vishwakarma (िवश्वकमार् / വിശ*കർ,) – The Divine Architect. Vishwakarma is the divine architect and celestial engineer in Hindu mythology. He is revered as the creator of the universe's grand structures, weapons, and divine cities. His name is a compound of: Vishwa (िवश्व) – Universe Karma (कमर) – Work or action. Iconography &

Depiction: Usually depicted with four arms, holding a book, a measuring scale, a pot, and tools. Sometimes shown riding a white elephant (Airavata). Wears a crown and adorned with ornaments, symbolizing his divine craftsmanship.

Vishwakarma's creations and contributions Swarga Loka: The grand palace of Indra in heaven Dwarka: The magnificent city of Lord Krishna

Lanka: Originally built for Kubera, later taken by Ravana

Kailash Mansion: The abode of Lord Siva

Vajra (Thunderbolt): Weapon of Indra, made from Rishi Dadhichi's bones

Pushpaka Vimana: The first known flying craft in mythology, as edited by VK Madhav Mohan

[137] Vajrayudha (वज्रायुध) – The Thunderbolt Weapon of Indra. Vajrayudha (वज्रायुध), also known as Vajra (वज्र), is the divine thunderbolt weapon of Indra, the king of gods in Hindu mythology. It is one of the most powerful celestial weapons, often described as indestructible (Vajra means "hard" or "unyielding") and unstoppable. Origins of Vajrayudha: The weapon was crafted by Vishwakarma, the celestial architect. Made from the bones of Sage Dadhichi, who

The Devas met Dadhichi and sought his body.

The great sage did not attach any value to his body.

He concentrated his Atma on Ishvara and in that state, renounced his body.

Vishwakarma gathered up his bones and built the Vajrayudha.

Devendra armed himself with the Vajrayudha and along with the Devas went into battle with Vrtrasura.

Vrtra and his cohorts used all sorts of weapons. Devas broke every one of them. Then the Asuras started pelting stones and trees.

When that proved futile, they abandoned Vrtra and ran for their lives. They have to be brought back.

Their cloudy valour has to be restored and made to burn bright again. The battle has to be resumed, Vrtra was determined to do all of that.

"Fellow warriors, if we are born, death is inevitable. We must welcome a death that is glorious and righteous. There are two kinds of noble death. One, during Tapas and the other, in battle. Let us embrace death in battle."

---

sacrificed himself so that Indra could have a weapon to defeat the demon Vritra. The story of its creation is mentioned in the Rigveda, Mahabharata, and Puranas. 3. Symbolism of Vajrayudha : Unbreakable Determination – Symbolizes unshakable strength and righteousness. Divine Power – Represents spiritual energy that destroys ignorance and evil. Protection & Justice – Indra wields Vajrayudha as the protector of dharma (cosmic order). Modern-Day Influence: The term Vajra is used in the Indian military (e.g., Vajra tanks, Vajra missiles) as a symbol of indestructible strength. Used metaphorically for unshakable resilience and divine force. Conclusion: Vajrayudha is not just a weapon but a symbol of divine justice, indestructible strength, and the victory of righteousness over evil. It continues to inspire warriors, spiritual seekers, and even modern defence strategies, as edited by VK Madhav Mohan

Vrtra's exhortation had no effect on the cowardly, fleeing Asuras. They continued running away.

Vrtrasura faced the Devas alone.

When he roared many of them fell unconscious, so terrifying was that roar.

He crushed the fallen Devas underfoot like an elephant in heat tramples a Ramacha[138] grove.

Devendra ran up and attacked the Asura with his mace.

Vrtrasura grabbed the mace and landed atremendous blow on Airavata[139].

The gigantic four tusked elephant was flung as far a distance as travelled by seven consecutive arrows.

And so was Devendra thrown, who was mounted on it.

VrtrasuraknewthatDevendrahadcomeintothepossessionof Vajrayudha.

And also, that Vajrayudha could kill him.

Yet the valiant Asura was not bothered at all. "Devendra, you have severed the head of your teacher. You are shameless and merciless. Your heart is as hard as stone. I am going to tear apart that heart with this spear or else you will have to use Vajrayudha which is full of Lord MahaVishnu's divinity and grace. My Atma

---

[138] Ramacha – Refers to the medicinal plant Plumbago zeylanica, commonly known as Ceylon Leadwort or Wild Leadwort. In Ayurveda, it is valued for its medicinal properties, especially in treating skin diseases, digestion issues, and inflammation, as edited by VK Madhav Mohan

[139] Airavata is a divine, white elephant in Hindu mythology, known as the vahana (mount) of Indra, the king of the gods. It is often depicted as a massive, majestic elephant with multiple trunks and is sometimes said to have four tusks. Airavata is believed to have emerged during the Samudra Manthan (churning of the ocean) and is considered a symbol of strength, purity, and divine authority.

will willingly merge with Bhagavan," so saying Vrtra prayed to Bhagavan.

And then he threw the spear with a mighty scream. Devendra cut the spear and with it the hand that held it too. Vrtra's courage was undiminished.

With his other hand he heaved a heavy iron pestle and smashed Devendra.

That hand too was severed by Devendra. Blood spurted like a river.

Unbearable pain!

Paying no heed to any of that, Vrtra opened his huge mouth wide and swallowed Airavata and along with it, Devendra too!

Devendra used Vajrayudha again, tore asunder Vrtra's stomach, jumped out, and decapitated him.

Vrtra's Atma went straight to Vaikuntha.

Despite being an Asura and having fought Devendra, how did that happen?

We can be astonished.

But if we know the story of his prior life the astonishment will disappear. In his previous life Vrtra was Chitraketu.

Chitraketu was a king endowed with every virtuous quality. He had just one problem, he had no son.

One day, Angiras Maharshi arrived.

"O King, why do you seem worried?" the Maharshi asked him. "Revered Maharshi, I have every good fortune except the fortune of having a son.

Please help me have at least one son," Chitraketu pleaded with the Maharshi.

"You will have a son. He will give you both happiness and sorrow," said the Maharshi who then proceeded to conduct a Homa.

From the mantra he produced the purest rice and gave it to the King.

The King then offered the rice to his first Queen, Kritadyuti. Kritadyuti ate the rice, became pregnant and later, gave birth. How quickly everything changed!

Sadness gave way to happiness but happiness was limited only to Chitraketu and Kritadyuti. The other queens who did not have children became jealous. They conspired and committed a terrible crime.

Secretly, they fed poison to the baby and killed him! Chitraketu and Kritadyuti were devastated.

How long they had waited for a son. Eventually they did get a son who died at such a tender age.

The King and Queen beat their breasts and cried out in pain. Then too, Angiras Maharshi arrived and along with him, Narada Maharshi.

They taught Chitraketu mantras to overcome his grief.

Chanting and repeating those mantras Chitraketu worshipped Lord MahaVishnu.

Lord MahaVishnu was pleased and blessed Chitraketu.

As a result, Chitraketu became a Vidyadhara[140].

He travelled far and wide aboard an aircraft, singing praises of Bhagavan. Unfortunately, however, he once also insulted Siva.

Siva and Parvati were angered and cursed him, "Let this fellow be born as an Asura forthwith."

And, Chitraketu was born as Vrtra.

Though he was an Asura wasn't he, a Vishnu Bhakta in his previous birth? Because of that Vishnu Bhakti he obtained entry into Vaikuntha!

Devendra killed Vrtra and won a famous victory. Did this end Devendra's difficulties? No.

There is a great sin called Brahma Hatya[141].

---

[140] The term Vidyadhara comes from Sanskrit, where: Vidya" (विद्या) means knowledge, wisdom, or mystical sciences and Dhara" (धर) means one who holds or possesses. Thus, Vidyadharas are beings who possess and protect
divine knowledge, magical powers, and mystical wisdom. They appear in Hinduism, Buddhism, and Jainism with slightly different roles.
Vidyadharas in Hinduism
•Vidyadharas are semi-divine beings who reside in the Himalayas or in celestial realms.
•They are known as guardians of knowledge, magic, and mystical sciences.
•Often depicted as flying beings with superpowers, they are also associated with Gandharvas (celestial musicians) and Yakshas (nature spirits).
•They appear in epics like the Ramayana and Mahabharata.
As Edited By Vk Madhav Mohan
[141] In Hindu Dharma, Brahmahatya (-ബ.ഹത1 / ब्रह्महत्या) refers to the grave sin (Mahāpāpa - മഹാപാപം / महापाप) of killing a Brahmin (Brahmana), who is traditionally considered a custodian of Vedic knowledge and spirituality. Mahāpāpa (Great Sin) of Brahmahatya It is regarded as one of the five great sins (Pancha Mahāpātaka -

പ6 മഹാപാതകം) in Hindu scriptures. The sin of Brahmahatya is believed to bring severe karmic

consequences, including suffering in hellish realms (Naraka) and rebirth in lower forms. In some texts, it is described as a sin comparable to killing one's own guru, parents, or a cow (Gohatya). Consequences of Brahmahatya: Ancient scriptures like the Manusmriti, Garuda Purana, and Mahabharata describe severe spiritual, karmic, and worldly punishments. It is said that a person who commits Brahmahatya carries the burden of the sin for several births unless purified through extreme penance. The 5 Great Sins, Pancha Mahatapa are: 1.

Brahmahatya (-ബ.ഹത1 / ब्रह्महत्या) – Killing a Brahmin (a learned Vedic scholar or spiritual teacher).

Considered the worst sin, leading to intense suffering in hell (Naraka). Severe karmic burden for multiple births unless purified through extreme penance. 2. Surāpāna (സുരാപാന / सुरापान) – Drinking intoxicating liquor (Surā).

This refers specifically to consuming prohibited alcohol (Surā) that clouds judgment and spiritual awareness. Considered a sin because it corrupts the mind and consciousness, leading to further immoral acts. 3.Steya

(സ്ടേഒതയം / स्तेयं) – Stealing or theft. Particularly stealing from temples, Brahmins, or sacred offerings.Taking

wealth dishonestly is believed to bring severe karmic retribution. 4.Guru Talpa Gamana (ഗുരു തൽപ ഗമനം / गुरु तल्पगमन) – Committing adultery with a Guru's wife (or any highly respected woman). Considered a betrayal of

Dharma and sacred relationships. Those guilty of this sin are said to suffer endlessly in lower realms. 5. Mahā Vishwāsa Bhanga (മഹാ വിശ*ാസഭംഗം / महा विश्वासभंग) – Betraying or deceiving someone who has complete

trust in you. This includes acts like breaking trust, cheating, false witness, or betraying one's protector. The Garuda Purana states that such acts destroy one's spiritual merit and bring great misfortune. Consequences of Pancha Mahāpātaka:

•These sins are said to cause birth in hellish realms (Naraka).

•The sinner may suffer countless rebirths in lower life forms like insects or animals.

•A person who commits these sins carries a heavy karmic burden and faces obstacles in spiritual progress.

As Edited By Vk Madhav Mohan

That sin took a female form- the unsightly form of Chandali[142].

She was suffering from severe tuberculosis. Clothes were smeared with blood, grey hair strewn wildly. Fishy odour emanating from her exhalations. A very unpleasant woman!

She moved close to catch hold of Devendra. Devendra panicked and tried to escape.

Wherever he ran, Brahma Hatya followed. He dived into Manasasaras (Mansarovar)[143], entered the Lotus flower, hid in its stem, and prayed incessantly to Lord MahaVishnu. A thousand years passed.

During all this time Swarga was ruled by a King named Suharsha[144]. Eventually, Devendra returned to Swarga and conducted an Ashwamedha Yaga.

Brahma Hatya was banished forever.

---

[142] In ancient Hindu society, Chandāli referred to a woman from the Chandala community, which was traditionally considered a lower or outcast group engaged in tasks like cremation and handling dead bodies, as edited by VK Madhav Mohan

[143] Manasa Sarovar (मानस सरोवर / മനസാസരോവസ്) refers to the sacred lake located in Tibet, near Mount Kailash. It holds deep religious, spiritual, and cultural significance in Hinduism, Buddhism, and Jainism. Meaning & Etymology. The name "Manasa Sarovar" comes from Sanskrit:"Manasa" (मानस) – Meaning mind or consciousness.

"Sarovar" (सरोवर) – Meaning lake. It is often interpreted as "The Lake of the Mind", symbolizing purity,

enlightenment, and spiritual reflection. Religious Significance: Believed to be created by Lord Brahma from his mind (Manas) for the gods. Considered abode of purity and is associated with Lord Siva and Goddess Parvati. Mentioned in Puranas as a sacred place for liberation (Moksha). Taking a dip in the lake is believed to cleanse all sins and bring spiritual enlightenment, as edited by VK Madhav Mohan

[144] Suharsha's story is told in MaliBharatam

The only reason for that was Vishnu Bhakti!

There is a dynasty, Vamsa, named Surya Vamsa[145]. It is a Vamsa adorned by Vishnu Bhakta's.

Let me tell you the story of some of them.

Remember Lord MahaVishnu's Matsyavatara that occurred a long time ago?

Satyavrata from that age was born again as Vaivasvata Manu.

Vaivasvata Manu is the progenitor of the Surya Vamsa.

---

[145] Surya Vamsa (सूयर वंश / സൂര്യവംശം), also known as the Solar Dynasty, is one of the two principal Kshatriya dynasties in Hindu Itihasas and Puranas. The other is the Chandra Vamsa (Lunar Dynasty). Origins of the Surya Vamsa: Founder: Vivasvan (Surya Deva) – the Sun God. His son Vaivasvata Manu (the progenitor of mankind in the current cycle of creation) was the first human ruler. Ikshvaku, Manu's son, became the first king of the Ikshvaku Dynasty (Surya Vamsa).

Famous Kings of the Surya Vamsa

The Ikshvaku lineage, or Surya Vamsa, is renowned for its great rulers:

1.Ikshvaku – The first king of the dynasty.

2.Harishchandra – Known for his extreme truthfulness and integrity.

3.Sagara – The ancestor of Bhagiratha, who brought the Ganga to Earth.

4.Bhagiratha – Performed severe penance to bring the Ganges from heaven.

5.Raghu – Established the Raghuvamsha (a sub-lineage), after whom the Ramayana's dynasty is also called Raghu Vamsa.

6.Aja – Grandfather of Lord Rama.

7.Dasharatha – The father of Lord Rama.

8.Lord Rama – The greatest king of the Surya Vamsa and the seventh incarnation of Lord Vishnu.

9.Lava & Kusha – Sons of Rama, continued the dynasty.

Characteristics of the Surya Vamsa

• Kings of this lineage were known for their righteousness (Dharma), truthfulness, and valor.

•Many performed Ashwamedha Yagnas (Horse Sacrifices) to establish their sovereignty.

•The Ramayana extensively describes the greatness of Surya Vamsa. As Edited By Vk Madhav Mohan

Initially, the great Vaivasvata Manu had no children. He conducted a Yaga to have a son.

Vasishta Maharshi supervised the Yaga.

Though he wanted a son, his wife Shradha desired a daughter. The priests conducted a Homa for the Queen.

As a result, a daughter was born. Vaivasvata Manu was astonished.

"O Guru, the result is the opposite of what we expected. It is sad. How did this mistake happen?" he asked Vasishta Maharshi. Vasishta examined the matter with his divine vision.

He saw the reason clearly. "This was done by the priests. But do not worry. With the power of my Tapas, I will convert the female into a male," said Vasishta Maharshi with certainty.

Vasishta possesses the divine power of Vishnu Bhakti. He applied that power.

The baby girl became a baby boy. He was named Sudyumna.

After a long time Sudyumna became a female again. How did that happen?

All we can say is that it was the play of destiny! There is a forest reserved especially for Siva.

Whichever man enters it becomes a woman immediately. But Sudyumna was not aware of this.

He was out hunting, on horseback. Many attendants were accompanying him. What happened when they entered the forest? Every one of them became women.

Even the stallions changed into mares!

Sudyumna wanted to become a man again.

Vasishta Maharshi prepared to help him fulfil that desire. Maharshi knew that this was possible only if Siva was pleased so he went about propitiating Siva. But Siva had difficulty in changing a decision he had made a long time ago.

Bhagavan found a solution.

Sudyumna would be a man one month and then a woman the very next month.

Every month he would alternate between being a man and a woman. That arrangement would continue!

The King was switching between being a male and a female. So, the subjects were not very satisfied or pleased.

What did Sudyumna do then?

He left the country and went into the forest to perform Tapas. Vaivasvata Manu now wanted other children.

To propitiate Lord MahaVishnu, he performed Tapas. As a result, he had ten more sons, one of them was Prashadhra.

Prashadhra was entrusted with a special responsibility. According to his father's instructions, he had to protect the cows.

Every night he would fight off sleep and stand guard in the Goshala[146].

One night, he made a big mistake.

---

[146] Goshala (गोशाला) is a Sanskrit term meaning "shelter for cows" (Go = cow, Shala = shelter). In Hindu tradition, a Goshala is a protective sanctuary where cows are cared for and protected, often run by religious or charitable organizations. Significance of Goshala: Cows hold a sacred status in Hinduism, often referred to as "Gomata" (divine mother). Protecting cows is considered punya (meritorious act) and is linked to dharma (righteous duty). Scriptures like the Śrīmad Bhāgavatam, Manusmṛti, and Mahābhārata emphasize cow protection, as edited by VK Madhav Mohan

It was pitch dark everywhere and raining heavily suddenly a leopard bounded in. The cows panicked. The leopard caught hold of a cow. The poor cow began to cry loudly.

Prashadhra heard the commotion and ran to the source of noise. He realised that a leopard was in the Goshala.

He swung his sword at the leopard. The blow glanced off the leopard and landed heavily on a cow. The leopard was only injured slightly. It ran away, bleeding from the ear but the cow's head was severed.

Of course, it is true that this was not deliberate.

Be that as it may, the Guru of the dynasty, Vasishta Maharshi cursed him. "Let Prashadhra become a Sudra[147]."

Prashadhra's heart was brimming with Vishnu Bhakti. So, he did not feel any grief even after being cursed. He wandered around many places eventually he found himself in a forest.

---

[147] Śūdra (शूद्र) is the fourth varṇa (social class) in the traditional Vedic Varna System of Hindu society. The term appears in the Vedas, Manusmṛti, Bhagavad Gītā, and Śrīmad Bhāgavatam, among other scriptures. Traditionally, Śūdras were responsible for service-oriented and labor-based roles such as: Farming, Artisanship, Craftsmanship & Serving the other varnas (Brahmins, Kshatriyas, and Vaishyas). Ṛg Veda (Purusha Sūkta - 10.90.12): The four varṇas are described as emerging from Puruṣa (the Cosmic Being):

•Brahmins (priestly class) from the head.

•Kṣatriyas (warrior class) from the arms.

•Vaiśyas (merchant class) from the thighs.

•Śūdras (working class) from the feet.

•This allegory symbolizes societal interdependence, not inherent inferiority.

Śrīmad Bhāgavatam specifies that anyone, regardless of birth, can attain liberation through bhakti (devotion to God).... as edited by VK Madhav Mohan

There he was trapped in a forest fire and renounced his body. Saryati is one of Prashadhra's brothers.

He is a scientist and also a scholar of Vedanta[148]. King Saryati had a daughter named Sukanya.

Once, he went into a forest, Sukanya and her companions accompanied him.

The maidens were frolicking with youthful zest. They spotted an anthill.

They could see a pair of shining objects inside the anthill like fireflies.

What could they be?

Sukanya was overcome with curiosity. She broke a twig and poked.

Blood began to ooze from the anthill! What were those shiny objects?

The eyes of a Maharshi!

Chyavana Maharshi was performing Tapas. The anthill had formed around him.

Saryati was gripped by fear. Won't the Maharshi be furious? If he is, he will spew out a curse and if he does that all will be lost. So, the Maharshi had to be pacified.

---

[148] Vedanta (वेदान्त) – The Philosophy of Ultimate Knowledge. Vedanta is one of the six major Darśanas

(philosophical systems) of Hinduism. It is based on the teachings of the Upanishads, which form the concluding part (anta) of the Vedas, hence the name "Vedanta" (meaning "the end of the Vedas" or "the essence of Vedic knowledge"), as edited by VK Madhav Mohan

To do that, Saryati offered his daughter in marriage.

Sukanya was young and beautiful while the Maharshi was ugly and old, shrivelled body, loose skin dangling from his frame. His hair, all white. No compatibility between husband and wife but to Sukanya her husband was God. She served her husband with devotion as a Pativrata[149].

---

[149] Pativrata (पितव्रता) – Meaning & Cultural Significance: The Sanskrit term "Pativrata" (पितव्रता) refers to a devoted and virtuous wife who is fully dedicated to her husband, upholding dharma (righteousness) in marriage. It comes from: Pati" (पित) – Husband "Vrata" (व्रत) – A vow or dedicated observance Thus, Pativrata means "a woman

who has taken a sacred vow of unwavering loyalty, devotion, and service to her husband." Pativrata in Hindu Scriptures & Epics. In Hindu mythology, Puranas, and epics like the Ramayana and Mahabharata, a Pativrata woman is glorified as one who exhibits unwavering loyalty, self-sacrifice, and spiritual strength.

A. Iconic Pativrata Women in Hindu Tradition

1.Sita (Ramayana) – Embodiment of patience, devotion, and loyalty to Lord Rama.

2.Draupadi (Mahabharata) – Fiercely loyal and protective of her husbands, especially Yudhishthira.

3.Savitri – Known for her unwavering devotion, she defeated Yama (the god of death) and brought her husband Satyavan back to life.

4.Anasuya – The wife of Sage Atri, known for her extreme purity and devotion.

5.Arundhati – The wife of Sage Vashistha, symbolizing perfect marital fidelity.

2.Characteristics of a Pativrata Woman

According to classical Hindu texts like the Manusmriti, Vishnu Purana, and Devi Bhagavata, a Pativrata is characterized by:

•Loyalty (Bhakti to Husband) – She considers her husband a divine presence in her life.

•Self-Sacrifice & Service (Seva) – She prioritizes her husband's needs over her own.

•Moral Strength (Dharma Rakshana) – She follows dharma and ensures the well-being of the

Once, the doctors of the Devas, known as Ashvis[150], visited Chyavana. They are endowed with wondrous powers. Yet, they were burdened with an important shortcoming. During Yagas they were not served Somarasa[151].

"You must give me good looks and youth. Then, I will present you with Somarasa," said Chyavana.

The Deva Vaidyas[152] held Chyavana's hand and took a dip in a deep pond they had created with their special powers.

What transformation was visible when they surfaced? Handsome, young men!

---

family.

•Purity & Chastity (Pativrata Dharma) – She remains devoted in mind, body, and spirit.

3.Pativrata and Spiritual Power (Shakti)

•Pativrata women are believed to possess immense spiritual energy due to their dedication.

•Their devotion is said to grant them mystical abilities (e.g., Savitri's power to bring her husband back to life). In many traditions, it is believed that a Pativrata's curse or blessing carries great power.

As Edited By Vk Madhav Mohan

[150] Ashvini Kumaras (अश्विनीकुमाराः): The divine twin horsemen in Hindu mythology, known as physicians of the gods.They are associated with healing, dawn, and speed. Their names: Nasatya and Dasra. Linked to Rig Vedic hymns and often invoked for health and vitality…ChatGPT 40 as edited by VK Madhav Mohan

[151] Somarasa (सोमरस) – The Divine Nectar in Vedic Tradition Somarasa (सोमरस) refers to the sacred drink of the gods, frequently mentioned in the Vedas, particularly in the Rigveda. It was considered a divine elixir that granted strength, immortality, and heightened consciousness. Meaning & Etymology

"Soma" (सोम) = The mystical plant or its extracted juice. "Rasa" (रस) = Juice, essence, or nectar.Somarasa literally

means "the essence or juice of Soma." as edited by VK Madhav Mohan

[152] Doctors, V.K.Madhav Mohan

Adorned with divine ornaments and clothes. All three were identical.

Sukanya was deeply troubled.

Which of the three was her husband?

She requested the Vaidyas to move aside so she could recognise her husband.

Her sincerity as a Pativrata pleased the Ashvis. Both of them moved aside, Sukanya recognised her husband.

After much time had passed, Saryati returned to the forest. What did he see then?

A radiant young man with his daughter! What is this?

Did Sukanya abandon Chyavana Maharshi? Did she accept another husband?

Saryati was overcome with anger but his daughter shared all that had happened. The father's misunderstanding cleared up.

Chyavana Maharshi got Saryati to conduct a Soma Yaga.

He presented the Ashvis, the Vaidyas of the Devas, with Somarasa as he had promised earlier.

Chyavana possessed so much Tapas Shakti that he could remove all shortcomings!

Ambareesha was one of Saryati's descendants. He was foremost amongst Vishnu Bhaktas.

Even Durvasa Maharshi had to taste defeat from him. Durvasa is quick to anger.

Once he is angry, he forgets everything else. No matter who, he curses them, and his curse becomes effective instantly. But all that did not work with Ambareesha.

Ambareesha had conducted numerous Ashwamedha Yagas. Despite that he had no wish to attain Swarga.

In his heart, Lord MahaVishnu was established permanently. Why then did he need Swarga?

Ambareesha observed the Dwadasi Vrita[153] for a whole year. He donated sixty crore[154] cows.

They were not cheap cows either. These were cows with horns encased in gold and hooves shod in silver. Not just did he donate, he distributed sweets to everyone too.

Then he proceeded to break his fast. That's when Durvasa Maharshi walked in.

Ambareesha welcomed him with all the appropriate ceremonies and invited him to eat.

Since bathing precedes eating, Maharshi went to the river Yamuna.

Parana breaking the fast needs to happen before the auspicious time specified for Dwadasi ends.

---

[153] Dwadasi Vrita, Dwadasi Vrata is a significant Hindu religious observance (vrata) performed on Dwadasi (the twelfth day of the lunar fortnight). It is closely associated with Ekadashi fasting and is considered the proper way to conclude the Ekadashi Vratam. Significance of Dwadasi Vrata

1.Parana (Breaking the Fast) – Those who observe Ekadashi Vratam (fasting on the 11th lunar day) should break their fast on Dwadasi in a prescribed manner, ensuring spiritual and physical well-being.

2.Associated with Lord Vishnu – It is believed that eating on Dwadasi pleases Lord Vishnu, as fasting beyond Dwadasi is not recommended.

3.Removes Doshas (Defects) – Dwadasi is considered an auspicious day for receiving divine blessings and for removing sins or negative karma.

4.Annadanam (Food Donation) – Many devotees perform charity, feed the poor, and donate food or grains as part of the vrata.

As Edited By Vk Madhav Mohan

[154] 1 crore is 10 million..so 60 crore is 600 million…V.K.Madhav Mohan

That is the rule.

At the same time, no one can proceed to perform Parana before the Maharshi eats, so Ambareesha waited but there's no sign of Maharshi returning. Time was running out, Dwadasi was almost over. Ambareesha was deeply concerned. There was no other way.

So, he drank a bit of water to break his fast and end the Dwadasi Vrita. That is exactly when Durvasa returned.

With his Yoga Shakti he realised what had happened. Ambareesha has drunk water!

"What a grave mistake have you committed? Before I have eaten you drank water, didn't you? That is insulting! I will show you your place!" Roaring in anger, Durvasa pulled out his matted hair and struck it on the floor.

Then and there rose a scary female form - Kritya[155] Kalagni[156].

With sword in hand, she jumped in front of Ambareesha. But he was unshaken and fearless.

How can those who are dissolved in Vishnu Bhakti be shaken or fearful? When His devotees are in danger, Bhagavan always sends help.

---

[155] Kritya: In ancient texts, Kritya is a supernatural female entity, often depicted as a vengeful spirit or an energy created through Tantric rituals. It is believed that certain mantras and rituals can invoke a Kritya to carry out specific tasks, such as revenge, destruction, or carrying messages. Some legends describe Kritya as an entity sent to punish wrongdoers, as edited by VK Madhav Mohan

[156] Kalagni: Kalagni is associated with Lord Siva in his destructive form. It symbolizes the fire of time that ultimately destroys everything at the end of a cosmic cycle (Kalpa, as edited by VK Madhav Mohan

His Divine Sudarsana Chakra arrived and reduced Kritya to ashes like a forest fire cremates a snake.

Durvasa was shocked and disoriented.

He had created Kritya out of his Tapas Shakti. Sudarsana had finished her off and now, it was speeding towards him.

He too was soon going to be reduced to ashes! Maharshi started fleeing for his life.

Sudarsana followed him relentlessly.

On land, in the sky, in Swarga, in other places Maharshi ran and ran.

Wherever he went, there too did Trichakra follow! Durvasa was overcome with panic and exhaustion. He ran to Brahma for help.

Could Brahma compete with Vishnu Shakti? Durvasa ran to Siva.

Siva too disengaged Himself but He gave Maharshi a direction, "Go and surrender to Lord MahaVishnu. He will surely protect you." Durvasa ran forthwith to Vaikuntha and fell at Lord MahaVishnu's feet. "O Bhagavan, I have erred. Please protect me," he cried.

"Durvasa, there are devotees who serve me even at the cost of their lives. I will never abandon them. Vidya and Tapas may provide Mukti. But in ill-mannered and arrogant people they will create opposite results. It is better for you to go and seek forgiveness from Ambareesha for your mistake," advised Bhagavan.

Durvasa had behaved badly with Ambareesha.

He had even tried to destroy him. And yet, now, he had to surrender to Ambareesha or else, he could lose his life!

Durvasa went immediately to Ambareesha.

He fell at Ambareesha's feet and sought forgiveness. Ambareesha is epitome of virtue.

He does not hold enmity towards anyone, even to Durvasa who tried to destroy him.

That great being prayed from the depth of his heart to Lord MahaVishnu, "O Lord of Everything, please protect Maharshi."

The prayer was from the most perfect devotee so it prevailed instantly.

Sudarsana calmed down and withdrew.

"O King, this is not just a wonder. It is a miracle. I have just experienced the greatness of Vishnu Bhakti," said Durvasa. Fearing the Trichakra, Durvasa had been running for a full year.

Only after that did he come to seek forgiveness from Ambareesha. For that entire year, Ambareesha had not eaten his meals.

Isn't it improper to eat when the Maharshi has not eaten?

He had subsisted only on water for all this time.

Only after he had fed Maharshi did Ambareesha eat. Durvasa blessed him, "Ambareesha, your greatness will be sung in praises even by the Devis. Your name and fame will be remembered and propagated by people forever."

Bhagiratha is yet another great King.

Bhagiratha is the one who brought Ganga Devi from Swarga to Bhoomi. That story needs to be told before we commence telling the story of Krishna.

Bahuka was a King from the Surya Vamsa. Enemies invaded Bahuka's kingdom.

The King was forced to retreat into the forest. The pregnant Queen was with her King.

The King passed away in the forest. The Queen gave birth to a son name Sagara. What happened when Sagara grew up?

He defeated the enemies, retrieved the Kingdom and ruled over it. Once, he commenced the Ashwamedha Yaga.

Suddenly, the Yaga horse went missing.

Devendran had stolen it and spirited it away but no one knew about it.

What is to be done if the Yaga horse goes missing? From somewhere, somehow, it needs to be found. Only then can the Yaga be completed.

Sumati is one of Sagara's two wives. Sumati has many sons, not a hundred or a thousand but sixty thousand! Sagara sent them to seek out the Yaga horse.

All sixty thousand of them together searched far and wide, throughout the earth.

They simply couldn't find the Yaga horse anywhere. They dug the earth and went down below together, there they saw the horse.

Devendra had brought it there and tied it up. A man was seated by the horse.

His eyes were closed, he was praying and chanting.

The sons of Sagara thought that he was the thief who stole the horse.

He's sitting in the guise of a Sanyasi as though he is not aware of anything!

Actually, he was not a Sanyasi but Kapila Maharshi! Sagara's sons prepared to kill him.

Maharshi opened his eyes and glanced at them. Instantaneously all of them were reduced to ashes! Sagara's other wife was Kesini.

She had only one son - Asamanjasa.

In his previous birth he was Yogeeswara. He had suffered Sansarga Dosha[157] in that life so he had to be born again, this time as Sagara's and Kesini's son. Asamanjasa remembered his previous life. That led him to decide that he would keep no contact at all with people.

He wanted people to despise him so that he could distance himself from everyone. So, he committed many wicked acts. Once he went to the banks of the river Sarayu, many children were playing there.

Asamanjasa threw them into the river.

Sagara banished his son from the land.

The children who fell in the river returned to their parents. That happened because of Asamanjasa's Yogic power.

It was then that Sagara realised the divinity of his son.

He was overcome with remorse but Asamanjasa was nowhere to be found. Anshuman was the son of Asamanjasa.

Sagara gave him an order. "Search out and bring back the Yaga horse."

Anshuman embarked on the search. He travelled the path dug by his father's brothers. After a while, he came upon the heap of ashes. He saw the horse and also Kapila Maharshi, deep in Tapas.

---

[157] In Hindu and Jain spiritual texts, Sansarga Dosha refers to the impurity that arises from bad company, association with sinners, or immoral influences. It is believed that being in the company of negative-minded or unethical individuals can lead to spiritual downfall.

Anshuman paid obeisance to the Maharshi with folded hands. Maharshi was pleased and told him,

"You may take your grandfather's Yaga horse. But only the holy waters of the Ganga can provide Sadgati[158] for those who have become ashes."

Now that the horse was retrieved, Sagara completed the Ashwamedha Yaga.

Then he anointed Anshuman as the King, performed Tapas and attained Paragati[159].

---

[158] Sadgati (सद्गति) – "Good Path" or "Liberation in a Relative Sense"
•Sadgati literally means "good movement" or "auspicious journey."

•It refers to an individual's progression toward a better state, often in terms of spiritual growth or rebirth in a higher realm.
• In Hinduism, Buddhism, and Jainism, Sadgati can mean attaining a favorable rebirth due to good karma, but it does not necessarily mean ultimate liberation (moksha).
Moksha is the ultimate goal of spiritual life in Hinduism, Jainism, and Buddhism.
•It refers to complete liberation from the cycle of birth, death, and rebirth (samsara).
• Unlike Sadgati, which still operates within the karmic cycle, Moksha signifies absolute freedom from all worldly attachments and suffering.
As Edited By Vk Madhav Mohan
[159] Sadgati (सद्गति) – "Good Path" or "Liberation in a Relative Sense"
•Sadgati literally means "good movement" or "auspicious journey."

•It refers to an individual's progression toward a better state, often in terms of spiritual growth or rebirth in a higher realm.
• In Hinduism, Buddhism, and Jainism, Sadgati can mean attaining a favorable rebirth due to good karma, but it does not necessarily mean ultimate liberation (moksha).

Only with Ganga water could the sons of Sagara obtain Sadgati. However, Ganga is in Swarga.

Ganga has to be brought to Bhoomi. And from Bhoomi she has to be taken to Patala. What a difficult task this is!

Anshuman could not do it neither could his son Dileepa. But Dileepa's son Bhagiratha did it.

Bhagiratha performed Tapas focused on Ganga Devi. Ganga Devi was pleased and manifested.

Bhagiratha requested Devi to come down to Bhoomi.

"When I drop down with immense force who has the strength to hold me? If there is no one strong enough, I will split Bhoomi and rush to Patala. Besides, there is another difficulty. When people drink my water and bathe in it, their sins seep into me. Where can I dispose of those sins?" asked Ganga Devi.

"Bhagavan Siva will hold you up, revered Devi. Lord Mahavishnu is established in Vishnu Bhaktas. When you touch their bodies, all sins will be removed," replied Bhagiratha.

Ganga Devi realised that Bhagiratha had spoken the truth.

Bhagiratha focused his Tapas on Siva. Siva was pleased and manifested.

He prepared to receive Ganga Devi by establishing Himself on a firm footing.

Moksha is the ultimate goal of spiritual life in Hinduism, Jainism, and Buddhism.

•It refers to complete liberation from the cycle of birth, death, and rebirth (samsara).

• Unlike Sadgati, which still operates within the karmic cycle, Moksha signifies absolute freedom from all worldly attachments and suffering.

As Edited By Vk Madhav Mohan

Ganga Devi rushed down onto Bhoomi with indescribable force. Siva absorbed her in the matted locks of the hair on his head.

Bhagiratha mounted a chariot as fast as the wind and led the way for her, Ganga flowed along this way.

She purified all the places on this route.

Eventually, she reached the place where the ashes were located, her waters drenched the ashes.

Those who had died attained Moksha.

SriKrishna Avatara

Vaivasvata Manu, Prashadhra, Saryati, Ambareesha, Sagara, Asamanjasa, Anshuman, Dileepa, Bhagiratha - these were just some of the Kings of Survya Vamsa.

There are many other great Kings too, but who amongst them all is the key leader who shines most brightly? None other than SriRama Himself.

Did Lord MahaVishnu not make the Surya Vamsa blessed in the form of SriRama?

In the same way He made the Yadu Vamsa, blessed in the form of SriKrishna.

A story unlike any other. A story that we can never stop wanting to hear. A story that overwhelms us whenever we listen. A story that fills our hearts with bliss. The sacred story of SriKrishna! Let me tell you that story!

Kamsa is the son of Ugrasena, the King of Bhoja. He is courageous, strong, and obstinate.

He is willing to do anything, even the harshest, cruellest acts however, he has great love for his younger sister.

Her name is Devaki. Vasudeva married Devaki.

The bridegroom went on a journey with the bride. They were travelling in a chariot.

Kamsa himself was the charioteer, so much was his affection for his sister.

The wedding party had just travelled a short distance with much excitement.

Then, "Kamsa, Devaki's eighth son will kill you," a disembodied, unseen, divine voice said.

Immediately, Kamsa's affection turned into hatred. "Oh, it seems that Devaki's son will kill me! That can happen only if a son is born to Devaki. If I kill her, no son can be born to her," with that intention Kamsa stopped the chariot and grabbed his younger sister by the hair.

He drew his sword to slit her throat.

Vasudeva was desperate to stop the killing, somehow. He begged and pleaded and reasoned with Kamsa.

Nothing worked.

Finally, an idea struck him.

"Kamsa, what did the divine voice say? Not that Devaki will kill you but that her son will. So, as soon as a son is born, I will hand him over to you. You can then kill him. Please do not kill Devaki." Kamsa saw reason in that.

"Only one of Devaki's sons will kill me. But I can kill all of them. That being so, there's no point in killing Devaki," he thought. He sheathed his sword.

Vasudeva went home along with his bride.

In due course they had a baby.

Vasudeva was grief-stricken.

How can he give up the infant to be killed? What could he do? Doesn't the promise have to be kept?

He went to see Kamsa, even though his heart was breaking.

Since Vasudeva did not break his promise, Kamsa was pleased. He said, "Vasudeva, the eighth child is supposed to kill me. Isn't that the prophecy? I'm concerned about him, not about this baby, so I'm not going to kill this one. You may take him back with you."

This goodwill was, however, short-lived. The reason was Narada.

The Maharshi met Kamsa and told him about what was to come. Devaki's eighth son is none other than Lord MahaVishnu.

Bhagavan's intention is to kill Kamsa along with several others! In his previous birth Kamsa was an Asura named Kalanemi.

Kalanemi was killed by Vishnu Bhagavan.

Kamsa's previous enmity flared up. He imprisoned Vasudeva and Devaki and killed their baby.

Not just that, he also threw his own father into the dungeons and usurped the throne.

Wasn't all this proof enough of his cruelty? Devaki had a second son, Kamsa killed him too. Devaki had a third son, he too was killed by Kamsa. Devaki had in all, six sons. All six were killed by Kamsa.

The grief of Devaki and Vasudeva can only be imagined! Devaki became pregnant with her seventh child.

Who was in her womb this time?

The serpent Adisesha [160] on whom the Lord MahaVishnu reclined! Lord MahaVishnu issued an order to Devi Yogamaya: "Rohini resides in Gokula. Go and transfer Devaki's foetus into Rohini's womb. Later, I will be born as Devaki's son. In the meanwhile, I want you to be born as the daughter of Nandagopa's wife, Yashoda."

---

[160] Adisesha: He is known as the king of serpents (Nāga Raja) and serves as the divine serpent on whom Lord Vishnu reclines in the cosmic ocean (Kṣīra Sāgara), as edited by VK Madhav Mohan

Devi followed the order.

As a result, Devaki's pregnancy vanished. Kamsa came to know of this development but he did not know the truth.

It was Bhagavan's secret so how could that wicked person know it? Devaki became pregnant again; Kamsa was waiting for it.

The younger sister's eighth son was about to be born. According to the prophecy this child was going to kill him.

Kamsa was constantly thinking about this child - while bathing, eating, walking, lying down, every single moment!

On a pitch-dark night, during a fearsome rainstorm, in a sparse jail cell, in human form, was born the Cause of The Universe!

A beautifully tender, flower-like body coloured a mystical blue, with the sacred Srivatsa[161] birthmark on His chest. The divine gem Kaustubha[162] around His neck, mace in one Hand and a conch in the other.

---

[161] Sacred Mark on Vishnu – Srivatsam is often depicted as a golden or white curl of hair on Vishnu's chest, sometimes represented as a subtle swirl or design. It symbolizes divine love, fortune, and the eternal connection with Goddess Lakshmi (who resides in Vishnu's heart). Srivatsam appears on many avatars of Vishnu, such as Krishna, Rama, and Narasimha, marking them as divine manifestations, as edited by VK Madhav Mohan

[162] Kaustubha is a legendary, divine jewel in Hindu mythology, most famously associated with Lord Vishnu. It is considered the most precious gem in the universe, symbolizing purity, divine authority, and spiritual radiance.Kaustubha emerged from the churning of the ocean of milk (Samudra Manthan), along with other divine treasures like Goddess Lakshmi, Amrit (nectar of immortality), and Airavata (Indra's elephant). The gods and demons fought over it, but it was ultimately accepted by Vishnu, as he was the only being worthy of wearing it. Vishnu wears Kaustubha on his chest, just above the Srivatsam mark. It symbolizes his supreme divinity and transcendental nature, as edited by VK Madhav Mohan

The Chakra in yet another Hand and the lotus, yellow silk and divine ornaments in the fourth.

The complete form of Lord MahaVishnu!

Bhagavan Himself born in human form? That too, as their own son!

Can there be a greater good fortune?

Vasudeva and Devaki were completely overwhelmed. Hot tears of devotion and happiness poured from their eyes. With quivering voices, they worshipped Bhagavan and extolled his greatness. "Take Me away from here. Get Me to Gokula. Lay Me down next to Yashoda. Mayadevi has been born as Yashoda's daughter. Bring her here," Bhagavan said to Vasudeva.

And then, suddenly, He hid his complete form and changed into a human baby.

Vasudeva took the baby in his arms. Many difficulties loomed in front of him. He's in a prison cell, his legs are in bound in shackles. The doors are bolted from outside, guards are posted. Darkness is everywhere, rain is falling incessantly. So many challenges!

But Bhagavan's powers are supreme!

So, every challenge is dissipated by them like dawn dispels darkness.

The shackles fell away from his feet, bolts slid open on their own. Doors swung open, guards fell into deep slumber.

The serpent Anantha arrived, spread his hoods, and held them aloft like umbrellas for Vasudeva.

Vasudeva carried the baby and came to the banks of the Yamuna. The swirling river gave way.

Vasudeva walked to the far shore and thereafter, reached Gokula.

He saw that everyone was fast asleep. He went near Yashoda, placed the baby he brought next to her. He took the baby girl into his arms, and made the return journey. Reached the jail cell, placed the girl child next to Devaki.

The shackles on his feet reattached themselves. Doors closed on their own. Everything was as before! Suddenly the baby girl let out a cry. The guards jerked awake.

A baby has been born to Devaki! They ran to Kamsa and informed him.

Kamsa jumped up and rushed to the jail cell.

"Elder brother, you have killed all my previous children. This is a baby girl. Please, I beg you, spare her at least!" beseeched Devaki. But Kamsa paid no heed. He stepped forward and grabbed the baby by her legs and smashed her on a rock! But the baby did not touch the rock. And then?

She slipped from Kamsa's hands. Rose into the sky and assumed a divine, radiant form. Just before vanishing she told Kamsa,

"You fool, your Kala, destroyer, has been born in another place!" Kamsa's brain was befuddled.

What's all this?

The prophecy was that Devaki's eighth son would kill him. But the eight child is not a son, it's a daughter!

The prophecy was wrong and now I hear that my destroyer is born elsewhere. So, one thing is certain, there is no danger from Devaki's children.

It was a mistake to have believed in the prophecy. It was wrong to have killed the children.

With that thought, Kamsa released Vasudeva and Devaki. What should I do next?

Kamsa consulted his ministers and well-wishers. And who are these ministers and well-wishers? Asuras born as human beings, people who hate Vishnu. Aggressive and cruel people.

It is now certain that Vishnu has been born on earth.

But where?

No one has a clue.

He has to be found and killed. How can that be possible?

A solution was come upon.

Rakshasas and Rakshasis are all Kamsas servants. They must fan out and kill every child born around this time. Vishnu is bound to be amongst them.

That will bring relief!

Meanwhile, what is the situation in Gokula?

Nandagopa is revelling in the happiness of welcoming the newborn baby!

Vedas are being chanted.

Auspicious musical instruments are ringing out. Every house has been swept and cleaned. Garlands, flowers, and flags are fluttering everywhere. Everyone is wearing festive clothes. Countless people are flocking to see the baby boy.

Actually, a baby girl had been born.

No one ever knew that Vasudeva had come and switched the babies. Bhagavan's pastime of Maya!

What else can we say? Many joyful days went past, Nandagopa travelled to Mathura.

Kamsa had to be paid money for protection, every year.

Vasudeva and Nandagopal were friends; they would talk about everything!

Vasudeva got news of Nandagopa's arrival in Mathura and went to meet him.

They were immensely happy to meet each other. Even so, Vasudeva mentioned a troubling matter, bad omens are visible.

Something untoward is going to happen in Gokula. Nandagopa needs to return home immediately.

Yes, a disaster is unfolding in Gokula. Poothana is a terrible Rakshasi.

Kamsa has given her an assignment. She has to wander all over the land and murder newborns and infants. She has a special technique to kill children.

Hiding her original form as a Rakshasi she assumes the form of a beautiful young woman.

She smears poison on her breasts. Taking infants in her arms she offers them her breasts. Infants who suckle, die!

No one in Gokula was aware of this. Poothana arrived in Nandagopa's house. She entered stealthily, took the baby in her arms.

What if a person picks up a snake thinking it is a rope? The snake will bite him to death!

Poothana's experience was similar! She offered the infant her breast.

A short while later she felt a numbness. Numbness changed into pain. Pain became unbearable. She tried to push the child away from her chest. No matter how hard she tried, the child would not budge.

The child had bitten deeply and was holding on with incredible strength. Her eyes bulged out, legs thrashed about, sweat drenched her, and she screamed loudly.

The child sucked the life out of her through her breast. That is, Bhagavan, in the form of a child!

Poothana fell dead! With death, her beautiful form changed.

The body reverted to its original form, the form of a Rakshasi. A cavernous mouth with wicked, long, curved fangs. Eyes like sunken, dry wells. Wild, brown hair.

She lay sprawled dead like a huge, black mountain.

The Gopis[163] who came there were terrified and confused. They saw Yashoda's baby playing on the chest of the Rakshasi! Rushing in, they swept the baby up into their arms.

By then Nandagopa had returned from Mathura. Didn't Vasudeva speak the truth?

Danger had been close and yet, disaster had been averted all because of Ishvara's blessings!

---

[163] Gopis .. Gopastrees of Vrindavan are considered the epitome of pure, selfless love (Prema Bhakti) for Lord Krishna. The term "Gopastree" refers to the cowherd women (Gopis) of Vrindavan, who were known for their unparalleled devotion (Bhakti) to Lord Krishna. The Gopis hold a sacred place in Hindu mythology, especially in Vaishnavism and Bhakti traditions. Their devotion was so intense that they forsook worldly attachments to be with Krishna, as edited by VK Madhav Mohan

Poothana's body was cremated by the Gopas[164]. From the smoke the scent of Akil[165] rose into the air. The Rakshasi had attempted to kill Bhagavan but it was Bhagavan who had killed her instead.

What happened when death occurred at Bhagavan's hands? All the sins of the sinner were destroyed.

Rohini's son was enchantingly fair and Yashoda's son, a radiant blue. Both children were extremely beautiful. A divine beauty that no one else has!

Another grave danger is impending. Yashoda laid the baby down to sleep. Then, she rushed off to take care of guests. A sudden loud noise!

Emanating from the place where the baby had been placed. Yashoda and others rushed in, panic-stricken.

What did they see?

A big cart lay smashed to smithereens. How did this cart come here? Who smashed it?

No one had any idea.

---

[164] The word "Gopa" (ഗോപാ) is derived from Sanskrit and means "cowherd" or "protector of cows." It holds deep cultural, spiritual, and historical significance, especially in Hindu traditions. The Gopas were the cowherd men and boys of Vrindavan, who lived alongside Lord Krishna during his childhood. They were simple, devoted, and engaged in cattle-rearing, playing a significant role in Krishna's Leelas (divine pastimes). Krishna himself is often called "Gopala", meaning "the protector of cows." as edited by VK Madhav Mohan

[165] Akil" refers to Agarwood, a rare and highly fragrant resinous wood derived from the Aquilaria tree.

It is used in perfumes, incense, and Ayurvedic medicine. Known as Oud in Arabic, it is one of the most expensive natural substances in the world due to its rich and long-lasting aroma. The fragrance of Akil is often associated with Divinity & Spirituality – Used in temples, meditation, and rituals for its calming and sacred aroma, as edited by VK Madhav Mohan

Sakatasura is one of Kamsa's henchmen. He was a magician who changed his form to a Sakata, a cart. His plan was to crush the baby to death under the cart. The baby just swiped the cart with his tiny foot and lo, the cart was broken to bits! There was an Asura named Trinavarta. He too was Kamsa's loyal servant.

He roared in as a whirlwind, spreading darkness. Kicked up a lot of dust, rained stones. Took the child and rose to the sky. The weight of the child increased, massively and quickly. Strong Trinavarta's strength was insufficient to bear the weight, his speed dropped.

The child was gripping his neck and the grip was tightening with every passing moment. Soon the Asura wasn't able to make a sound, unable to breathe.

His eyes bulged and he fell down, dead. Body was in parts. And the child?

Not even a scratch!

The Muni named Garga conducted the naming ceremony for the children.

Rohini's son was older. He was named Rama.

Rama was extremely strong (Bala), so he was known as Balarama.

Yashodha's son was named Krishna. He was usually known as SriKrishna.

Balarama and SriKrishna were at the stage at which they were crawling. How wonderful it was to see them crawling!

Mud or dirt did not bother them.

When they saw someone scary, they would crawl quickly to their mothers. The mothers would take them in their arms and offer their breasts.

When their teeth arrived?

The teeth would be visible when the babies smiled. The mothers would feel so much bliss!

In due course, the children could stand up and then walk. Sometimes they would grab the tails of calves. The calves would drag them along. When they grew up a little more?

The difficulties of the mothers were the real difficulties! Balarama and SriKrishna would not sit still for a moment. Will they fall into some danger?

They've got to be watched constantly.

Along with that, housework too needs to be done. Can both be handled?

On top of that, SriKrishna's mischief knew no bounds.

He'd go to neighbouring houses and create all kinds of unnecessary trouble.

The ladies of those households ignored it at first. Eventually, it all became too much for them.

They complained to Yasodha. SriKrishna would go to a house, he'd untie the calves.

They would drink the milk from their mother cows.

When it was time for milking, not a drop of milk would be available!

Some women would spot his pranks and scold him. As though he cared!

He'd listen to them and smile!

He'd do other naughty things elsewhere. Steal and drink milk and not leave anything for anyone else. Even if some milk was left over, he would not let it remain in the pot. He would give it all to the cats. If there was some quantity left over in the pot after the cats had their fill, SriKrishna would break the pots!

In some houses it would not be possible to steal milk. There, he would trouble the householders.

Sleeping children would be woken up and made to cry then he would run away.

In other places, he would do some other things. He would stealthily enter the larder.

There he would find urns full of butter and milk. They would be placed higher than he could reach. He would stand on a stool and try to reach the milk.

If that was still short, he would place a stone mortar on the stool.

And if even that too was short, would he give up and go his way quietly? No, not at all!

He would find a stick and poke a hole in the pot and catch the milk that poured out of the hole in his mouth and drink it up. If by chance he was caught in the act?

He would turn around and scold the householder! So many kinds of mischief would he do!

Even after the ladies complained, SriKrishna was not bothered. He pretended as though he knew nothing of it all!

Yashoda looked at her son's face. What innocent and tender beauty was seen on that face! She had to smile!

At another time Yashoda received yet another complaint. The complainants were Balarama and his playmates.

Apparently, SriKrishna had eaten mud! Yasodha caught hold of her son and held his hands together. "Why did you eat mud?" she asked angrily.

"Amma, I have not eaten any mud. These boys are lying just to see me being beaten up. If you don't believe me, you can check my mouth," replied SriKrishna.

"Fine, let me see. Open your mouth," Yashoda ordered. SriKrishna opened his mouth.

Yashoda peered in. Then, what did she see? Islands, rivers, mountains, oceans…everything that was happening on earth, and not just that, the sun, moon, stars, and all other celestial bodie, the entire Universe!

What is this? A dream? Magic? Madness?

Yashoda was transfixed in shock, awe, and amazement.

SriKrishna used VishnuMaya and Yashoda forgot everything she saw! Did SriKrishna become less mischievous?

On the contrary! Yashoda was once churning curds, SriKrishna ran up and grabbed the churning stick and insisted on drinking his mother's milk then and there. Yashoda stopped the churning.

She placed her son in her lap and offered her breast. That's when she saw that the milk on the stove is on the boil. She put her son aside and ran to remove the vessel of milk from the stove.

Oh, you should see SriKrishna's anger! He gnashed his teeth, smashed the pot of curds and te the butter made a day earlier.

Yashoda returned a moment later and saw the sight! SriKrishna was feeding a monkey with butter!

Yashoda was furious. She took a stick and rushed to beat her son. He just ran away!

The mother chased him. Both ran!

The mother's hair came loose while she ran, flowers in her hair scattered.

Not paying heed to all that she caught up with her son and grabbed him. What did SriKrishna do?

He rubbed his eyelids with his fingers, curled his lips into a cute pout, and started crying loudly.

When she saw her son crying, she just could not bring herself to beating him.

However, she was still angry. She prepared to tie him to the heavy stone mortar, but the rope was two lengths short. She added another rope. The longer rope was still two lengths short. Yashoda brought more rope but it was not long enough.

Many more ropes were brought to lengthen the original rope. They all fell short.

Then no more rope remained.

By now, Yashoda was sweating and panting.

When he saw his mother in discomfort, SriKrishna's heart melted. He had deliberately made the rope short.

Now, he couldn't trouble his mother anymore.

When Yashoda tried just once more, the rope became long enough.

She tied her son tightly to the mortar and went back inside the house. That circumstance arrived!

The circumstance when both received redemption from their respective curses.

Both were the sons of Kubera - Nalakubera and Manigreeva[166]. They were under the curse for a long time. Arrogance had overcome them.

From time to time, intoxication from alcohol would mix with arrogance. It was one such time, they were bathing in the Ganga, swimming, playing boisterously. Narada Maharshi was passing by.

He was not acknowledged or respected by the brothers. Narada Maharshi was angered and he cursed them to become Marutha[167] trees. But he also offered them redemption from the curse.

At a particular time, SriKrishna would descend to the earth and liberate them.

That is when they would revert to their original forms! SriKrishna was now ready to redeem the brothers.

Pulling the heavy stone mortar, he moved forward, stepped in between the two trees.

---

[166] The story of Nalakubera and Manigreeva teaches us that even the most arrogant souls can be redeemed through divine grace. It is a powerful lesson in spiritual humility, devotion, and Krishna's boundless mercy, as edited by VK Madhav Mohan

[167] The term "Marutha" (മരുത്) refers to the Terminalia arjuna tree, commonly known as Arjuna tree in English. It is a significant tree in Ayurveda, Indian mythology, and traditional medicine.Scientific Name: Terminalia arjuna.

Family: Combretaceae. Common Names: Malayalam: മരുത് (Maruthu) / അരജുന മരുത് (Arjuna Maruthu) It is

a tall, deciduous tree growing up to 20-25 meters in height. Considered sacred in Hindu traditions and is associated with Lord Vishnu. The Pandavas from the Mahabharata are believed to have stayed in forests with Marutha trees. These trees are highly valued in Ayurveda for various medicinal uses.

Environmental & Ecological Benefits :

Air Purification: Marutha trees help in improving air quality by absorbing pollutants. Soil Conservation: Their deep roots prevent soil erosion.

Supports Biodiversity: Provides shade and habitat for birds and insects, as edited by VK Madhav Mohan

The mortar was caught between the trees. SriKrishna pulled the mortar with all his strength.

The trees snapped and crashed into the ground with a loud noise. Nalakubera and Manigreeva stepped out.

They fell at SriKrishna's feet.

With great Bhakti, they worshipped him and vanished.

Having heard the loud noise, Nandagopa and others came quickly to investigate.

They saw SriKrishna amongst the broken, fallen trees. How did this happen?

From a distance, some Gopas had seen it all. They described how SriKrishna had toppled the trees and how two divine beings had emerged from them.

No one really believed all this. Srikrishna after all is a little child. And the trees? Well, they are huge! SriKrishna felled these trees?

How could anyone believe any of this? And yet everyone was concerned.

Nandagopa is the leader of Gokula. And Unni Krishnan?

He's the apple of everyone's eye!

Dangerous situations are occurring one after another. What is the solution?

The Gopas sought the opinion of Upananda.

He was the elder amongst all of them.

In intelligence and wisdom, he was superior to all. He instructed them on the remedy.

Pootaana, Sakatasura, Trinavarta, from all these enemies SriKrishna has been saved. And now, also, from the fall of these massive trees. This is all by the grace of Ishvara.

However, more misfortunes may occur so it is necessary to depart from Gokula as quickly as possible. We must shift our residence to Vrindavan.

Vrindavan is a beautiful place. It is ideal for our cattle too.

Nandagopa and the other Gopas respected and accepted that opinion. Everyone went to Vrindavan and started living there.

Balarama and SriKrishna grew up. They became old enough to graze the calves, both had a lot of friends.

These friends also had a lot of calves. All of them used to go together to places with an abundance of grass. There, the calves would be let loose to graze.

Much excitement would follow after that. They would run around ringing little bells, throw stones at targets, play the flute, imitate bird calls, snort like bulls, play hide and seek, stage mock fights with each other. So many games, so much fun!

So much joy and excitement! So much noise and hustle and bustle! There too enemies lay hidden.

Kamsa's henchmen were in search of SriKrishna. If found, they will only be satisfied by killing him. Most of them were sorcerers, Vatsasura was one of them.

He spotted the children playing.

Changed his form into that of a calf and joined the rest of the calves. He believed that no one would recognise him but that belief was wrong. How can Bhagavan be fooled?

SriKrishna pointed him out to his elder brother. Went close to the Asura.

Suddenly He grabbed him by the hind legs, twirled him round and round with great speed and threw him on top of a tree.

The fruits from the tree fell in a heap.

Along with the fruits, Vatsasura's dead body too crashed to the ground. Another time, the children went to the lake.

They first made the calves drink water; then they too drank. Bakasura had concealed himself there in the form of gigantic crane.

He rushed out, picked up SriKrishna in his huge beak and swallowed. He had no idea about the strength of Bhagavan!

Suddenly he felt this throat burning.

He spat SriKrishna out.

Then, he tried to stab SriKrishna to death with his beak.

SriKrishna tore apart the beak like tearing up a blade of wild grass. Alpasura was the brother of Pootana and Bakasura.

He was bent upon seeking revenge from SriKrishna for killing his siblings.

He assumed the form of a serpent as long as a Yojana[168] and lay in the path of the Gopa boys.

His mouth was wide open, a trap.

Unknowingly, the Gopa boys walked into the trap. Bhagavan grew in size from within the serpent's neck. Alpasura's throat became jammed shut.

---

[168] A "Yojana" is an ancient Indian unit of distance, roughly equal to 8-12 kilometers (5-7.5 miles) depending on different texts.

His breath was blocked.

He twisted and turned and thrashed his tail before dying and thus, the Gopa boys were saved.

Srikrishna never tried to harm anyone.

Many powerful forces tried to kill him but they all met their end. Like moths which came too close to a flame.

The Gopas and Gopis were amazed!

Bhagavan's pastimes are strange and mysterious.

I want to see and test them first hand, Brahma thought and readied himself.

The Gopa boys were all together.

They made the calves drink water from the river then they were allowed to wander into the forest to eat grass. The Gopas sat on the sandbank.

They'd brought rice and curry with them.

Everything was spread out and they began enjoying the meal. How tasty every dish was!

SriKrishna told so many entertaining stories! No one knew how much time had passed.

Where are the calves that wandered into the forest? They have to found and brought back or slse, there would be big trouble. The children were deeply worried. "All you, eat your meals. I will find the calves," said SriKrishna and went into the forest.

The calves were nowhere to be found.

He went back to his friends.

How terrible! Now, even his friends are missing! He searched everywhere but they were not found. SriKrishna thought for a moment then He knew.

Brahma had hidden all of them so a reverse ploy had to be played!

SriKrishna changed Himself into many Gopa boys and calves. That is, the missing Gopa boys and calves!

Identical to the originals!

Even the mothers of the Gopa boys couldn't spot the difference. All of them reached home.

The copies were so true to the originals in every way that no one knew! One year passed, Brahma came to take a peek.

The Gopa boys and calves that he had hidden are now here! Brahma was amazed.

When he looked again, carefully, he saw, clearly!

Every one of them was a Vishnu Rupa, the form of Vishnu.

See the greatness of SriKrishna, who is Lord MahaVishnu Himself? Brahma praised, glorified, and worshipped Him with folded hands.

Remember the place near the forest, where a year previously all the boys had eaten together? SriKrishna went to that very place.

All the Gopa boys and calves that Brahma had hidden were all present there.

The boys did not realise that they had been there for a full year. It was as if only a moment had passed!

Days passed with excitement and enthusiasm.

Balarama, SriKrishna and their friends grazed cattle, danced, sang, played and laughed a lot together.

The All Powerful was living a simple village life! A palm grove was not too far away.

Plenty of fruits from the palm tree used to fall on the ground. The children loved these fruits but no one could enter the grove.

A Rakshasa named Dhenuka lived there. He had many servants and attendants, all of them were in the form of donkeys.

The children were desperate for the palm fruit but they dare not venture into the grove.

What could they do?

SriKrishna and Balarama went into the palm grove. The super strong Balarama shook the palm trees.

Ripe palm fruits fell in copious quantities from the trees. The noise from all this fell on Dhenuka's ears.

Its first time that human beings have entered his forest. Dhenuka charged in and aimed a kick at Balarama's chest.

The kick that could have killed anyone else had no effect on Balarama.

Not only that, he grabbed the Asura donkey's hind legs, swung them around at great speed and heaved skyward, with that his life ended.

The body landed on top of a palm tree, that tree broke and fell on another tree and that tree too fell on yet another. Trees fell on top of each other.

Many palm trees collapsed onto the ground. The donkey leader's death was witnessed by all.

Immediately, all the donkey servants rushed in to do battle.

Balarama and SriKrishna caught each one by the hind legs and smashed it to death against the trees.

Not one Asura donkey was left alive.

How convenient it became for the Gopa boys!

Now, whenever they felt like eating palm fruit, they could enter the grove and eat to their heart's content!

Srikrishna and his companions were enjoying themselves on the banks of the river Kalindi.

On that day, Balarama had not accompanied them. Everyone except SriKrishna drank water from the river so too did the cows.

Instantly, every one of them, all the children and all the cows, fell dead. Within the river Kalindi is a deep hole.

That was the home of the highly venomous serpent, Kaliya. His venom had made the water boil with toxicity.

Just a whiff of the poison was sufficient to kill any creature. Flying birds would fall dead, their wings burnt. Every tree except a solitary Kadamba[169] tree had dried up. Kaliya's venom was that deadly!

Kaliya has to be taught a lesson, decided SriKrishna!

With a mere glance he brought his friends and cows all back to life. Then he tied his waistband tightly, climbed on top of the Kadamba tree, dived into the river, and swam around noisily.

---

[169] The Kadamba tree is associated with Lord Krishna. It is believed that Krishna used to play his flute and dance with the Gopis under the shade of Kadamba trees in Vrindavan. The Kadamba tree (കദംബ മരം), scientifically known as Neolamarckia cadamba, is a fast-growing, evergreen tree native to South and Southeast Asia, as edited by VK Madhav Mohan

Hearing the commotion Kaliya got up and looked around and spotted the noise maker.

Do you know what that fearsome serpent did?

He bit SriKrishna in all his vulnerable spots and wound himself tightly around him.

The light in everyone's eyes, the tender Kanna[170], was caught in the midst of the coils of the terrifying serpent.

The children who watched this horrendous scene from the shore screamed in fear and agony.

Who can bear to see this sight?

At that exact same time in Vrindavan signs of impending danger began to be seen.

Many people experienced a quivering on the left side of their body.[171] Kollimeen[172], a type of fish, began to fall from the sky.

The earth started shaking. SriKrishna must be in danger! Everyone raced to the river.

---

[170] Kanna is a loving and endearing name for Lord Krishna, especially used in South India. It is a short form of Kannayya or Kannan, derived from Tamil and Telugu traditions. Why is Krishna Called Kanna? The name comes from

"Kannan" (கண்ணன் in Tamil), meaning "the one with beautiful eyes" (derived from "Kannu" meaning eye).

Krishna's mesmerizing eyes are often described in devotional literature. Childhood Affection – The name Kanna is often used in a motherly or friendly tone, showing the close bond devotees feel with Krishna as a divine child (Bala Krishna), as edited by VK Madhav Mohan

[171] Some believe that the left-side quivering warns of upcoming dangers, obstacles, or negative events, as edited by VK Madhav Mohan

[172] In Malayalam, "Kollimeen" (കൊക്കാഡ൦മീൻ) refers to a predatory fish or a carnivorous fish that preys on smaller fish and aquatic creatures. The term is commonly used in Kerala to describe aggressive or large fish species.

Inside, they were all burning up with terror and worry!

Only one person wasn't panic-stricken - Balarama. He knew, exactly, what was happening but he did not say anything to anyone. All he did was to smile.

Those who rushed to the banks of the Kalindi, what did they see? SriKrishna was in the middle of the river, in the grip of Kaliya!

All those who saw that fell unconscious.

When they regained their senses, all of them burst into tears and cried their hearts out.

Nandagopa and Yashoda tried to jump into the river. Yashoda was prevented by the Gopis and Nandagopa, by Balarama.

Everyone stood transfixed, gazing at SriKrishna, with their hearts trembling in desperation and fear.

What does it matter, how many times Kaliya bites or how much he tightens his coils?

What harm can come to SriKrishna? Bhagavan, in a flash, made his body bigger.

Kaliya's body now got squeezed, harder and harder.

He was forced to release his grip. The serpent snarled loudly, snorted venomous fire from his nose, made his forked tongues dart about, and spread out all his hoods.

He looked at SriKrishna carefully, with focused attention. Around him moved SriKrishna.

Kaliya followed him, round and round, to catch him.

But no matter how many times Kaliya went around, he just couldn't catch SriKrishna.

He became tired.

SriKrishna jumped up on his heads.

Standing on those heads, SriKrishna began to dance. What beauty and rhythm, so enchanting and endearing was SriKrishna's dance.

All kinds of divine beings descended from the sky to witness this cosmic spectacle.

These are Bhagavan's feet on Kaliya's many heads!

Can we imagine their strength and weight?

Kaliya did not have the wherewithal to absorb the force of those steps. Blood gushed from the serpent's mouths and noses, every upright hood collapsed in disarray. Kaliya's wives ran to SriKrishna in panic.

"O, Bhagavan! Protect us, protect us!" they beseeched. All merciful, compassionate Bhagavan stopped dancing.

Kaliya realised that this is none other than Lord MahaVishnu. "Bhagavan, you have the power to punish and protect. You are the foundation of the entire Universe. Whatever is your desire, I will obey without question," said Kaliya, having shed all his arrogance.

"Kaliya, you cannot stay here anymore. Take your wives and children and go to Ramanaka Island in the ocean. You came here from there because of your fear of Garuda, isn't it? From now, you need not have that fear. Your heads have the mark of my feet. When Garuda sees them, he will never trouble you again," SriKrishna assured Kaliya.

Kaliya and his wives performed Puja to Bhagavan.

They offered gems and garlands and other valuables to Bhagavan. Then, they took leave and proceeded to Ramanaka Island.

At that moment, Kalindi river was cleansed of all venom. Kaliya had reason to fear Garuda[173]!

Garuda is the born enemy of serpents and a very powerful enemy at that!

He was preparing to annihilate the entire lineage of serpents. What if Garuda was propitiated?

Then, perhaps, they could receive a lease of life.

To do just that, the serpents had conducted a sacrifice. A sacrifice once in a month, on every new moon day.

The sacrifice was offered not by Kaliya but the other serpents.

"I'm very strong; my venom is the most toxic; why then should I fear Garuda?"

This was Kaliya's state of mind.

Not only did he not offer the sacrifice but he also ate the sacrificial rice that the other serpents had offered.

When he learned about this, Garuda was furious. He flew in to confront the upstart.

The arrogant Kaliya spread his many hoods, extended his tongues, revealed his poison fangs and tried to bite.

---

[173] Garuda (ഗരുഡൻ) is a mythological bird and a prominent figure in Hindu, Buddhist, and Jain traditions. He is revered as the vahana (vehicle) of Lord Vishnu and symbolizes strength, speed, and protection. Garuda was born from Vinata, one of the wives of Sage Kashyapa. His birth was extraordinary, and he possessed immense strength from a young age. Garuda's mother, Vinata, was enslaved by her co-wife Kadru (mother of serpents). To free her, Garuda stole the Amrit (nectar of immortality) from the gods. Impressed by his power, Vishnu made Garuda his vahana and granted him eternal protection. Garuda is often depicted carrying Vishnu on his back. He represents devotion, speed, and divine service, as edited by VK Madhav Mohan

What then did the supreme bird do?

He stretched out his left wing and struck Kaliya.

Garuda has a fearsome beak and claws as hard as diamonds but he did not use any of those.

Just his left wing was sufficient to vanquish Kaliya! But that too was so very powerful.

Kaliya could not bear the pain inflicted by the blow. It was certain that he would die from the beating so he simply turned tail and fled.

The flight ended in the waters of the Kalindi.

Garuda could never come to the Kalindi river, only Kaliya knew this secret.

Garuda had been cursed by Saubhari Muni.

Once, the Muni was performing Tarpana in the Kalindi river. Garuda began picking up fish from the river and eating them. Saubhari Muni prohibited him from doing this but Garuda disregarded the Muni and continue eating the fish. In fact, he even ate the King of the Fish.

The enraged Muni cursed him.

If Garuda dared to return to the Kalindi ever again he would die. After being so cursed, Garuda had never come back nor would he ever return to the Kalindi. So, Kaliya made Kalindi his home.

After seeing Kaliya off, SriKrishna came ashore.

Yashoda, Rohini, Nandagopa, the Gopas, the Gopis, how overjoyed were they all!

Every one of them took turns in hugging and embracing SriKrishna. Everyone was overwhelmed with happiness, even the cows and calves!

Vrindavan!

Gardens brimming with beauty, trees standing, holding green umbrellas spread out. No heat could not seep in even during hot summers. The ground, covered with green grass like green silk draped over the land.

Countless flowers bloomed in myriad colours, a feast for the eyes in every direction.

Cool, gentle breeze wafted in, laden with the fragrance of flowers. Bees, buzzing about feasting on honey[174].

Birds, many kinds, flying around, singing songs.[175]

Vrindavan was endowed with a forested beauty that cannot be described in words.[176] Where the Gopa children played out their pastimes, Srikrishna, Balarama, and their companions were all together.

They would don peacock feathers, flower garlands, and tender blossoms.

Singing songs, dancing, and wrestling, so many ways in which they entertained themselves.

---

[174] Beautifully poetic and allegorical original in Malayalam, written by Mali: "Thenundu murandukondu

mandunnundu vandukal..V.K.Madhav Mohan.. page 83, MaliBhagavatam, July 2019 Edition, DC Books. First published: December 1968

[175] Beautifully poetic and allegorical original in Malayalam, written by MaliVakkukondu varnikkan vayyatha

vanabhangiyanu Vrindavanithil..V.K.Madhav Mohan.. page 83, MaliBhagavatam, July 2019 Edition, DC Books. First published: December 1968

[176] Beautifully poetic and allegorical original in Malayalam, written by MaliVakkukondu varnikkan vayyatha

vanabhangiyanu Vrindavanithil..V.K.Madhav Mohan.. page 83, MaliBhagavatam, July 2019 Edition, DC Books. First published: December 1968

They would hold hands and move fast round and round in circles. They would pluck unripe fruits and throw them at each other. Blindfold touch, frog jump, back and forth on swings. Ha! What commotion in Vrindavan!

But there too the aggressive Asuras were lying in wait, seeking an opportunity to kill SriKrishna.

A fellow named Pralamba disguised himself that too as a Gopa boy.

The Gopas thought that he was one of them.

Only SriKrishna knew the truth. The children got ready to play, they divided themselves into two groups. Balarama was the leader of one group.

The other group was led by SriKrishna.

Both the groups had agreed that the losers would carry the winners on their backs.

The game was hard fought. Balararama's group won.

The losers began to carry the winners.

SriKrishna too was carrying one of the members of his elder brother's group.

Balarama was being carried by Pralamba disguised as a Gopa boy. Pralamba's aim was to carry SriKrishna but he did not get SriKrishna.

Even if he had, it was doubtful whether he could have killed SriKrishna.

For the time being he could take Balarama to a secluded place and kill him.

That was Pralamba's secret intention.

Balarama, who had divine powers, understood. He increased the weight of his body.

Pralamba found it difficult to carry Balarama.

He reverted to his Asura form and shot skyward. Balarama's hand was as strong and hard as a diamond. Curling that hand into a fist he punched Pralamba's head, the head was smashed.

Pralamba vomited blood and fell dead.

SriKrishna performed the extraordinary feat of drinking fire, just like drinking water.

Once, the cattle which were out grazing went missing. The Gopa boys went in search.

Crushed grass and hoof marks indicated the direction in which the cattle had gone.

Following this trail, the boys reached a dense forest. The cattle had entered this forest while grazing.

The boys started leading them out of the forest. Suddenly, a forest fire broke out.

In no time at all, the raging fire closed in from every side.

There was no way for the boys to escape. They would surely be burnt to death.

Everyone shouted and cried for SriKrishna. Only SriKrishna had the ability to save them. SriKrishna asked them all to close their eyes, everyone obeyed.

Shortly afterwards, they opened their eyes. And then?

There was no sign of the forest fire, SriKrishna had drunk the forest fire.

It was just that they had not had seen this feat.

The realisation that Balarama and SriKrishna are incarnations of the Devas took root in the minds of the Gopas.

The music of SriKrishna's flute!

How can we ever describe the sweetness of that music?

Bhagavan's red lips would rest lightly on the flute. It would be filled with His breath.

His fingers would dance to a rhythmic beat and then divine music would rise from the flute.

Hearing it, the trees would shed tears of bliss. Peacocks would spread their wings and dance.

Deer would worship Bhagavan with the flowers of their adoring looks. Cows would drink in the bliss-filled nectar with their ears held aloft.

Birds would find seats quietly among the leaves of trees.

The river would hold out its hands in the form of waves and offer lotuses at the Divine Feet.

The moving and unmoving aspects of Nature would be thrilled. Vrindavan would transform into heaven on earth!

Every Gopi maiden had a desire - to become SriKrishna's wife at one time or the other, to achieve that aim all of them undertook the Katyayani Vrita[177], a month-long vow along with Devi Puja.

---

[177] Katyayani Vrat is a sacred ritual and fasting practice dedicated to Goddess Katyayani, a powerful form of Durga or Shakti. It is especially observed by young girls and unmarried women who seek blessings for a good husband, marital happiness, and prosperity. This vrata is prominently mentioned in the Bhagavata Purana (Srimad Bhagavatam). Goddess Katyayani is the sixth form of Durga and

The maidens would bathe in the Kalindi just before daybreak.

They would make a mud idol of Devi on the shore of the river and offer Puja to it with great devotion, that was the daily routine.

One day, the maidens got into trouble.

They removed all their clothes, placed them on the shore and went into the river.

After a while they noticed something. SriKrishna was sitting atop the Kadamba tree and all their clothes were in his possession!

The maidens were overcome with embarrassment and shyness. They begged Him to return the clothes.

He gave the garments back only after they came ashore! Nandagopa was organising a Yaga and Puja on a grand scale. Everyone was busy and the atmosphere, chaotic.

"Acha[178], for whom is this, Puja? What is the aim of the Puja?" asked SriKrishna innocently, as if he didn't know.

"Son, this is for Devendra. Clouds provide water to human beings. Devendra is the Lord of Clouds. Therefore, we must pay obeisance to him. We have been conducting this Puja for many years," said Nandagopa. SriKrishna made some very important observations.

"Acha, human beings do many things, karmas. They experience the fruits of those actions. Devendra does not have the capability to

---

is believed to remove obstacles in marriage and bless devotees with happiness and strength. She is also worshipped as the warrior goddess who destroyed Mahishasura. According to Srimad Bhagavatam (10th Canto), the young Gopis of Vrindavan observed Katyayani Vrat by worshipping the goddess on the banks of Yamuna River to seek Lord Krishna as their husband, as edited by VK Madhav Mohan

[178] Acha..Father, in Malayalam..V.K.Madhav Mohan

change the fruits of action. We are cowherds. Cows are our wealth. And this Prashadhra Mountain protects our cows. So, it is for our cows and Govardhana Mountain that we must do Puja. This is my opinion," said SriKrishna.

My son's opinion is right, realised Nandagopa. He prepared to act on this opinion.

The cows were fed sumptuously.

Collecting all the Gopas, Nandagopa and companions reached the foot of Govardhana Mountain.

Praying to the mountain, they performed the Pradakshina.[179]

---

[179] The term "Pradakshina" is derived from two Sanskrit words: Pra (प्र) – "forward" or "in favor of" Dakshina

(दिक्षण) – "right" or "south" (symbolizing auspiciousness). Pradakshina (Sanskrit: प्रदिक्षणा) refers to the act of

circumambulating (walking around) a sacred object, deity, temple, or shrine in a clockwise direction. Since the right side is considered sacred, the devotee keeps the deity or sacred object to their right while walking around it. This represents the belief that God is at the center of existence and that devotees revolve around this divine force with humility and devotion.

Types of Pradakshina

1.Temple Pradakshina – Walking around the main deity or sanctum sanctorum in a Hindu temple.

2.Peepal Tree Pradakshina – Circumambulating the Peepal tree, considered sacred in Hinduism.

3.Mountain Pradakshina – Pilgrims walk around sacred mountains, such as:

•Arunachala Hill (Tiruvannamalai) – Girivalam (14 km)

•Govardhan Parikrama (Uttar Pradesh) – Govardhan hill circumambulation

• Mount Kailash Parikrama (Tibet) – Considered one of the holiest pilgrimages.

4.River Pradakshina – Devotees circumambulate sacred rivers such as the Narmada Parikrama.

5.Deity-Specific Pradakshina – For example, devotees of Lord Ganesha perform 21 pradakshinas as a mark of devotion.

As per the set rituals, they offered Naivedya[180]. Srikrishna took a divine form and shouted,

---

6.Saptapadi (Seven Circumambulations in Marriage) – In Hindu weddings, the bride and groom walk around the sacred fire (Agni), making vows.

As Edited By Vk Madhav Mohan

[180] Naivedya :Naivedya refers to the sacred food offering made to a deity in Hinduism before it is consumed as

Prasadam (blessed food). It is an essential part of worship, symbolizing devotion, gratitude, and the offering of one's best to the divine. Meaning & Significance: The word Naivedya comes from Sanskrit: Nai (नै) – "belonging to" Vedi (वेद्य) – "knowledge" or "offering". It signifies surrender and devotion, where devotees offer food to God

before partaking. It is believed that offering food removes ego (as food is a basic necessity of life) and fosters a sense of gratitude.

Types of Naivedya Offerings: Naivedya can range from simple food items to elaborate dishes, varying by region, festival, and deity.

1.Sattvik Naivedya (Pure & Simple Food): Cooked without onion, garlic, or tamasic (impure) ingredients. Common offerings:

•Rice, dal, vegetables (without onion & garlic)

•Fruits

•Milk, curd, ghee, honey

•Coconut

•Dry fruits & nuts

2.Specific Naivedya for Different Deities

•Lord Ganesha – Modak, ladoo, durva grass

•Lord Vishnu/Krishna – Panchamrit, butter, sweets like Peda

•Lord Siva – Bael leaves, bhang, milk, fruits

•Goddess Lakshmi – Rice kheer, coconut, sweet dishes

•Goddess Durga – Puri, halwa, chana, jaggery

•Lord Hanuman – Jaggery, gram (chana), banana, boondi ladoo

Procedure of Offering Naivedya:

1.Preparation with Purity – The food is prepared in a clean manner with devotion.

2.Placing the Naivedya – It is arranged on a clean plate or banana leaf.

"I am Govardhana," and then ate the Naivedya.

All who witnessed were united in their belief, "the mountain has accepted our Puja."

Everyone bowed with Bhakti to the divine form.

The anger that overcame Devendra is the real anger!

The Puja and Yaga meant for him have been disrupted by the Gopas. What arrogance!

And that too, on the opinion of a mere boy! So, then, they have to be shown their place. He summoned the clouds.

"You must destroy the Gopas and their cows," he ordered. The clouds obeyed their Master's order.

They squeezed in, layer upon layer and spread out in the sky. Ear splitting thunder boomed out.

Blinding flashes of lightning danced about. Rain started falling, not ordinary rain.

Each drop like a giant pillar.

3.Invocation Mantra – A prayer or mantra is chanted while offering.
4.Symbolic Offering – The food is symbolically offered to the deity, usually by placing a Tulsi leaf on
it.
5.Silent Absorption – It is believed that the deity absorbs the essence of the food.
6.Distribution as Prasadam – After the offering, the food is distributed as prasadam to devotees.
Scientific & Philosophical Aspects:
•Encourages mindful eating and gratitude.

•Promotes sharing and community bonding.

•Many of the foods offered have Ayurvedic benefits, enhancing health. As edited by VK Madhav Mohan

Withoutinterruption,withoutblocks,pouring,forceful,continuous rainstorm!

Accompanied by howling gale force winds.

The Gopas and cows were drenched and shivering. Water was rising in all four directions.

Hills and holes were indistinguishable. There was no place to sit or sleep.

All were shaken and fearful.

If this continues, death is certain. It feels like the Pralaya[181]. Everyone crowded around SriKrishna and cried, "Protect us, protect us." What is the reason behind this fearsome rainstorm?

Devendra's anger at the disruption of the Puja. Of course, SriKrishna is aware of this.

It is absolutely necessary to puncture Devendra's arrogance. So, what did Bhagavan do?

He ripped out Govardhana, took it in one Hand and held it up like an umbrella! "Take refuge under the mountain. Bring all the cattle too. Have no fear that the mountain will fall. I will protect everyone!" Said SriKrishna to the Gopas. Everyone stood under the mountain.

The rainstorm continued fiercely.

A day passed, then two, then seven.

Still, Bhagavan was unmoved and unshaken. He could stand like that forever, Devendra realised this.

---

[181] Pralaya is a Sanskrit term meaning dissolution, destruction, or the end of a cosmic cycle in Hinduism, particularly in cosmology and mythology. It signifies the periodic destruction and recreation of the universe as part of an eternal cycle.

He had no power to defeat SriKrishna.

It was a gigantic blunder have thought otherwise. Devendra ordered the clouds to disperse.

The rainstorm ceased and the sky cleared.

The Gopas and their cows stepped out. SriKrishna set Govardhana down.

Nandagopa, Yashoda, Rohini, all lovingly embraced Him.

Others performed Abhiksekam[182] on Him with milk and curds (yogurt)[183].

---

[182] The Sanskrit word "Abhishekam" (जिअभषेकम्) means "bathing" or "anointing". It is a sign of reverence, similar to how a king was anointed during coronation in ancient India. Abhishekam is performed to invoke divine energy and purify both the devotee and the temple environment. The pouring of sacred substances represents the devotee's surrender and offering to God.

Types of Abhishekam & Their Significance

Different substances (Dravyas) are used in Abhishekam, each carrying spiritual and health benefits:

Dravya (Substance) & Significance

Water (Jala)Purification and removal of sins

Milk (Dugdha) Peace and prosperity

Honey (Madhu) Sweetness and harmony in life

Ghee (Clarified Butter)Strength, health, and divine blessings

Curd (Dahi)Good fortune and progeny

Sandalwood Paste (Chandanam) Cooling effect and mental peace

Panchamrit (Milk, Curd, Honey, Ghee, Sugar)Divine nourishment and fulfillment of wishes

Coconut Water Removes negative energies and enhances positivity

Lemon JuiceDissolves negative karma Turmeric Water Auspiciousness and prosperity Rice FlourFertility and abundance Deities and Their Specific Abhishekams

•Lord Siva – Abhishekam is most common in Siva temples. Milk, water, and Bilva leaves are poured over the Siva Linga.

•Lord Vishnu – Usually Panchamrit Abhishekam with milk, honey, and ghee is performed.

• Goddess Durga/Kali – Kumkum (vermillion), turmeric, and milk Abhishekam are done for prosperity and protection.

•Lord Hanuman – Abhishekam with Sindoor (vermillion) and mustard oil is common.

•Lord Ganesha – Milk and durva grass are used for blessings.

• Navagrahas (Nine Planets) – Different grains, flowers, and colored substances are offered to please the planetary deities.

How Abhishekam is Performed in Temples

1.Preparation – Devotees bring sacred items like milk, honey, and flowers.

2.Invocation of Deity – Mantras and prayers are recited by priests.

Divine beings showered flowers from the sky and chanted stotras184. A grand demonstration of happiness, gratitude, and Bhakti!

Devendra also arrived.

He was feeling deep remorse.

Arrogance had disappeared like the sunset, head was bowed in contrition.

He fell at SriKrishna's feet.

"Bhagavan, I did not know your strength. I was drunk on arrogance. I have committed a grave mistake. Please forgive me. Bless me so that I am never arrogant again." Devendra pleaded with folded hands.

"Devendra, because of the arrogance caused by your fame you had forgotten Me. That is why I disrupted your Puja. Now, you may go back to Swarga," SriKrishna directed.

3.Offering of Substances – Sacred liquids are poured over the idol or Linga.

4.Chanting of Vedic Mantras – Special mantras, like the Rudram Chamakam for Lord Siva, are recited

5.Completion & Aarti – After the Abhishekam, the deity is adorned with fresh clothes and flowers, followed by aarti and prasadam distribution.

As Edited By Vk Madhav Mohan

[183] Famous Abhishekam Rituals in India

•Mahakaleshwar Abhishekam (Ujjain) – Bhasma (sacred ash) Abhishekam to Lord Siva.

•Tirupati Balaji Abhishekam – Performed every Friday with milk and sandalwood.

•Rameshwaram Abhishekam – One of the most sacred Siva Linga abhishekams.

•Kashi Vishwanath Abhishekam – Rudrabhishekam with Ganga water.

•Puri Jagannath Snana Yatra – A grand bathing ceremony of Lord Jagannath before Rath Yatra. As Edited By Vk Madhav Mohan

184 A Stotram is a hymn of praise dedicated to a deity, sage, or cosmic principle in Hinduism. These verses, usually written in Sanskrit, express devotion (bhakti), gratitude, and adoration, often accompanied by deep spiritual meaning.

Kamadhenu performed Abhishekam on Bhagavan with her own milk and Devendra performed the Abhishekam with water from the Ganga scooped up by Airavata in his trunk.

Meanwhile, SriKrishna also came to be known by another name: Govinda.

The Gopas had been thinking that SriKrishna had divinity in Him. He's at a tender age.

And yet so many amazing things has He done! So many powerful Asusras has He sent Kala's way.

The fierce serpent Kaliya's arrogance was subdued. Now, he's picked up the mountain and held it up.

As effortlessly as an elephant lifts a lotus flower.

The realisation that SriKrishna is none other than Lord MahaVishnu became established in their hearts.

One day Nandagopa went into the river and disappeared.

Where did he go? What happened? No one knew.

Everyone was helpless with worry.

Only SriKrishna understood the actual situation. Varuna's servants had taken Achan[184].

Bhagavan immediately appeared in Varuna's capital.

"I want to see SriKrishna and fulfil the objective of my life. Srikrishna will certainly come in search of Achan!"

That is why Varuna had taken Nandagopa. SriKrishna fulfilled Varuna's desire and left with His father.

---

[184] Achan..Father..in Malayalam…V.K.Madhav Mohan

Sharad Kaalam[185], autumn arrived.

Thefullmoon,SharadPurnima [186] , hadrisenandwasshining magnificently.

Vrindavan was bathed in the soft moonlight. SriKrishna stood alone in the glow.

His lips were caressing the flute.

Divine music began to gush from the flute.

The Amruta of sound spread all over Vrindavan.

It seeped into the hearing and consciousness of the Gopis.

Their souls were powerfully drawn to it like a magnet attracts iron.

Those who were milking cows, eating their meals, cooking rice, serving food, all of them stopped what they were doing.

Their feet took them to where the divine music was coming from.

The love and Bhakti for SriKrishna had made them forget everything else. So much excitement all around!

The most beautiful of the beautiful Gopis were around the most handsome of the handsome, SriKrishna like the full moon in the midst of stars.

The excitement quickly gave way to sadness. SriKrishna disappeared from where He was standing. Where did Bhagavan, the

---

[185] Sharad Kalam (शरद् कालम्) refers to the autumn season in the traditional Indian calendar. It is one of the six seasons (Ritus) described in Hindu scriptures and Ayurveda, occurring between mid-September and mid- November.
[186] Sharad Purnima – A full moon night associated with Lord Krishna's Raas Leela and Goddess Lakshmi's blessings.

Embodiment of Love, go? The Gopis were bewildered, they simply did know.

They started crying uncontrollably and sobbing. They began trudging back home. SriKrishna was nowhere to be found.

The Gopis had a bit of pride.

That pride needed to be removed. That is why SriKrishna had vanished.

There were no places the Gopis did not search.

Their dark, tear-soaked eyes looked frantically hither and tither. But the dark blue-cloud coloured heart-stealing form did not bless those longing eyes.

The Gopis ran here and there in a frenzy, desperately repeating the question to all and sundry, "Did you see Krishna, did you see Krishna?"

They posed the question to the trees, flowers, and deer. None of them answered.

The Gopis broke down with unbearable sorrow.

Suddenly, SriKrishna manifested, drenching the eyes of the Gopis with Amruta.

Sorrow turned to bliss in an instant! Bhagavan embraced His devotees tenderly.

As many SriKrishna's appeared as there were Gopis! Gopis on either side and SriKrishna in the centre!

Like a sapphire in the middle of a necklace of golden beads.

Song and dance and fun and games continued without a break till daybreak!

Dangerous situations arose frequently.

Nandagopa was on the banks of the river Saraswati. He was performing Puja to Lord Siva and Devi Parvati. He had also been undertaking a Vrita[187].

One night, a dreadful event occurred. Nandagopan was deep in slumber.

He was captured and swallowed by a fierce serpent. Nandagopa screamed for help.

The Gopas ran to his rescue.

They started hitting the serpent with flaming torches. The huge serpent was not bothered at all.

By then, SriKrishna arrived. Bhagavan did not hit the serpent.

Instead, He just touched it gently with His foot. An amazing event occurred.

The serpent transformed into a divine form and was subdued. Sudarsana was a Gandharva.

He was exceedingly handsome, much more so than anyone else. He was also arrogant about his good looks.

Once he came upon some Maharshi's who were ugly and unkempt. The pompous Sudarsana made fun of their appearance.

The Maharshis cursed him and made him into a serpent.

With just a touch of SriKrishna's divine feet he obtained redemption.

---

[187] The word "Vritam" (-വ്രതം in Malayalam, व्रतम् in Sanskrit) refers to a religious vow, observance, or disciplined practice undertaken for spiritual or moral reasons. It often involves fasting, prayers, rituals, or self-discipline to achieve a sacred goal, as edited by VK Madhav Mohan

Sankhachooda was one of Kubera's attendants. A gem was embedded in his head.

He once committed an act of aggression. SriKrishna and Balarama were relaxing in the forest. The Gopi women were with them.

Sankhachooda kidnapped some of the Gopis. Terrified, they cried out for help.

SriKrishna and Balarama gave chase to Sankhachooda.

When he found that he was about to be caught, he released the women and ran faster.

Balarama stood guard over the women. SriKrishna chased down Sankhachooda and ripped off his head.

From the head, He prised out the gem and offered it to His elder brother. The cruel Arishtasura prepared to kill SriKrishna.

He took the form of a huge ox.

Mistaking him for a mountain, the clouds sat upon the bull. The bull was that big!

Snorting fiercely, raising its tail, screeching loudly and lowering its horns the bull raced towards Gokula.

The Gopas were frightened.

SriKrishna caught hold of both the horns and hurled the bull far into the distance.

The bull rose up and charged SriKrishna again.

SriKrishna held it by the horns and flipped it onto the earth and kicked it repeatedly like wet clothes being beaten clean.

Then He ripped out the horns and smashed the bull. Vomiting blood, Arishtasura sprawled dead.

Around this time Narada Maharshi went and met Kamsa. Maharshi told Kamsa a secret that he had known nothing about. Balarama and SriKrishna are not the sons of Rohini and Yasodha. Actually, they are the sons of Devaki.

It was Vasudeva who brought SriKrishna to Gokula. Kamsa was overcome with anger, he was ready to cut Vasudeva's throat.

Took his sword and left to kill Vasudeva.

However, Narada Maharshi stopped him. Kamsa did not kill Vasudeva.

Yet, he imprisoned him in the dungeons and Devaki too.

Kamsa was not satisfied, though.

Somehow, (Bala)Rama and Krishna have to be killed. How can this be achieved?

A strategy dawned on Kamsa.

He had two servants who were ace wrestlers - Chanoora and Mushtika. No one could win against them.

Balarama and SriKrishna should be made to fight against them. The wrestlers would kill them both.

There was absolutely no doubt about that. But the wrestling match was a second option. Before that, another ploy had to be tried.

Kamsa could use his giant, killer-elephant, Kuvalayapeedha to kill them. If that didn't work, he could try the wrestling match.

One or the other method would definitely succeed if he conducted the Dhanur Yaga[188].

Kamsa organised the Dhanur Yaga quickly.

He would now have to ensure that the RamaKrishnas, Balarama and SriKrishna would attend.

He instructed Akrura: go to Gokula, convince both and bring them. Akrura had known much earlier that SriKrishna is Lord MahaVishnu Himself.

He was steadfast in his Bhakti towards Bhagavan. It was just that he had concealed it in his heart.

Kamsa had decided one other thing.

He would get his servant Kesi to kill SriKrishna.

If he could do that, none of the other actions would be necessary. The Asura, Kesi, assumed the form of a very large horse.

The mane and hair on his body could even disperse the clouds!

The gigantic horse came up and aimed a kick at SriKrishna.

He dodged with lightning speed, grabbed the legs and heaved; the horse fell far away.

It got up and raced in again.

---

[188] Dhanur Yaga refers to a sacrificial ritual or event associated with bows (Dhanus) in Hindu mythology. It is most famously linked to King Kamsa's wrestling festival in Mathura, where he planned to kill Lord Krishna and Balarama. part of the event, a huge ceremonial bow (Dhanus) was placed in Kamsa's court for worship. When Krishna entered the arena, he effortlessly lifted and broke the mighty bow, shocking Kamsa and his ministers. This act symbolized the destruction of Kamsa's power and the impending downfall of his rule. Soon after, Krishna defeated Kamsa's strongest wrestlers and later killed Kamsa himself, liberating Mathura,as edited by VK Madhav Mohan

SriKrishna thrust his left hand into the horse's mouth. The divine hand grew rapidly in size.

Kesi was suffocated.

His eyes went up and around and legs became paralysed. SriKrishna pulled out his hand.

The Asura had died already.

Another Asura too died at the divine hands in a different way.

The son of Maya, Vyomasura experienced such a death. Vyomasura abducted a few Gopa boys and held them in a cave. Then he closed the mouth of the cave with rocks.

Bhagavan came to know of this and rushed to rescue the boys.

He caught the Asura, flung him to the ground and strangled him to death and freed His friends.

Akrura was travelling to meet SriKrishna. His mind was beset by so many thoughts! How many good deeds might have I done!

I am now about to receive the fruit of those deeds - the divine Darsana[189] of SriKrishna.

Is there a greater good fortune than this? No.

There is not going to be much more delay.

I'm going to fall at the divine Feet and worship Him. In that instant, all my sins will be wiped clean, the purpose of my life will be fulfilled.

In one way, Kamsa's order was beneficial.

---

[189] "Darśana" means having a sacred vision of a deity or a saint. It is a key part of temple visits, where devotees seek divine blessings by seeing the deity (Murti, as edited by VK Madhav Mohan

How else would I have been able to obtain this opportunity?

Bhagavan's tender form sparked waves of emotion and beauty
- oh, how clear they were in Akrura's mind!

A peacock feather tied within curly blue hair, blue forehead with
a Tilak[190], eyes that far surpass the beauty of a lotus, a nose that is
the definition of elegance, tender lips from which divine melodies
arise[191], and the enchanting smile that blossoms and blooms on
them. How many times have I seen all this in my mind's eye!

Now, it is time for me to see them with the eyes in my body.
Time for the vision of grand good fortune!

As a messenger of the wicked Kamsa, will Bhagavan doubt me?
Why am I fearful of this?

Can Bhagavan not see inside and outside alike with His eyes?

---

[190] The word "Tilak" (തിലക് in Malayalam, तिलक in Sanskrit) refers to
a sacred mark applied on the forehead in Hinduism. It is worn as a symbol of
devotion, spiritual significance, or cultural identity. Commonly applied during
pujas, rituals, and temple visits. Symbolizes the third eye (Ajna Chakra), wisdom,
and divine energy.
Different Types of Tilak Based on Traditions
Urdhva Pundra: (Vertical Tilak) Two or three vertical lines on the forehead
(usually with a central red or yellow mark) denotes Vaishnavism (Followers of
Lord Vishnu & Krishna).
Tripundra: (Three Horizontal Lines)Three horizontal lines of sacred ash
(vibhuti), often with a red dot in the center ; denotes Shaivism (Followers of Lord
Siva)
Red Kumkum Dot: (Bindi / Tilak) Married women wear it as a sign of
prosperity and auspiciousness; denotes Shaktism
Chandan Tilak: (Sandalwood Paste) Cooling effect, used by saints & priests;
Common in various sects
Yellow & Red Tilak : (Haldi-Kumkum) Symbolizes auspiciousness, victory,
and honorApplied in religious ceremonies & greetings, as edited by VK Madhav
Mohan
[191] Chenthondikkindalundakkunna chenchundukal..MaliBhagavatam, 1968
Edition, DC Books, pa 91..V.K.Madhav Mohan

What should I do when I reach Him?

I will fall at those sacred Feet and do Namaskaram. Bhagavan will cast a glance laden with compassion at me. He will raise me up from His feet.

On my head He will place his sin-dispelling Hands and then He will embrace me.

I will be immersed in the sea of bliss!

Akrura travelled far in the kingdom of imagination. His journey was coming to an end.

Bhagavan's footprints began to be visible. Akrura was overcome with emotion.

He alighted from the chariot and rolled in the dust, the pure, divine dust in which Bhagavan's footprints had been imprinted.

Soon the kingdom of imagination became real. Bhagavan's form came into view.

Akrura's eyes filled up and overflowed, a thrill of devotion shot through his entire body. His ability to speak evaporated.

He ran and prostrated at Bhagavan's feet.

Bhagavan helped him up, caressed him gently, embraced him firmly, following Him, so too did Balarama. Together, both of them led Akrura inside. Made him sit on the sacred seat, washed his feet, served food, and Tamboolam[192] too.

---

[192] he word "Taamboolam" (താംബൂലം in Malayalam, ताम्बूलम् in Sanskrit) refers to the traditional offering of betel leaves, areca nut, and slaked lime, often accompanied by other auspicious items. It is a symbol of hospitality, prosperity, and blessings in Hindu culture, as edited by VK Madhav Mohan

Akrura spoke about the reason for his visit. SriKrishna had understood everything.

He decided to go to Mathura.

Many things had to be accomplished in Mathura, the most important being the killing of Kamsa.

Many Gopas too prepared to travel.

They carried pots filled with curds and butter. These were to be offered to Kamsa.

After all, isn't Dhanur Yaga is being conducted? Srikrishna, Balarama and Akrura travelled together. They were all in the same chariot.

In the afternoon, SriKrishna and Balarama got down from the chariot. They drank water from the Kalindi river and returned to the chariot.

Akrura too went to the river and bathed. When he chanted mantras and took a dip, he could see SriKrishna and Balarama underwater! Rising to the surface, he looked at the chariot.

Both of them were still seated in the chariot!

Was it just his imagination that he saw them underwater? To crosscheck, Akrura took a dip again.

There, this time he could see clearly, Lord MahaVishnu and Adisesha! The greatness of Bhagavan!

All Akrura could do was to worship and surrender completely! It was late when they reached Mathura.

Akrura requested that they stay at his home.

Bhagavan agreed to do that after killing Kamsa. The next day, SriKrishna went around to see the city.

Balarama and some companions went with Him.

Gopuras [193] , Torana [194] , palatialhouses,grainstorehouses, soldier's barracks, marketplaces, broad roads, how wonderful they all were!

Many citizens saw SriKrishna and Balarama.

Once they were seen no one could take their eyes off! The divine beauty and attraction were irresistible.

They came upon a washerman.

He was the one who washed Kamsa's clothes. Many colleagues accompanied him.

Everyone carried big bundles of clothes.

"Please give us the washed clothes," SriKrishna requested them.

The haughty washerman was angry and contemptuous.

"Oh, the forest and mountain dwellers want to wear the Maharaja's clothes! You want to feel that you're wearing silk garments? If you care for your life run far away from here. Or else the King's soldiers will break your bones," he said dismissively. Shouldn't this effrontery be punished?

---

[193] The word "Gopura" (ഗോപുരം in Malayalam, गोपुर in Sanskrit & Tamil) refers to the ornate, towering entrance gateway of a Hindu temple. It is an important architectural feature, especially in South Indian Dravidian-style temples…

[194] The word "Torana" (തോരണം in Malayalam, तोरण in Sanskrit) refers to a sacred or decorative gateway, arch, or festoon used in Hindu, Buddhist, and Jain traditions. It is commonly seen in temples, palaces, and homes, symbolizing auspiciousness, welcome, and protection, as edited by VK Madhav Mohan

SriKrishna ripped off the washerman's head and threw it on the ground. The man's colleagues dropped the bundles of clothes and fled.

SriKrishna and Balarama wore the best clothes from the bundles.

They gave the Gopas all the clothes they wanted and threw the rest away.

SriKrishna was seen by workers without haughtiness too. A tailor presented Him with especially decorated clothes.

Beautiful flower garlands were presented by a garland seller. SriKrishna and Balarama walked away, adorned with all of this.

A young woman approached with a vessel full of sandalwood paste. She was beautiful but was bent over and walking with difficulty.

"Who are you and for whom is the sandalwood paste? Give it to me," said SriKrishna.

"I am Teevraka, the Dasi[195] who applies sandalwood paste. Kamsa Maharaja prefers my sandalwood paste.

---

[195] Dasi (ദാസി) is a term historically used in India, particularly in Sanskrit, Malayalam, and other Indian languages, to refer to a female servant, maid, or attendant. In its simplest sense, a Dasi refers to a maidservant or

female slave, often serving in the homes of royalty, nobles, or wealthy individuals.The male equivalent is "Dasa" (ദാസൻ), meaning a servant or devotee. In spiritual and bhakti traditions, "Dasi" refers to a devoted female

follower or servant of God. Examples include Sita (as Rama Dasi) or Meera Bai (as Krishna Dasi), symbolizing complete surrender and devotion to the divine. In historical India, some Dasis were associated with temples as Devadasis (literally meaning "servants of God"). Devadasis were trained in classical dance and music and were dedicated to temple rituals. Over time, the system deteriorated, and many Devadasis faced exploitation of many kinds, as edited by VK Madhav Mohan

However, you are the one who deserves it," the woman with a stoop replied.

She extended the vessel towards SriKrishna.

SriKrishna and Balarama smeared the sandalwood paste on themselves. A suitable reward had to be provided to Teevraka, isn't it?

SriKrishna stepped on her feet and pressed.

Then, with His divine Hands He held her hands and stretched them upwards.

Instantly, Teevraka was free of her stoop and stood up straight. Then, she was endowed with so much beauty!

Dhanur Yaga was being conducted.

The ceremonial bow was placed for Puja. It was a special bow, studded with gems.

Many soldiers stood guarding it.

SriKrishna and Balarama entered the premises. The soldiers tried to stop both of them.

Brushing them aside, SriKrishna raised the bow in his left hand, stood it up on the floor, bent it and strung it and then broke it!

Like a tusker snapping a length of sugarcane!

The bow had been placed for Puja, the guards rushed in with great anger.

SriKrishna and Balarama each took a piece of the broken bow and beat the guards to death.

And then, nonchalantly, they walked out to see the sights!

That night was indeed a dark night for Kamsa, a night full of fears. So many bad omens had occurred!

When he looked at the mirror his head was not visible. When he looked at the moon and fire, each seemed double. When he stepped on mud, no footprints could be seen.

When he slept, nightmares would bring Pretas who would cling to him, various kinds of nightmares in which he walked around naked and similar ones.

The wrestling match was to be held in the morning. Toranas had appeared.

Garlands with many kinds of flowers had been hung. Flags were fluttering in the breeze. Countless charming colourful canopies had been set up. Seats had been arranged all around.

Ministers, prominent citizens and spectators were all filling the arena. Kamsa was present in his royal pavilion.

The battleground is in the centre. Drumbeats are beginning!

The wrestling match, hand to hand combat, is all set to commence.

Chanoora and Mushtika entered the arena along with Sala, Tosala and other fighters.

Every one of them is strong and courageous.

They were all roaring and slapping their thighs in anticipation. Only the (Bala)RamaKrishnas were yet to arrive.

They arrive, but entering the arena is a problem!

Just outside the Gopura, confining the space, is stationed the killer elephant - Kuvalayapeedha.

The mahout has positioned the killer elephant to kill. "Move the elephant aside, make way for us. Else, I will kill the elephant and you," said SriKrishna. The mahout, of course, did not comply.

Instead, he directed the elephant to attack SriKrishna.

Theelephantmovedforward,extendedhistrunkandgrabbed SriKrishna.

SriKrishna slipped out of the elephant's grasp and landed a blow on its forehead.

Then, he slipped in between its legs.

The elephant caught SriKrishna again with its trunk. Srikrishna escaped again and moved to the rear.

He pulled the elephant by its tail.

To get at SriKrishna, the elephant kept turning round and around. In a flash, SriKrishna spun to the front.

The elephant tried to catch Him.

Just as he was about to be caught, SriKrishna changed direction and avoided capture.

Then, He pretended to fall.

The elephant thrust with his tusks. SriKrishna rolled away.

The tusks struck the ground!

The battle raged for some more time.

Finally, SriKrishna decided that enough was enough. He held the elephant's trunk and pulled hard.

The elephant fell, head over heels.

SriKrishna tore out the tusks and beat the elephant to death and the mahout too.

SriKrishna heaved one tusk on to his shoulder, Balarama took the other one.

Drenched in blood both of them burst into the arena!

The spectators had heard about SriKrishna and Balarama.

After all, isn't everyone praising the beauty and courage of both the brothers?

Their beauty far exceeded what people had heard.

As for their courage, that was going to be revealed very soon. Chanoora was the foremost amongst the wrestlers.

He challenged the RamaKrishnas.

"Maharaja desires to know how good are your combat skills. That is why you've been brought here. Come, let's begin the battle!"

In jest SriKrishna asked, "We are Balas, young boys and you are Balavan, very strong. How can we do battle with you?"

"G r e a t ! Aren't you the boy who killed the killer elephant who was as strong as a thousand elephants? And, is the boy who has earned a reputation for strength, Balarama the one without strength?[196] Krishna, you fight with me and Balarama will fight against Mushtika," said Chanoora.

Two bouts at the same time! Legs and hands intertwined. Bunched fists slamming into each other, bent knees pounding one another. Head butting. Deft moves and powerful throws. Clinching and sweating.

Pulling forward, shoving back. Pushing into the ground and so both the battles raged. Srikrishna's hands were hard as diamonds.

The blows from those hands weakened Chanoora. With all his strength he struck SriKrishna in the chest.

Will an elephant be shaken if it is hit by a flower garland? Chanoora's punch had the same effect on SriKrishna.

---

[196] Balavan ennå peredutha Balaramano balamillatha balan ? ..MaliBhagavatham, p 95, 1968 Edition, DC Books.

Bhagavan suddenly grabbed Chanoora, twirled him around and flung him hard onto the ground.

Chanoora breathed his last!

Meanwhile, Mushtika suffered a terrible beating at the hands of the powerful Balarama.

He vomited blood and died.

Kooda arrived in the arena.

Balarama cocked his left hand and hit him. Kooda collapsed and died.

Sala and Tosala closed in around SriKrishna. SriKrishna kicked Sala to death.

Then he caught Tosala by the legs and tore in two. The other combatants simply ran away.

If they had stayed, they too would have died. All the prominent fighters have been killed. Kamsa was confused and maddened.

He shouted frenzied orders to his soldiers, "Chase away Rama and Krishna. Tie up Nandagopa. Kill Vasudeva. And also, my father who has sided with my enemies."

Hardly had he finished speaking when SriKrishna appeared in front of him.

Kamsa picked up his sword and shield.

SriKrishna gripped Kamsa by the hair and felled him. Then He sat on his body and killed him in an instant.

Kamsa had eight brothers, all eight rushed in anger. Balarama killed all eight of them.

Remember, Vasudeva and Devaki were in the dungeons? SriKrishna and Balarama freed them.

"Acha, Amma, you had to suffer because of us. We were in another place. We did not have the good fortune of enjoying the tender love of parents. Please forgive us for our inadequacies," SriKrishna requested them. Do you know what Vasudeva and Devaki did?

They made both their children sit in their laps. Kept embracing them tighter and tighter, rained kisses on their heads, and bathed them in tears.

They couldn't find words, so overcome were they with emotion.

Kamsa had usurped the kingdom from his father Ugrasena. SriKrishna made Ugrasena rule as the King.

Many righteous people had left the kingdom in fear of Kamsa. They were all brought back by Bhagavan.

No one had to fear Kamsa anymore! Srikrishna decided to live in Mathura.

He had to part from Nandagopa and Yashoda.

They had raised him with love and tenderness all this while. SriKrishna and Balarama were deeply saddened.

How can the sorrow of Nandagopa and Yashoda be described? Both the boys are so very close to their hearts[197]. How can they be apart?

Gokula without the brothers? Unthinkable! But what could anyone do?

---

[197] "Kannilunnikal aanu unnikal randum"...MaliBhagavatam p 96, 1968 Edition, DC Books..V.K.Madhav Mohan

Shedding rivers of tears Nandagopa and Yashoda bid goodbye. Balarama and SriKrishna commenced their education, Sandeepani Maharshi was their Guru.

He was born in Kasi[198] and lived in Avanti.

---

[198] Kasi is Varanasi or Benaras. The ancient and sacred city in India, known for its spiritual significance, temples (especially Kashi Vishwanath), and connection to Hinduism, moksha (liberation), and pilgrimage as edited by VK Madhav Mohan

Balarama and SriKrishna went there, both of them served their Guru with Bhakti. He taught them - Vedas[199], Upanishads[200],

---

[199] he Vedas (वेद) are the most ancient and revered scriptures of Hinduism, considered the foundational texts of Indian philosophy, spirituality, and knowledge. They are believed to have been revealed (Śruti) to ancient sages (Rishis) and passed down orally before being written down in Sanskrit. The Vedas are composed in poetic and hymn form and serve as the source of various branches of Hindu thought, including rituals, philosophy, and sciences.

The Four Vedas

The Vedas are divided into four main texts:

1.Rgveda (ऋग्वेद) •The oldest and most important Veda.•Composed of hymns (Suktas) dedicated to deities like Agni (fire),

Indra (rain), Varuna (cosmic order), and Soma (ritual drink).•Contains over 10,000 verses in 1,028 hymns.•Discusses cosmology, philosophy, and the nature of existence.

2.Yajurveda (यजुर्वेद) • Focuses on rituals, ceremonies, and sacrificial rites.•Divided into two versions: Shukla Yajurveda

(White) and Krishna Yajurveda (Black).•Provides mantras and procedures for performing Vedic sacrifices (Yajnas).

3.Sāmaveda (सामवेद) •Known as the "Veda of Melodies."•Contains hymns mainly from the Rgveda but arranged for chanting in musical form. •Forms the basis for Indian classical music. •Associated with devotional and ritualistic singing.

4.Atharvaveda (अथर्ववेद) •Deals with everyday life, healing, magic, and practical knowledge.•Contains hymns for protection, health, success, and social harmony. •Less ritualistic than the other Vedas and closer to folk traditions.

Structure of the Vedas :Each Veda consists of four major parts: 1.Samhitas (संहिता) – Collection of hymns, prayers, and mantras. 2.Brahmanas (ब्राह्मण) – Ritualistic and ceremonial instructions.3.Aranyakas (आरण्यक) – Philosophical and symbolic interpretations of rituals.4.Upanishads (उपिनषद्) – Mystical and philosophical teachings on the self (Ātman) and ultimate reality

(Brahman).

The Upavedas (Subsidiary Vedas) The Vedas also have four Upavedas, which are applied knowledge branches:

1.Ayurveda – Medicine and health. 2.Dhanurveda – Warfare and military science.3.Gandharvaveda – Music, dance, and fine arts.4.Arthashastra – Governance, politics, and economics.

The Vedangas (Auxiliary Sciences) To assist in the study and application of the Vedas, six Vedangas (limbs of the Vedas) were developed: 1.Shiksha –

Phonetics and pronunciation. 2.Vyakarana – Grammar (e.g., Pāṇini's Ashtadhyayi). 3.Chandas – Metrics (poetic meter).4.Nirukta – Etymology (study of words and their meanings).5.Kalpa – Rituals and ceremonies.6.Jyotisha – Astronomy and astrology Significance of the Vedas •Considered Apauruṣeya (not of human origin) and revealed to Rishis. •Form the foundation of Hindu dharma (Sanatana Dharma).•Have influenced Indian philosophy, culture, and sciences.•Continue to be recited and studied in temples and Vedic schools (Gurukuls).

as edited by VK Madhav Mohan

[200] The Upanishads (उपिनषद्) are the philosophical and mystical texts of Hinduism, forming the core of Vedanta (the "end of the Vedas"). They explore profound spiritual concepts such as the nature of the self (Ātman), the ultimate reality (Brahman), karma, rebirth, and liberation (Moksha). The Upanishads mark the transition from Vedic ritualism to spiritual philosophy, focusing on self-realization and inner knowledge.

Origins and Structure •The Upanishads are part of the Shruti (revealed texts) and belong to the last section of the Vedas.•They are attached to the four Vedas (Ṛgveda, Yajurveda, Sāmaveda, Atharvaveda). •The name Upanishad means "sitting near" (upa = near, ni = down, shad = sit), referring to the intimate teacher-student dialogues on deep spiritual truths.

Major Upanishads: There are over 200 Upanishads, but 13 principal ones are most significant:1.Īsha Upanishad – Discusses the all- pervading nature of Brahman and the balance between action and renunciation. 2.Kena Upanishad – Explores the nature of the mind, consciousness, and the supreme knowledge beyond the senses. 3.Kaṭha Upanishad – Contains the famous story of Nachiketa and Yama (the Lord of Death), discussing the immortality of the soul. 4.Praśna Upanishad – A Q&A dialogue on the origin of the universe, Prana (life force), and meditation. 5.Muṇḍaka Upanishad – Introduces the idea of Para Vidya (higher knowledge of Brahman) and Apara Vidya (worldly knowledge). 6.Māṇḍūkya Upanishad – Describes the four states of consciousness: Waking, Dreaming, Deep Sleep, and Turiya (pure awareness).7.Taittirīya Upanishad – Explains the five koshas (sheaths) of human existence and the importance of bliss (Ananda).

8.Aitareya Upanishad – Discusses creation theory and the emergence of the soul. 9.Chāndogya Upanishad – Contains the famous "Tat Tvam Asi" ("You Are That") teaching, emphasizing the unity of Ātman and Brahman. 10.Bṛhadāraṇyaka Upanishad – The longest Upanishad, covering deep metaphysical ideas and Yajnavalkya's teachings on the Self. 11.Shvetāshvatara Upanishad – Introduces theistic concepts, discussing Ishvara (personal God), yoga, and karma12.Kaushītaki Upanishad – Explores the journey of the soul after death. 13.Maitrī Upanishad – Discusses duality, mind control, and meditation.

Key Teachings of the Upanishads

1.Brahman: The Ultimate Reality

•Brahman is the absolute, infinite consciousness beyond time, space, and causation.

•It is the source of all creation, present everywhere but beyond human perception.

2.Ātman: The True Self

•Ātman is the eternal soul, pure consciousness within every being.

•Realizing "Ātman = Brahman" leads to Moksha (liberation).

3.Maya: The Illusion of the World

•The material world is Maya (illusion), created by ignorance.

•Only true knowledge (Jnana) can remove ignorance and reveal the real self.

4.Karma and Rebirth

•Every action (karma) has consequences, leading to rebirth (samsara).

•Liberation (moksha) ends the cycle of birth and death.

5.Meditation and Self-Inquiry

•Meditation, inner reflection, and self-inquiry are emphasized to realize Brahman.

•Aum (ॐ) is considered the cosmic sound that represents ultimate reality.

6.Guru-Shishya Tradition

•Spiritual wisdom is transferred through guru-disciple relationships.

•True knowledge comes not from books but through deep experience and guidance.

The Upanishads are the foundation of Vedanta philosophy.
as edited by VK Madhav Mohan

Dharmasastras[201], Nyayasastras[202], Rajaniti[203], Ayudhavidya[204] and many other things.

Such was their intellect and memory that they only had to hear something once to understand, assimilate and remember forever.

After the education was completed, Dakshina[205] had to be provided. They asked the Guru what Dakshina they could offer.

---

[201] Dharmaśāstras (धर्मशास्त्र) are ancient Hindu texts that define and guide the ethical, moral, social, and legal duties (Dharma) of individuals and society. These texts provide rules on law, justice, governance, family life, caste duties, and spiritual responsibilities. They form the foundation of Hindu law and have influenced Indian jurisprudence over centuries, as edited by VK Madhav Mohan

[202] Nyāyaśāstra (न्यायशास्त्र) – The Science of Logic and Reasoning: The Nyāyaśāstra (also called Nyāya Darśana) is one of the six classical schools of Indian philosophy (Shad Darshanas). It is the science of logic, reasoning, debate, and epistemology (the study of knowledge). Nyāya provides a systematic method for acquiring valid knowledge and distinguishing truth from falsehood, as edited by VK Madhav Mohan

[203] Rajanīti (राजनीति) – The Art of Governance and StatecraftRājanīti refers to the principles of governance, administration, diplomacy, military strategy, and ethics in politics. It is the ancient Indian science of statecraft, guiding rulers on how to govern effectively, maintain order, and protect their kingdom…ChatGPT 40 as edited by VK Madhav Mohan

[204] Ayudhavidya (आयुधविद्या) is the ancient Indian science of warfare and weaponry. It is a branch of Dhanurveda (धनुर्वेद), which is one of the traditional Upavedas (subsidiary Vedas) associated with the Yajurveda. Ayudhavidya encompasses various aspects of martial arts, including the use of traditional weapons like swords, bows, spears, and maces, as well as unarmed combat techniques, as edited by VK Madhav Mohan

[205] Dakṣiṇā (दिक्षणा) – The Sacred Offering of Gratitude and Duty: Dakṣiṇā refers to the act of offering or giving in gratitude, as a form of duty or honor, often given to a guru, priest, or as a religious offering. It is an essential part of Vedic culture, Hindu rituals, and ethical living, symbolizing respect, learning, and the fulfillment of one's obligations.Meaning and Significance •Derived from the Sanskrit root "dakṣi", meaning "worthy," "capable," or "fitting". •It is not a transaction but an offering of gratitude—a spiritual and ethical duty.•Mentioned in the Vedas, Upanishads, Dharmaśāstras, and Puranas as a means to sustain knowledge, dharma, and societal harmony, as edited by VK Madhav Mohan

"I want my son back, alive. He had drowned in the ocean," replied Sandeepani Maharshi.

Is this possible for any ordinary person to accomplish?

But is there anything impossible for SriKrishna and Balarama? They went to the ocean.

Varuna arrived to greet and pay respects to them. SriKrishna asked him to return the Guru's son.

Varuna then told them what had actually happened.

The child was taken not by him but by the Asura named Panchajana. He was living in the ocean in the form a conch.

SriKrishna dived into the ocean and killed Panchajana. He took the conch named Panchajanya from his body but the Guru's son was not found.

Bhagavan rose from the ocean.

Along with Balarama, He went to the capital city of Yama. He sounded the conch loudly.

Recognising the sound of Bhagavan's conch Yama arrived immediately. SriKrishna told him the reason for His arrival.

The Guru's son was indeed present in Yama's capital. Yama handed the boy over to SriKrishna and SriKrishna took him back to Sandeepani Maharshi.

The Maharshi's joy knew no bounds.

He blessed his disciples with all his heart. They returned to Mathura.

Udhava was the chief amongst the Ministers. He was intelligent, righteous and full of Bhakti. SriKrishna despatched him to Gokula.

Comfort and console my parents, friends and the Gopis - that was Bhagavan's instruction to Udhava.

How can they be comforted and consoled? They were living in extraordinary grief because of separation from SriKrishna.

Gokula was shrouded in desolation as though life had deserted it. SriKrishna was a feast for the eyes.

His music was soothing to the ears. SriKrishna's form was now, no longer visible. Srikrishna's music was now, no longer heard.

Not for a moment could separation from SriKrishna be endured. Can separation forever even be imagined!

SriKrishna was in everyone's consciousness, every moment.

Everyone's heart was pounding in desperation all the time. Udhava attempted to pacify them but how could they find peace?

SriKrishna had a close relationship with the Pandavas. Their mother Kunti was Vasudeva's sister.

SriKrishna had the deepest affection for his aunt and her sons. "Akrura, please go to Hastinapura. After Pandu passed away, Kuntidevi is in great difficulty. Dhritarashtra is partial towards his own children. Inside his heart he harbours enmity towards the Pandavas. Please return after enquiring about the true and complete state of affairs," Bhagavan instructed Akrura.

Akrura stayed for a few days in Hastinapura.

He learned everything about the situation there. The Pandavas followed the path of Dharma.

The citizenry had great affection for them but Duryodhana and his brothers had undying hatred towards them. The despicable brothers had the backing of their father.

They had inflicted many atrocities on the Pandavas.

And they would continue to do so.

Kuntidevi was helpless and suffering unending, tearful grief.

SriKrishna was the only hope and shelter for Kuntidevi and the Pandavas. Akrura counselled Dhritarashtra,

"Pandu was your younger brother. After his death you are now the Maharaja. Please consider the Pandavas as your sons. Conduct your reign with righteousness, Dharma. Then, your name and fame will live forever. Otherwise, the world will disrespect you. And you will tumble into Naraka." Akrura's counsel was wise and correct.

Not that Dhritarashtra was unaware of this. Pandavas are the sons of his younger brother.

He ought to nurture affection towards them and consider them as his own sons.

All that was true.

Yet, Dhritashtra had overwhelming, excessive love towards his own offspring.

That love had led him to the wrong path. SriKrishna had many enemies.

Many of them SriKrishna had already dispatched to the Land of Kaala[206]. But many powerful adversaries remained.

Foremostamongstthemwastheall-powerfulRajaofMagadha, Jarasandha.

Jarasandha bore undying hatred and enmity towards SriKrishna for a special reason.

---

[206] Death..V.K.Madhav Mohan

SriKrishna was the killer of Kamsa. Jarasandha was the bosom friend of Kamsa.

Not just that, he was also the closest relative of Kamsa. Kamsa's wives, Asti and Prapti, were Jarasandha's daughters.

After the death of their husband, they were living with their father. Jarasandha had resolved, SriKrishna had widowed his daughters. He must pay!

Jarasandha was determined to extract revenge from SriKrishna!

SriKrishna too was prepared. Jarasandha was sure to attack.

That would, in a way, be advantageous.

Jarasandha commanded a huge following of wicked people. Only if they are destroyed will Bhoomi be relieved of distress. As many as possible should be killed in that first attack.

But Jarasandha should be spared.

He will then lead a second attack by the villains. Jarasandha should still be untouched but the villains would all be killed.

When this happened repeatedly, most of the wicked would have been eliminated.

Jarasandha would then be killed by someone else. This was the plan that Bhagavan had designed.

Jarasandha attacked with a huge army.

The Yadava army faced the attack head-on. The battle was ferocious.

SriKrishna's and Balarama's skill and valour were incomparable. Jarasandha's entire army was wiped out and he alone remained alive. Balarama caught hold of Jarasandha and prepared to kill him when SriKrishna stopped him.

Wouldn't Srikrishna's intention be impeded if Jarasandha had been killed?

The defeat did not cow Jarasandha down.

He regrouped and staged a second attack on a massive scale. This time too his army was destroyed.

He attacked a third time.

Then too he suffered defeat and destruction. Jarasandha attacked 17 times!

Every time his experience was not different. Jarasandha prepared for the 18th attack.

This time he had readied an army that was bigger than ever before.

In addition, the Mlecha[207] army had also joined battle against SriKrishna. Kalayavana, Chief of the Mlecha army was feared by the entire world.

---

[207] The Mlecha Army refers to the foreign or non-Vedic tribes that participated in battles during the Mahabharata era. The term "Mleccha" was used in ancient Sanskrit literature to describe people who did not follow Vedic culture, spoke different languages, or came from distant lands. They were often depicted as powerful warriors but were considered outsiders by the mainstream Vedic kingdoms.

Mlechas in Jarasandha's Army

Jarasandha, the King of Magadha, had a massive and diverse army, which included many Mlecha warriors. He had alliances with several non-Aryan tribes and brought them into his battles against Krishna and the Yadavas. Some of these Mlecha forces were:

•Shakas (Scythians)
•Yavanas (Greeks)
•Kambojas (Central Asian warriors)
•Kiratas (tribes from the Himalayan region)
•Pulindas and Nishadas (forest-dwelling tribes)

Jarasandha had decided to follow just behind him. SriKrishna spoke to Balarama, "Dear elder brother, we are going to be busy fighting Jarasandha. He will seize the moment to either kill or capture our relatives. We must not allow him that opportunity. So, let us build an impregnable fort." That was how Dwaraka was built.

It was constructed by the Architect of the Devas, Vishwakarma[208]. The ocean surrounded it on all sides.

These Mlecha warriors were known for their fierce combat skills and unconventional warfare techniques. Jarasandha used their military strength in his 17 attacks on Mathura, making his invasions particularly difficult for Krishna and the Yadavas to resist.
as edited by VK Madhav Mohan
[208] Vishwakarma is the celestial architect and divine engineer in Hindu mythology. He is credited with designing and constructing some of the most magnificent cities, palaces, and divine weapons in the universe. He is considered the chief architect of the Devas (gods) and the builder of celestial cities, palaces, and divine weapons.

He is often depicted as a skilled craftsman with multiple tools in his hands, symbolizing his mastery over architecture, engineering, and craftsmanship. He is also known as the Divine Carpenter and Blacksmith, creating weapons for gods like Vishnu, Siva, and Indra.

Famous Creations by Vishwakarma

1.Sudharma Sabha (Assembly Hall of Dwaraka): •Vishwakarma built the Sudharma Sabha, the grand royal court of Krishna in Dwaraka. It was a divine hall, always pleasant in all seasons and a symbol of justice and righteousness.

2.Dwaraka – Krishna's City: After Krishna decided to leave Mathura due to constant attacks from Jarasandha and Kalayavana, Vishwakarma was tasked with creating Dwaraka.•He built it as a fortified, island city, making it unconquerable. The city was filled with golden palaces, vast gardens, and intricate designs, making it one of the most glorious cities in Hindu mythology.

3.Indraprastha: The Pandavas' Capital.When the Pandavas were given Khandavaprastha, it was an arid, barren land. Krishna advised them to seek Vishwakarma's help, and he transformed it into Indraprastha, a grand and prosperous city. The Maya Sabha (royal court of the Pandavas), which later played a crucial role in the Mahabharata, was one of his finest creations.

Its beauty was beyond description. Extraordinarily strong and unshakeable. SriKrishna was given various gifts by the Devas.

Devendra presented the assembly hall named Sudharma[209]. Varuna gave horses that ran faster than thoughts and Kubera infinite riches.

Dwarakapuram shone with all these priceless treasures. Two chariots descended from Vaikuntha.

They brought armour and weapons.

4.Lanka (Ravana's Golden City): Originally built by Vishwakarma for Lord Siva, Lanka was later given to Kubera (the god of wealth). Ravana, Kubera's half-brother, took it over and turned it into his grand kingdom.

5.Swarga Loka (Indra's Heaven): Vishwakarma built Amaravati, the heavenly city of Indra, filled with celestial palaces and gardens.

6.Divine Weapons: •Vajra (Indra's thunderbolt) – Made from Sage Dadhichi's bones. •Pushpaka Vimana – A flying chariot used by Ravana and later by Lord Rama. •Trishul (Siva's trident) – One of the most powerful weapons in Hindu mythology.

As edited by VK Madhav Mohan

[209] Sudharma Sabha Mandapam (സുധർ, സഭാമ്ജപം) was the royal court and assembly hall of Lord Krishna in Dwaraka. It was renowned for its grandeur, divine architecture, and righteous governance. Sudharma was originally located in Indraloka (the abode of Lord Indra). It was later gifted by the Devas to Krishna when he established Dwaraka. This sabha (assembly hall) symbolized justice, wisdom, and dharma (righteousness). It was magnificent and celestial, constructed with divine materials. The hall was designed to be comfortable in all seasons, never too hot or too cold. It was a place where important discussions, legal matters, and strategic decisions were made. Krishna, along with the Yadava elders, ministers, and warriors, held court here to govern Dwaraka. Many crucial events of the Mahabharata took place in Sudharma Sabha. The messengers of the Pandavas and Kauravas

visited Krishna here. Krishna's famous preparations for the Kurukshetra war and his role as a peace messenger were all discussed in this hall. The name Sudharma (സുധർ,) itself means "supreme righteousness". It was considered

a hall where truth, justice, and wisdom prevailed. Unlike the Kaurava Sabha (Hastinapura's court), which was filled with deceit, Sudharma Sabha was a place of fairness and divine rule, as edited by VK Madhav Mohan

One chariot for SriKrishna and the other for Balarama.

With Yogashakti, Bhagavan populated Dwaraka with His own people. Then, unarmed, he stepped outside the city.

He ran into Kalayavana.

Kalayavana tried to capture SriKrishna.

Pretending to be afraid SriKrishna started running away. Kalayavana chased, in hot pursuit.

Twisting and turning, darting this way and that, SriKrishna stayed just in front, within touching distance.

SriKrishna found a cave and sprinted into it.

Kalayavana entered it and searched frantically for SriKrishna. He saw a man sleeping on the floor.

He mistook the man for SriKrishna and stamped hard with his foot. The man woke up, opened his eyes and looked up.

Kalayavana was burnt to ashes in a white flame. Who was the sleeping man?

The son of Mandhata Maharaja[210], Muchukunda. Why was Muchukunda sleeping in the cave?

To know the answer, we must go long back in time. The Devas were desperate in their fear of the Asuras.

They sought help from the great, valorous warrior, Muchukunda.

------

[210] Muchukunda's father was King Mandhata, a legendary ruler of the Ikshvaku dynasty in Hindu mythology. He was a Chakravarti (universal ruler), known for his great valor, righteousness, and devotion to dharma. He ruled over the entire world and was considered an incarnation of Vishnu's divine power.He was a devotee of Lord Vishnu and performed great yajnas (sacrificial rituals) to maintain dharma, as edited by VK Madhav Mohan

He accepted their request, went to Swarga and removed the menace of the Asuras.

After that, he lived on in Swarga. Much time elapsed.

Devas said to him, "O King, you have done us a great favour. Now you may return to Bhoomi. It is a long time since you came here. Your wives, sons, ministers and friends are no longer alive. Time has taken them away. Time, after all, is most powerful. In any case, please ask for a boon. We are only too happy to grant it." Muchukunda asked for the boon.

"For a very long time, I have been enduring countless sufferings. I can't bear the fatigue anymore.

I need deep, undisturbed slumber.

Those who disturb my slumber must be reduced to ashes." The Devas were pleased to grant the boon.

"With just a look anyone who wakes you will become ashes".

Comfortable, deep sleep, that was Muchukunda's aim.

The found a cave and went to sleep.

That was the sleep that Kalayavana had interrupted. So, is it any wonder that he was reduced to ashes?

Muchukunda saw a Tejasvi in front of him. Who was it?

He was not sure.

Surya? Chandra?

It was certain that this was not Surya or Chandra or Indra, Vishnu Bhagavan!!

"Yes, I am Lord MahaVishnu. I've come to bless you. Ask for your boon," SriKrishna told him.

"Prabhu, I only need to worship You and serve You. I hereby surrender and seek refuge in You," Muchukunda said with folded hands.

He circumambulated Bhagavan. Prostrated at the Divine Feet.

Rose and travelled to the North to perform Tapas.

Now that Kalayavana was finished, SriKrishna slaughtered the Mlecchas.

He confiscated all their wealth and prepared to return to Dwaraka. Then, Jarasandha launched his 18th attack.

Feigning to be cowardly, SriKrishna and Balaraman began to run away. Jarasandha made fun of them and laughed loudly in contempt.

He followed them along with his soldiers.

The RamaKrishnas climbed the mountain named Pravarshana. Pravarshana had a special quality.

Devendra used to make it rain everyday there.

Jarasandha and his soldiers searched all parts of the mountain. But they could not find any sign of the RamaKrishnas.

Jarasandha suspected that they were hidingsomewhere in the mountain.

So, he gathered firewood and set fire everywhere.

Meanwhile, unseen by anyone, theRamaKrishnas came down the mountain and returned to Dwaraka.

Jarasandha thought that they had been consumed by the fires. With happiness he went back to Magadha.

Balarama got married.

Who was the bride?

The daughter of Raivata, King of Anarta, Revati and SriKrishna's bride? Rugmini.

Difficulties arose, very many.

Only if these were removed could the wedding proceed. Bhishmaka was the King of Vidarbha.

He had five sons, and just one daughter, Rugmini.

There was no maiden who could compare with Rugmini's beauty, grace and behaviour.

The eldest of her brothers was Rugmi.

He had decided to give Rugmini in marriage to Shishupala, the King Chedi.

Shishupala was Jarasandha's close friend and SriKrishna's implacable enemy.

But Rugmi's desire was not Rugmini's desire.

Rugmini was always performing Puja to SriKrishna after accepting Him as her husband. She was caught in a terrible situation.

SriKrishna had to be somehow informed of the matter. Won't Bhagavan save her?

A trusted Brahmin was her servant.

Rugmini despatched the Brahmin without anyone's knowledge. The Brahmin went to Dwaraka and told SriKrishna about the matter. He handed over Rugmini's message.

SriKrishna had to reach Kundhinapura and take Rugmini away with Him. How could He do that?

Rugmini had thought of a way.

Rugmi had fixed the marriage with Shishupala.

On the day before the marriage, she would step out of the palace. She would go to Ambika Temple to pray.

SriKrishna should seize that opportunity to put her in the chariot and whisk her away.

If He did not do that?

She would kill herself - she had conveyed that strongly in the message.

SriKrishna had decided a long time ago to marry Rugmini.

He assured the Brahmin that He would certainly fulfil Rugmini's desire. He ordered his charioteer Daruka to ready the chariot.

SriKrishna had four fast, divine horses.

Would He need much time to reach Kundhinapura? Isn't it the wedding of the Princess?

Multicoloured flags were fluttering everywhere. Streets had all been swept and watered.

Tendrils of Akhil smoke and fragrance wafted from houses. Women and men were all dressed up in finery.

Mantras, homes, donations were all happening according to established guidelines.

Countless guests were present.

Many Kings had arrived; their families and armies too. Hustle and bustle and noise!

Celebrations and commotion everywhere! But Rugmini's attention was not on any of this.

She had despatched the Brahmin with her message to SriKrishna.

She had hoped that SriKrishna would come.

But he had not come, yet. Doubts sprouted in her mind.

Could SriKrishna have seen any faults in her? Is he deliberately staying away?

Is the Brahmin embarrassed to tell her? Doubts nourished sorrow.

Hot tears shimmered in Rugmini's eyes. Suddenly, her left eye and left hand quivered. Rugmini felt that this was an auspicious sign. That feeling was correct.

The Brahmin arrived.

Happiness was visible on the messenger's face. A smile played on his lips.

He informed Rugmini that SriKrishna would indeed take her away. How relieved she was!

Not much later, Balarama and SriKrishna arrived.

Bhishmaka received them with due respect and welcomed them as per tradition; and made arrangements for their stay to be comfortable.

The citizens all went to see SriKrishna and pay their respects.

Their eyes were not satisfied no matter how much they saw Him! Finally, that moment arrived - the moment specified in the message. Rugmini left for Ambika Temple.

Armed guards protected her. Many women accompanied her, carrying puja materials. Drumbeats began and so did the music.

Rugmini reached the temple.

She conducted puja in the proper manner. Afterwards, she came out of the temple.

Her eyes anxiously scanned the scene. The Kings were all present.

Is SriKrishna amongst them? He is! Of course He is!

Everything followed in a flash.

SriKrishna came to her, took her into the chariot and drove away. Jarasandha and his companions were amongst the invitees

Jarasandha's companions, meaning people who hate SriKrishna. Isn't their friend Shishupala, Rugmini's bridegroom?

And yet, this cowherd had kidnapped the bride! Right under their noses!

While all the mighty warriors watched, motionless, with wide open eyes! What a public humiliation! Revenge!

Pay back must be extracted, in huge quantities, from the perpetrator.

All of them donned their battle armour in a hurry, formed up their armies and set off in pursuit of SriKrishna.

Srikrishna and his Yadavas turned around and battled them. Jarasandha, Shishupala and their companions were roundly defeated! Shishupala was devastated.

His bride was stolen by SriKrishna.

Not just that, he and his friends were beaten badly. What an insult, what a loss of face!

Sad, indeed!

Jarasandha tried to console Shishupala. "My friend, don't be sad. Look at my situation. I attacked SriKrishna eighteen times. Seventeen times was I defeated! Only the eighteenth time was I able to taste a small victory. Why did we lose this time? Only because time favours that cowherd now. We too will enjoy good times. We too will win then. We must think of that and take comfort.”

Shishupala and his friends returned to their respective kingdoms. Only one person was not satisfied or consoled.

He was seething!

Not anyone else, but Rugmi!

“My sister has been kidnapped by SriKrishna”. The anger was a raging fire.

In front of everyone, for all to hear, he took a vow, “Without killing SriKrishna, without getting Rugmini back I will not set foot in this capital city.”

He took up arms, rallied his army and reached SriKrishna. “You lowly being, stop and face me for a moment. Where do you think you are going, stealing my sister? Release her to me. Or else, die under my arrows,” Rugmi raged. SriKrishna and Rugmi closed in for battle.

SriKrishna broke Rugmi’s bow. Rugmi took up another bow.

SriKrishna broke that too. Rugmi grabbed a third bow, that too was broken.

Rugmi took up a sword and jumped down from his chariot and approached SriKrishna like a moth drawn to a flame.

SriKrishna broke Rugmi’s sword and shield with his arrows and then raised his sword.

He was about to slash Rugmi’s throat when Rugmini screamed, “Don’t.” SriKrishna did not have the heart to ignore Rugmini’s entreaty so he did something else.

He shaved off Rugmi’s hair and moustache.

Did Rugmi not take a vow that he would not return to his capital without killing SriKrishna and bringing back Rugmini?

And that too in full public view?

He could not kill SriKrishna and neither could he retrieve Rugmini. How could he then go back?

He built a new city and lived there, a city named Bhojakada. SriKrishna and Rugmini reached Dwaraka.

Their wedding was celebrated with great pomp and splendour. The joy of the people of Dwaraka knew no bounds!

A son was born to Rugmini, Pradyumna. Do you know who he was, actually? None other than Kamadeva.

Once upon a time Siva was displeased with Kamadeva.

He opened his Third Eye[211].

---

[211] Siva's Third Eye: Symbolism and Meaning: Lord Siva's Third Eye is one of the most powerful symbols in Hindu mythology, representing wisdom, destruction, higher consciousness, and inner vision. It is often depicted as a vertical eye on Siva's forehead, different from his two physical eyes.

1. Symbolic Meanings of Siva's Third Eye 1.Divine Knowledge & Inner Vision: Unlike the two external eyes that see the material world, the third eye symbolizes inner perception, spiritual wisdom, and enlightenment. It represents transcendence beyond illusion (Maya) and the ability to see the truth beyond appearances. 2.Destruction of Ignorance & Evil: Siva's third eye is known as the "Eye of Fire" or "Jñāna Netra" (Eye of Knowledge). When opened, it burns away evil, ignorance, and desires, symbolizing the destruction of ego and impurities. Example: When Kamadeva (the God of Love) tried to distract Siva with lust, Siva opened his third eye and reduced him to ashes. 3.Time & Cosmic Balance :Siva's third eye is believed to be linked to time and cosmic order. It symbolizes his ability to maintain balance between creation, preservation, and destruction. 4.Awakening of Higher Consciousness: The third eye is associated with the Ajna Chakra (the sixth chakra in Yoga and meditation), which governs intuition, wisdom, and awareness. In spiritual practices, activating the third eye (Ajna Chakra) is believed to lead to enlightenment and divine perception.

Fire leapt out from the eye and cremated Kamadeva's body. To regain a body, he had to take birth.

Kamadeva was born as the son of SriKrishna and Rugmini.

It was not yet ten days since Pradyumna's birth when disaster struck. Sambhara was a wicked, strong Asura…and also a magician.

He snatched Pradyumna and threw him into the sea. Did Pradyumna drown in the sea? Not at all.

He ended up in the stomach of a large fish.

The fish was caught in a fisherman's net. The fisherman offered the fish to Sambhara. Sambhara's cooks cut open the fish.

Inside was a human baby!

One of the women, Mayavati, knew who the baby was. She was living as a cook.

Actually, she was not a cook and her name was not Mayavati.

---

2. Stories & Mythological References :1.The Burning of Kamadeva (God of Desire)When Goddess Parvati was trying to attract Siva's attention, Kamadeva shot an arrow of love at him. Enraged, Siva opened his third eye and burned Kamadeva to ashes. This symbolizes victory over desires and attachment. Siva and the Tripura (Three Demon Cities) When three demon kings (Tripurasura) built three flying cities (Tripura) that could only be destroyed with a single arrow, Lord Siva used his third eye to burn them down, restoring balance in the universe. This represents the destruction of arrogance, ignorance, and materialism.

3. Connection to Meditation & Spirituality : The third eye (Ajna Chakra) is the center of intuition, clarity, and self-realization. Meditation and yoga aim to activate the third eye to gain insight beyond ordinary perception. It is believed that those who awaken their third eye gain wisdom, deep understanding, and connection with the divine. Siva's Third Eye is not just a symbol of destruction— it is a representation of awakening, knowledge, and transcendence. It teaches that true vision is not just seeing with the eyes, but perceiving reality with wisdom and understanding.

As edited by VK Madhav Mohan

She was Ratidevi, Kamadeva's wife! Remember, Siva had vaporised Kamadeva?

Awaiting the birth of her husband was Ratidevi in the guise of a cook. Pradyumna grew very quickly into a youth.

A youth whose beauty mesmerised the eyes that saw him. That was no surprise.

Can anyone be more beautiful than Kamadeva? Pradyumna prepared to eliminate Sambhara.

The brave young man armed himself and confronted Sambhara and criticised him roundly for his actions and challenged him to fight. Sambhara was aroused like a snake which had been trampled.

He swung a blow with his mace.

Pradyumna blocked the blow with his own mace and launched a counter blow.

Sambhara felt the power of his adversary.

The magician that he was, he rose into the sky and fought with magic. That did not work against Pradyumna.

Sambhara's head was severed and felled by the son of SriKrishna. Pradyumna and Rati travelled in the sky like clouds and lightning moving together.

When they reached Dwaraka, their beauty astonished everyone. This youth was an exact image of SriKrishna.

The very same complexion, the same expressions and beauty! Rugmini's mind went back in time.

Her son had gone missing just a few days after he was born. What if he was alive?

He would look exactly like this young man. Is he actually our son?

Rugmini was overcome by doubt.

SriKrishna, of course, knew everything.

Still, He said nothing.

That was when Narada arrived.

The Maharshi narrated the story of Pradyumna. The son she had given up for dead had returned! Rugmini's joy can only be imagined!

One day, on the street, there appeared a man who was radiating light. IIis effulgence was so intense that it was impossible to look at him.

Someone informed SriKrishna that Suryadeva had descended from the sky.

Not Suryadeva but Satrajit, said SriKrishna.

How did Satrajit come to possess so much radiance? He was a devotee of Suryadeva.

Suryadeva presented him with a gemstone. Syamantaka was the name of the gemstone. Radiance was not the only speciality of Syamantaka. It would produce eight bhaaras[212] of gold every day. Satrajit wore the Syamantaka around his neck.

SriKrishna had once before, requested Satrajit to give Him the gemstone.

Syamantaka was requested not for Himself but for the Yadava King, Ugrasena.

Satrajit turned down the request.

He did not know that his refusal would cause a calamity.

---

[212] Bhaara..Large measure, as edited by VK Madhav Mohan

Satrajit had a younger brother named Prasena.

Prasena went hunting, wearing the Syamantaka around his neck.

A lion killed Satrajit, took the gemstone and climbed the mountain. Nearby lived Jaambavan.

Remember, long, long ago SriRama manifested on earth? Jaambavan was his servant.

During SriKrishna Avatara, too the noble monkey was alive though he was very old by then.

Jaambavan killed the lion and took possession of the gemstone. What an apt toy for children!

No one knew anything about any of this. Satrajit was in grief.

Someone had murdered his brother in the forest.

Who could the killer be?

Satrajit's memory turned to SriKrishna. "SriKrishna had once asked for the Syamantaka. I did not give it to Him then. SriKrishna has borne anger in mind for that rejection. So, SriKrishna has killed Prasena," that became Satrajit's belief. He confided in a friend, that friend told another.

He shared it with yet another. And then?

A rumour sped across the entire land.

"The one who killed Prasena and stole the gemstone is SriKrishna".

Ill fame had spread.

It had to be removed. But why did it happen?

The reason had to be determined first.

Srikrishna took some of his companions and went to the forest. There He came upon the dead body of Prasena.

It was that Prasena had been killed by a lion.

The lion's pug marks extended deep into the forest. Following them, the lion's body too came into view. Who killed the lion?

SriKrishna thought for a moment. The truth dawned clearly in His mind. Bhagavan found Jaambavan's cave. He asked His companions to wait outside and entered the cave alone. He walked a long distance and saw a monkey-child

The monkey-child was playing with Syamantaka. SriKrishna approached it.

The monkey-child shrieked in fright.

Hearing the cry, Jaambavan raced to the rescue. He saw the human who had entered the cave.

In anger, he initiated battle.

Stones and trees were his weapons.

Though he was old, Jaambavan was extremely strong. SriKrishna's strength was, of course, indescribable.

One day passed. Then two, then three. The battled raged for twenty-eight days!

SriKrishna's thundering strikes weakened Jaambavan. The great monkey had never lost a battle until then.

For the first time in his life, he had been vanquished and that too by a human being.

Who is this man? For sure, not an ordinary person.

Jaambavan concentrated his mind on this question. The truth was then revealed.

This is none other than Lord MahaVishnu! He had incarnated as SriRama.

And now, He has incarnated as SriKrishna! Jaambavan did Namaskaram[213] repeatedly.

Srikrishna caressed His devotee fondly and told him the reason for His arrival.

Jaambavan handed over Syamantaka to Bhagavan. And along with it, his daughter Jaambavati too.

SriKrishna emerged from the cave with Jaambavati and Symantaka. His companions were nowhere to be seen.

They had waited for twelve days since He had entered the cave. SriKrishna had not returned.

They were convinced that He was no more.

With the heaviest of hearts, they went back to Dwaraka. Vasudeva, Devaki and Rugmini, can we even imagine their grief? All of them went to Durga Temple and worshipped Devi.

Devi's divine voice could then be heard, "You will see SriKrishna soon."

Shortly thereafter SriKrishna appeared along with the gemstone and the gem of a woman, Jaambavati.

---

[213] Namaskaram: Namaskaram (നമസ്കാരം / नमस्कारम्) is a respectful greeting in Malayalam and Sanskrit, commonly used in South India. It is equivalent to "Namaste" (नमस्ते) in North India.

Meaning & Usage:

•Derived from Sanskrit: "Namah" (नम:) = Bow, Salutation "Karam" (करम्) = Action or Gesture

Together, "Namaskaram" means "I bow to you with respect." Used as a formal greeting in Kerala, similar to how "Namaste" is used in Hindi-speaking regions, as edited by VK Madhav Mohan

Everyone was intoxicated with happiness. Satrajit was summoned to the royal assembly.

Srikrishna narrated the story of the retrieval of Syamantaka.

Satrajit realised the magnitude of his blunder.

Had he not created infamy for SriKrishna with his false accusations? To atone for his mistake Satrajit presented Syamantaka to SriKrishna. Not just that, he offered his daughter Satyabhama too.

Srikrishna refused to accept Syamantaka but he did not reject Satyabhama.

Syamantaka was coveted by a man named Satadhanva. SriKrishna and Balarama left for Hastinapura.

Seizing the opportunity, Satadhanva murdered Satrajit in his sleep then he made off with Syamantaka.

Satyabhama couldn't bear her sorrow and hatred for her father's murderer.

She rushed to Hastinapura and poured out her grief to her husband. SriKrishna returned to Dwaraka with Balarama and Satyabhama.

The panic stricken Satadhanva entrusted Syamantaka to Akrura and fled.

Bhagavan ferreted out Satadhanva and killed him..and gave Syamantaka to Akrura.

Did not Rugmini, Jaambavati and Satyabhama earn the good fortune of becoming the wives of Bhagavan?

That good fortune smiled on five more exquisite maidens[214].
Kalindi was one of them.

SriKrishna met the Pandavas. Oh, how happy was Kuntidevi!

---

[214] SriKrishna had eight principal wives, known as the Ashtabharyas (അഷ്ടഭാരികൾ / अष्टभायार्:). These queens were not just consorts but also symbolized different aspects of devotion, power, and dharma. The Ashatbharyas were:

1.Rukmini,Daughter of King Bhishmaka of Vidarbha; Krishna abducted her from her Swayamvara to save her from an unwanted marriage with Shishupala.

2.Satyabhama,Daughter of Satrajit of Dwarka: Krishna married her after he returned the Syamantaka jewel and proved his innocence.

3.Jambavati,Daughter of Jambavan: ,Krishna fought and defeated Jambavan to win the Syamantaka jewel, after which Jambavan gave Jambavati as a bride.

4.Kalindi,Daughter of Surya (the Sun God: Krishna found her praying for him by the Yamuna River and married her.

5.Mitravinda,Princess of Avanti, sister of Vinda & Anuvinda: Krishna abducted her from her Swayamvara because her brothers were forcing her into another marriage via a rigged Swayamvara

6.Nagnajiti (Satya),Daughter of King Nagnajit of Kosala: Krishna won her hand by taming seven wild bulls in a challenge set by her father.

7.Bhadra,Daughter of King Dhrishtaketu of Kekaya: She was Krishna's cousin and chose him as her husband in a peaceful marriage.

8.Lakshana (Madhavi),Daughter of King Brihatsena of Madra: Krishna won her hand by defeating many kings in a Swayamvara.

The Ashtabharyas were not just wives; they represented different qualities and aspects of devotion, love, power, and dharma. Each marriage happened under unique circumstances, showing how Krishna's life was filled with both divine and human experiences.

•Rukmini – Symbol of Bhakti (pure devotion).

•Satyabhama – Symbol of Shakti (power, pride, and material wealth).

•Jambavati – Represents patience, loyalty, and sacrifice.

•Kalindi – Symbolizes asceticism and unwavering love.

•Mitravinda – Represents love and commitment despite opposition.

•Nagnajiti (Satya)– Symbolizes dharma and Krishna's warrior prowess.

•Bhadra – Symbol of family ties and peaceful companionship.

SriKrishna was her beloved nephew.

The time together was joyful and exciting!

SriKrishna had boundless love for the Pandavas but Arjuna was His dearest friend.

Once, both of them went hunting. Arjuna saw a beautiful young woman. "Who are you? Who is your father? Where are you coming from?" asked Arjuna.

"I am the daughter of Suryadeva, Kalindi. I'm performing Tapas to make SriKrishna my husband," the damsel replied.

Arjuna informed SriKrishna about the matter.

SriKrishna accepted Kalindi and returned with her and Arjuna. He stayed for some more time with the Pandavas.

It was during this stay that Khandvadaaham[215] occurred.

After that, Bhagavan, along with Kalindi, left for Dwaraka. Mitravinda was a princess who resided in Avanti.

She desired to be SriKrishna's wife. However, the wedding was obstructed.

---

[215] Detailed in MaliBharatam. Khandava (खाण्डव / ഖുഡവ) – Name of a dense forest near the present-day Delhi region. Daha (दाह / ദാഹം) – Burning or destruction by fire. The Khandava forest was burned down by Krishna and Arjuna to fulfill the request of Agni (the fire god), who was suffering from indigestion after consuming excessive ghee from sacrifices. Agni sought to burn the forest to regain his strength, but Indra (the god of rain and the protector of the forest) tried to stop it. Krishna and Arjuna fought Indra and other celestial beings, ensuring that Agni could complete the burning of the forest. Takshaka (the serpent king) managed to escape. Mayasura (a demon architect) was saved by Arjuna and later built the grand Maya Sabha for the Pandavas. The destruction of the forest led to the rise of Indraprastha, the glorious kingdom of the Pandavas, as edited by VK Madhav Mohan

Her brothers, Vinda and Anuvinda did not approve. They were close friends of Duryodhana.

Duryodhana had hated SriKrishna for a long time.

Vinda and Anuvinda organised a Swayamvara[216] for their sister.

---

[216] Swayamvara (स्वयंवर / സ*ൡ൦൨ൟൠ൦) – The Ancient Practice of Bride Choosing. Swayamvara is a Sanskrit word meaning "self-choice of a husband" (स्वयं = "self" + वर = "groom"). It was an ancient Indian tradition where a princess or noblewoman would select her husband from a gathering of eligible suitors.
Historical & Mythological Significance
1.Process of Swayamvara

•The father (often a king) would invite eligible princes and warriors to compete for the bride's hand.

•The event often involved tests of valor, strength, or skill (such as archery or combat).

•The woman had the right to choose her preferred groom, either based on the contest or personal preference.
2.Famous Swayamvaras in Indian Epics
Sita's Swayamvara (Ramayana)

•King Janaka organized a Swayamvara for his daughter Sita.

•The challenge: Lifting and stringing Lord Siva's divine bow.

•Only Lord Rama succeeded, and Sita garlanded him.
Draupadi's Swayamvara (Mahabharata)

•Princess Draupadi had a challenge:Princess Draupadi had a challenge: shooting an arrow at a rotating target by looking at its reflection in water.

•Many kings, including Karna and Duryodhana, tried and failed.

•Arjuna, disguised as a Brahmin, succeeded and won Draupadi's hand.
Damayanti's Swayamvara

•Damayanti, a princess, fell in love with King Nala through a divine connection.

•Even though gods attended her Swayamvara, she chose Nala, proving the power of love over divinity.

SriKrishna came for the Swayamvara, took Mitravinda and married her[217]. The King of Ayodhya, Nagnajit, had a daughter named Satya.

He would give his daughter in marriage only to a man who executed an act of valour.

The King had sworn an oath to that effect.

The act of valour specified was to subdue and tie up seven bulls.

Ordinary men could not hope to accomplish it because the bulls were far too big, strong and aggressive.

Many Kings tried their strength, not one succeeded.

That was when SriKrishna arrived.

He took seven forms and subdued the seven bulls, pierced their noses, inserted ropes and tied them up.

The wedding of SriKrishna and Satya was conducted in the most auspicious manner.

The Kings who had lost face in their fight with the bulls confronted SriKrishna.

---

as edited by VK Madhav Mohan

[217] Mitravinda's Swayamvara & Krishna's Role: Mitravinda loved Krishna and wanted to marry him. However, her brothers, Vindhya and Anuvindhya, were against the match because they were loyal to Duryodhana and the Kauravas. They arranged a swayamvara, but rigged it so that she could not choose Krishna. Instead of letting her choose freely, her brothers forced her to marry a prince of their choice. Seeing this injustice, Krishna stormed the swayamvara, defeated her brothers, and abducted Mitravinda. After this, Krishna took her to Dwaraka and married her, as edited by VK Madhav Mohan

He scattered them in all directions like a lion chases away lesser animals.

Princesses Bhadra[218] and Lakshana[219] of the Kingdoms of Kekaya and Madra respectively were just two of the most beautiful wives of SriKrishna.Thousands of enchanting women also enjoyed the very same good fortune after the killing of Narakasura[220].

---

[218] Bhadra was a princess of the Kekaya kingdom and one of the Ashtabharya (eight principal wives) of Lord Krishna. She was the daughter of King Brihatsena of Kekaya and was Krishna's cousin (as her mother was Krishna's paternal aunt). Unlike some of Krishna's other marriages that happened through swayamvara or conquest, Bhadra and Krishna's marriage was one of love and mutual choice. She is sometimes associated with Shantidevi, a name found in Jain texts as one of Krishna's consorts…
As edited by VK Madhav Mohan
[219]

[220] Narakasura (നരകാസുരൻ / नरकासुर) was a powerful demon king in Hindu mythology, known for his
tyranny and oppression, particularly against celestial beings and women. His defeat by Lord Krishna and Goddess Satyabhama is celebrated as Narakasura Vadham, which is linked to Diwali (Deepavali) celebrations in India. Narakasura was born to Bhudevi (Mother Earth) and Lord Varaha (an incarnation of Vishnu). According to another version, he was the son of Hiranyaksha, the demon slain by Vishnu in his Varaha avatar. Although born with divine blessings, he was corrupted by power and arrogance, becoming a tyrant. He ruled Pragjyotishapura (modern-day Assam) and became an extremely powerful asura (demon). He acquired a boon from Lord Brahma that he could only be killed by his mother, Bhudevi (which he assumed made him invincible). He ruled Pragjyotishapura (modern-day Assam) and became an extremely powerful asura (demon).His unpardonable atrocities included: conquering Indra's heaven and stealing the divine earrings of Aditi, the mother of the gods. Kidnapping and imprisoning 16,100 princesses in his palace and spreading chaos and destruction across the three worlds. The gods pleaded with Lord Krishna to stop Narakasura. Krishna, along with his wife Satyabhama, marched to Pragjyotishapura on Garuda (his celestial mount). Krishna fought Narakasura's army, which included powerful demons like Mura (whom Krishna killed, earning the name 'Murari'). During the battle, Narakasura struck Krishna, and Satyabhama (his mother's incarnation)

Narakasura was the son of Bhumidevi. He was an evil tyrant, even the Devas could not stand up to him. There was no limit to the plunder and murder that he committed.

Devendra's seat on the Meru Mountain, Aditi's earrings and Varuna's celestial umbrella[221] were all looted by him.

Narakasura's depredations became unbearable. Devendra complained to SriKrishna about Narakasura. Bhagavan mounted Garuda and set out.

He took Satyabhama along with Him. Pragjyotisha[222] was Narakasura's Kingdom. It was remote and inaccessible.

Towering mountains surrounded it. Deep ravines lay beyond the mountains. Further, blazing fires burned, followed by whirlwinds whirling like wheels.

---

retaliated and killed him—thus fulfilling the prophecy that he could only be slain by his mother. Before dying, Narakasura repented and requested that his death be celebrated as a festival of joy—which became Deepavali (Diwali) in some traditions.In South India, Naraka Chaturdashi (the second day of Diwali) commemorates Krishna's victory over Narakasura. Narakasura represents arrogance, greed, and unchecked power, while Krishna and Satyabhama symbolize Dharma (righteousness) and divine justice. His story is a reminder that even the strongest must face the consequences of their actions…ChatGPT 4o as edited by VK Madhav Mohan

[221] The celestial umbrella of Varuna is a divine artefact mentioned in Hindu mythology. It was one of the many treasures stolen by the demon king Narakasura, who ruled Pragjyotishapura (modern-day Assam).The umbrella was a magical, divine parasol belonging to Varuna, the god of the oceans and water. It was said to possess mystical powers, possibly providing protection, control over water, and divine authority. Like Indra's Vajra (thunderbolt) and Surya's golden chariot, Varuna's umbrella was a symbol of power, as edited by VK Madhav Mohan

[222] Present day Assam, as edited by VK Madhav Mohan

And finally, Murasura's[223] defences filled with traps, illusions and magical warriors and weapons.

Enemies could be restrained and overpowered by these defences but what could restrain or overpower SriKrishna?

---

[223] Murasura: Murasura was a powerful Asura (demon) and a key general under Narakasura, ruling the fortified city of Pragjyotishapura (modern-day Assam). His defenses were some of the most formidable barriers ever described in Hindu mythology. Murasura was Narakasura's chief general and protector of Pragjyotishapura, the demon capital. His defensive strategies included a combination of physical barriers, magical traps, and supernatural forces. Key Elements of Murasura's Defenses 1. Five Layers of Fortification: The city was surrounded by five layers of ramparts made of iron, stone, and mystical barriers. These walls were enchanted, making them nearly impenetrable by conventional forces. 2.Surrounding Moats & Water Defenses: Deep moats filled with water encircled the city, making it difficult for enemies to approach. Magical creatures guarded the waters, preventing invaders from crossing. 3.Automatic Flying Weapons: The fort was guarded by magical, self-operating weapons that could attack intruders automatically. These included arrows, spears, and fireballs that rained down upon anyone approaching the city. 4.Armies of Demon Warriors:Thousands of asuras and demonic soldiers stood ready to defend the city. These warriors were trained in mystical warfare and deception.Illusions & Maya (Magical Traps) :The entire city was covered by layers of illusion (maya) that could confuse and mislead intruders. Attackers would see phantom armies, false doors, and endless mazes that made it impossible to find the real entrance. Murasura personally challenged Krishna, but Krishna killed him instantly with his Sudarshana Chakra. After Murasura's death, Krishna earned the title 'Murari', meaning "the slayer of Mura."The fortifications represent the arrogance of evil rulers, believing themselves invincible. Krishna's victory symbolizes Dharma (righteousness) triumphing over Adharma (evil). The breaking of the five fortifications is seen as the destruction of illusion, ignorance, and ego. Murasura's defenses were among the most elaborate and mystical barriers in Hindu mythology, but Krishna, the supreme strategist, overcame them effortlessly. This battle is commemorated during Diwali (Naraka Chaturdashi), celebrating the victory of good over evil.
As edited by VK Madhav Mohan

Bhagavan shattered the mountains with his mace.[224]

Then he absorbed into His Trichakra the water in the moats, wind in the whirlwinds and fire in the infernos.

He blew the conch named Panchajanya.

The five headed Murasura was the toughest of the tough. Brandishing his three-pointed spear, he rushed in to do battle. He hurled his spear at Garuda, Srikrishna sliced the spear with His arrows.

---

[224] Sri Krishna's Mace – Kaumodaki (െകൗേമാദകി / कौमोदकी) Lord Sri Krishna's mace is called Kaumodaki (െകൗേമാദകി / कौमोदकी), a divine weapon of immense power. It is one of the primary weapons of Vishnu, which Krishna, as an avatar of Vishnu, wielded during battles.Kaumodaki was not an ordinary weapon but a celestial gada (mace) gifted by the gods. It was created by Vishwakarma, the divine architect of the gods, and bestowed upon Lord Vishnu. The name "Kaumodaki" means "the one that brings joy and exhilaration." It symbolizes divine strength, dharma (righteousness), and cosmic justice. While Sri Krishna is most often associated with the Sudarshana Chakra, he also wielded Kaumodaki in battles, including: 1. The Battle Against Narakasura: During the war against Narakasura and his general Murasura, Krishna used Kaumodaki to crush enemy warriors and elephants. The mace was said to be so powerful that a single strike could shatter mountains.
2. Krishna's Role in the Mahabharata War: As a non-combatant charioteer (Sarathi) for Arjuna, Krishna did not directly fight. However, at one point, in a moment of divine fury, Krishna lifted Kaumodaki and charged at Bhishma, but was stopped by Arjuna. 3. Destruction of Demonic Forces: Krishna used Kaumodaki to defeat several asuras (demons) in different battles, including Paundraka Vasudeva, who falsely claimed to be Vishnu. Symbol of Power in Vishnu Iconography → In Vishnu's traditional four-armed form, he holds Sudarshana Chakra, Shankha (conch), Padma (lotus), and Kaumodaki (mace). Unstoppable Force → No enemy, no matter how powerful, could withstand a direct blow from Kaumodaki. While Sudarshana Chakra was used for precision attacks, Kaumodaki was the weapon of brute force and destruction, as edited by VK Madhav Mohan

Then he pierced each of Murasura's five faces with an arrow. Mura hit SriKrishna with his mace.

SriKrishna cut the mace into three pieces.

And then He severed all five heads with the Trichakra. Murasura had seven sons.

All seven and their soldiers attacked SriKrishna. SriKrishna despatched them all into the other world.

It was time for Narakasura himself to come to the battlefield. He did so at the head of his army.

Elephants in Musth[225] which had been born in the ocean were part of the force, SriKrishna started to annihilate the army of the enemy. Garuda drove away the elephants using his beak and claws.

Narakasura stabbed Garuda with his spear but Garuda brushed it off. Then, Narakasura tried to hurl the spear at SriKrishna.

Bhagavan beheaded him with the Trichakra. Remember all the articles Narakasura had looted?

His mother, Bhumi Devi, offered them all to SriKrishna.

---

[225] The Malayalam phrase "Mada Ana" (മദ ആന) translates to "Musth Elephant" in English. It refers to a male elephant in a state of musth (മദം / Madham), which is a condition of heightened aggression and dominance due to increased testosterone levels.Mada (മദ) → Madness, intoxication, or musth (a state of heightened aggression in elephants). Ana (ആന) → Elephant. Mada Ana refers to a male elephant that is in musth, often seen during

mating seasons or when asserting dominance. Characteristics of a Musth Elephant:•Highly aggressive and uncontrollable. •A dark liquid called temporin oozes from its temporal glands. •It often charges at anything in its path, making it extremely dangerous. Used in Kerala temple festivals, but musth elephants require strict supervision to prevent accidents. "Mada Ana or Musth Elephant" is often used metaphorically to describe a person who is arrogant, aggressive, or out of control, like a musth elephant.

As edited by VK Madhav Mohan

She chanted hymns praising Bhagavan and revered Him with intense Bhakti.

She pleaded with Bhagavan to save and protect her son's son. Bhagavan accepted the plea.

Narakasura's palace held over ten thousand princesses. They were being held prisoner by the tyrant of tyrants.

Every one of the Princesses harboured a desire to become SriKrishna's wife.

Bhagavan sent them all to Dwaraka.

Not only that, all of Narakasura's wealth, chariots, horses, four-tusked elephants were also transported to Dwaraka.

Subsequently, He went to Swarga and returned the earrings to Aditi.

Meanwhile, Satyabhama expressed a desire to possess the Parijata[226] flower.

------

[226] Parijatam (പാരിജാതം / पारिजात) – Meaning & Significance Parijatam (പാരിജാതം / पारिजात) refers to the divine Parijata tree, a celestial flowering tree in Hindu mythology, known for its fragrance, beauty, and symbolic significance. Scientifically known as Nyctanthes arbor-tristis, also called Night-flowering Jasmine or Coral Jasmine. Blooms at night and sheds its flowers at dawn, symbolizing impermanence and divine beauty. Native to South Asia,
especially India, Nepal, and Southeast Asia.Used in Ayurveda for its medicinal properties (for treating fever, arthritis, and skin diseases). Common Names: Parijat (Hindi / Sanskrit) – पारिजात• Pavizhamalli (Malayalam) – പവിഴമല്ലി•Sephali / Shefali (Bengali) – শেফালি •Harsingar (Hindi) – हरिसंगार. The Parijata tree originated during
the Samudra Manthan (Churning of the Ocean) and was gifted to Indra, the King of Gods. Indra planted it in Swarga (heaven), making it a celestial tree.
Famous story of the conflict between Krishna's two wives, Satyabhama and Rukmini:

SriKrishna pulled out the Parijata tree and placed it on Garuda's back. Devendra and the rest of the Devas were not prepared to give up the Parijata.

They tried to prevent SriKrishna from taking the tree but they could not do so.

Bhagavan reached Dwaraka and planted the Parijata in Satyabhama's Garden.

Bees had followed Parijata all the way from Swarga, so attached were they to the fragrance and nectar of the flowers.

Over ten thousand Princesses had been brought to Dwaraka.

Srikrishna made Himself into those many forms and married every one of the Princesses.

Bhagavan's domestic life was filled with comfort and well-being. Rugmini nursed a strong belief that SriKrishna loved her the most. That belief also caused a bit of pride.

SriKrishna decided to douse the pride.

•Satyabhama, Krishna's fiery and proud wife, wanted proof of Krishna's love.

•Krishna brought the Parijata tree from Indra's garden to plant in her palace.

•Indra opposed this, leading to a battle between Krishna and the gods.

•Krishna defeated Indra and brought the tree to Earth.

•To balance things, Krishna planted the tree in Satyabhama's garden, but its flowers fell in Rukmini's courtyard – symbolizing that Krishna's heart always belonged to Rukmini.

Moral of the Story:

•The Parijata tree represents divine love, desire, and spiritual wisdom.

•Material beauty fades, but spiritual devotion lasts forever.

As Edited By Vk Madhav Mohan

Rugmini and SriKrishna were both in the bridal chamber, under an elegant canopy.

Ornate oil and wick lamps were casting a soft glow. SriKrishna was reclining on the gemstone laden bed.

Rugmini was standing by His side, fanning Him with Venchamaram[227].

Dressed, adorned, and decorated, the beautiful lady was the very definition of grace, elegance, and charm.

SriKrishna played a prank. He said, "Rugmini, very many young suitors wanted to marry you. They were all Kings, brave and handsome. You rejected every one of them. Without considering your elder brother's wishes you accepted me, a trickster. I'm just a coward. Am I not hiding on this island fearing my enemies? I have powerful enemies - Shishupala, Jarasandha, Rugmi and many others. What you did was unfortunate."

Unexpected words!

Rugmini's manner changed. Her head drooped on its own, warm tears sprang from her eyes. She couldn't speak.

Her bangles loosened and fell from her hands. Vencharam slipped from her grasp.

---

[227] Venchamaram (ഭൗവെരാമരം) → A royal whisk (fan) made of white yak-tail hair, used in Indian royal and temple traditions. Rukmini (രുക്മിണി) → The consort of Lord Krishna, regarded as his principal queen and the

incarnation of Goddess Lakshmi.In Hindu mythology, Rukmini is Krishna's chief queen and is often depicted serving him with devotion and love. Fanning Krishna with a Venchamaram symbolizes her humility, service, and divine companionship. In temple murals and sculptures, she is often seen standing beside Krishna, gently waving a Venchamaram.

As edited by VK Madhav Mohan

Rugmini fell unconscious! The prank turned serious. SriKrishna jumped up, gathered Rugmini up in His arms and laid her down gently on the bed. Attended to her with utmost care. Rugmini regained consciousness.

"Wasn't I saying all that in jest? And you took it all so seriously!" SriKrishna said with the tenderest of tenderness. That is all it took for Rugmini to be consoled. Her sorrow vanished but the pride was diluted too.

SriKrishna had over ten thousand wives. Each wife had ten sons. How vast was His wealth in children! Anirudha was Rugmini's grandon - that is, Pradyumna's son.

Rochana was Rugmi's granddaughter. Anirudha married Rochana.

It is true that Rugmi carried vengeance in his heart for SriKrishna but he also had a lot of love for his sister.

That was the reason Rugmi agreed to the marriage. Balarama, SriKrishna and others attended the wedding.

After the ceremonies, everyone got together for the festivities.

Rugmi's close friend, the King of Kalinga was also in the group. The King of Kalinga had a mischievous idea.

He wanted to make Balarama look like a fool.

Balarama was very strong but he wasn't good at the game of dice.

Following the King of Kalinga's request, Rugmi invited Balarama to a game of dice.

They started playing. Balarama kept losing.

King of Kalinga laughed and sneered revealing his teeth. Balarama was not amused but he did not say anything and kept playing.

Balarama scored a victory. Rugmi argued that he had won. Balarama was annoyed yet he continued to play. Balarama won again.

Rugmi said, "This time too I am the one who has won. If there is a dispute, let mediators decide."

A voice from the heavens was heard. "Balarama has won. Rugmi is lying." Rugmi ignored the voice.

Instead, in a loud voice so everyone could hear, he said with contempt, "How can a forest dwelling cowherd like you be a good player of the game of dice?"Rugmi's friends burst out laughing. Balarama lost his temper.

He picked up an iron pestle and struck Rugmi. Rugmi died from the blow.

The King of Kalinga who had laughed and sneered fled in fright.

Balarama leapt up, caught him and smashed his teeth.

Rugmi's friends were beaten up too before they ran away. Srikrishna and Banasura engaged in battle.

Siva had to side with Banasura[228]. There was a special reason for that.

---

[228] Banasura was the son of Mahabali and the great-grandson of Prahlada. Banasura was a devout follower of Lord Siva and was granted a boon that made him nearly invincible. His story is prominently featured in ancient texts like the Bhagavata Purana, where he engages in a significant battle with Lord Krishna. In this tale, Banasura's daughter, Usha, falls in love with Aniruddha, Krishna's

Bana was the eldest amongst Mahabali's hundred sons. He was also the King of Shonitapura.

He was extraordinarily strong and hot-headed. On top of that, he also had a thousand arms. He propitiated Siva.

Siva told him to ask for a boon.

"I request you to guard my city," was the boon Banasura requested. Siva could not refuse.

Bana's strength and arrogance doubled. The insolent Asura once told Siva, "I have no equal. But my hands are itching for a fight. Please do battle with me."

Siva felt anger but he did not fight. However, he said, "At one time you will fight against someone equal to me. Your arrogance will then be extinguished."

Who is equal to Siva? SriKrishna, of course.

SriKrishna and Bana were about to engage. Bana had a daughter named Usha.

Hardly anyone was as beautiful as Usha.

She had a dream that a handsome young man had married her. When she woke up, she realised that it was only a dream.

She was disappointed.

Chitralekha, Usha's closest friend, was the daughter Bana's minister, Kumbhanda.

Chitralekha could draw wonderfully; she was also endowed with Yogic powers.

---

grandson, leading to a series of events culminating in a fierce confrontation between Banasura and Krishna. Ultimately, Banasura is defeated, but his life is spared due to his lineage and devotion, as edited by VK Madhav Mohan

She spoke to her friend, "Usha, I will find the husband that you dreamt about. No matter where he is in the three worlds I will fetch him. But I can do that only if know who he is. So let me draw pictures of many men. You can then identify him."

The artist Chitralekha drew pictures, one by one.

First, she drew pictures of the prominent amongst divine beings. Usha was sure that none of them was right.

Then Chitralekha drew pictures of great human beings. None of them were right, too.

Chitralekha began drawing pictures of people in Yaduvamsa.

The portraits of Balarama, SriKrishna and Pradyumna, one after the other.

None of them were right said Usha with certitude.

Yet, Pradyumna resembled the husband she saw in the dream.

When Pradyumna's son Anirudha's picture was drawn Usha immediately cried out with excitement,

"It's him, it's him, for sure!"

The person was recognised. That was a big thing. Now he needs to be brought to Usha.

Chitralekha used her Yogasidhi[229]. She flew fast through the sky. She reached Dwaraka at night. Lifted the sleeping Anirudha and returned to Shonitapura. She placed Anirudha next to Usha.

---

[229] The term "Yogasiddhi" is derived from Sanskrit, where "yoga" means union or discipline, and "siddhi" translates to perfection or accomplishment. Together, "Yogasiddhi" refers to the attainment of spiritual powers or accomplishments through dedicated yogic practices. In various traditions,

Anirudha began living with Usha in the Antahpuram[230]. Usha took great care to ensure that no one knew.

However, the guards were suspicious. They informed Bana.

He went into the Antahpuram. Anirudha was discovered!

Bana was overcome by uncontrollable anger. He and his soldiers went after Anirudha.

Along with his beauty Anirudha was also endowed with bravery.

He held them all at bay.

But Bana captured him with Nagapasa[231] and imprisoned him. Usha wept incessantly.

---

achieving Yogasiddhi involves intense meditation, ethical conduct, and the purification of the mind and body, leading to extraordinary abilities or profound spiritual insights, as edited by VK Madhav Mohan

[230] Antahpuram" is a term rooted in Sanskrit, translating to the "inner quarters" or "women's apartments" within a palace. These secluded areas were traditionally designated for the women of the royal household, ensuring their privacy and security, as edited by VK Madhav Mohan

[231] Nagapasha (Nāgapāśa) is a mystical weapon in Hindu mythology, often described as a divine noose made of serpents. It is associated with various gods and warriors and is known for its ability to bind enemies, rendering them immobile.Nāga" means serpent, and "Pāśa" means noose or trap. Together, Nagapasha refers to a serpent- noose weapon that entangles its target, much like a snake constricting its prey. The weapon is believed to be infused with the power of divine serpents (Nāgas) and could only be countered by specific mantras or divine intervention.The Nagapasha weapon is self-binding, meaning once it captures an enemy, they cannot escape unless the spell is broken. It paralyzes the victim, leaving them vulnerable in battle. The only way to nullify Nagapasha is through: Garuda's presence, as Garuda is the eternal enemy of snakes; Or Divine intervention, such as Rama's allies using specific mantras; Or A counter-weapon, such as Garudastra or Vishnu's Sudarshana Chakra. In the Ramayana, during the battle between Rama and Ravana, Indrajit (Meghnad), the son of Ravana, used the Nagapasha against Rama and Lakshmana. The weapon ensnared both Rama and Lakshmana, making them immobile. Seeing them trapped, Hanuman and

Meanwhile, what was the situation in Dwaraka? Anirudha was missing!

Where did he go?

No one had the faintest clue.

Four months later, the Narada Maharshi revealed the truth. SriKrishna and his army reached Shonitapura.

Bana's army faced off with the Yadava army.

The fiercest of battles commenced.

According to the boon, Siva had to protect Bana's city. So, Siva and his sons had to fight on Bana's side.

SriKrishna chased away Ganapati's Bhootas.[232]

Even Siva had to withdraw in the face of SriKrishna's power.

Garuda (the eagle mount of Vishnu) arrived. Garuda, being the eternal enemy of serpents, neutralized the weapon and freed Rama and Lakshmana. In the Mahabharata, Karna was given the Nagapasha (or Nagaastra) by the serpent king Takshaka to use against Arjuna. However, Karna failed to use it at the right moment during the Kurukshetra war, and his fate was ultimately sealed.

[232] Lord Ganesha, also known as Ganapati, is often depicted as the leader of a host of supernatural beings called Bhootas, Ganas, and Yakshas. These celestial attendants serve and accompany him, reinforcing his role as Ganapati, meaning "Lord of the Ganas" (divine hosts).Bhootas are ethereal beings, often described as spirits, goblins, or elemental forces that serve deities, particularly Siva and Ganesha. In the Siva Purana and Ganesha Purana, they are portrayed as part of Lord Siva's and Ganesha's divine entourage. Ganesha, being the commander of Siva's armies, leads these beings to maintain cosmic balance.

Types of Beings in Ganesha's Army

1.Ganas – Divine attendants of Siva, who follow Ganesha's command.

2.Bhootas – Mystical spirits, sometimes ghostly but benevolent under Ganesha's leadership.

3.Yakshas – Nature spirits, often associated with wealth and prosperity.

4.Pretas & Pisachas – Ghostly entities, sometimes mischievous but kept under control by Ganesha.

Subrahmania[233] battlefield, whofought against Pradyumna had to leave the Khambhanda met death at the hands of Balarama.

Bana armed himself with five hundred bows in five hundred arms. With the remaining five hundred arms he rained arrows.

SriKrishna destroyed all of Bana's bows and demolished his chariot.

Killed his charioteer and horses. Bana had to run for his life.

Siva had a terrifying servant - with three heads and three legs. Sivajwaram.[234]

He would burn everything wherever he went. He rushed to fight against SriKrishna.

---

[233]

[234] Sivajwaram is a personified form of extreme fever (Jvara) emanating from Lord Siva.

•He is a dreadful, three-legged, three-headed entity with fiery power, capable of burning entire armies.

•Created by Siva's intense heat, he represents fever, disease, and suffering.

•He was unleashed in battle to fight against Krishna's Narayana Jwaram (Vishnujwaram)

During the battle between Krishna and Banasura, Lord Siva sided with his devotee Banasura. To aid him, Siva released Sivajwaram, a terrifying force of fever and destruction.

•In response, Krishna created Narayana Jwaram, a divine cooling energy.

•Sivajwaram, despite his destructive power, could not withstand Narayana Jwaram.

•Overwhelmed by Krishna's cooling, peaceful energy, Sivajwaram surrendered to Krishna and sought refuge.

•Krishna, being merciful, granted Sivajwaram liberation from suffering.

Symbolic Meaning

•Sivajwaram represents intense suffering, fevers, and diseases—both physical and mental.

•Narayana Jwaram symbolizes divine grace, peace, and healing.

•The story shows that Krishna's divine energy can neutralize even the most destructive forces. As Edited By Vk Madhav Mohan

SriKrishna created Vishnujawaram[235] to negate Sivajwaram.

The clash was dreadful.

Eventually, Sivajwaram was on the verge of destruction.

That terrible creature fell at SriKrishna's feet and pleaded for protection. The very embodiment of compassion, Karunya Moorthi[236], Bhagavan, SriKrishna granted refuge. Bana reappeared on the battlefield.

---

[235] Vishnujwaram (also called Narayana Jwaram) is the personified form of cooling, divine energy that Lord Krishna (Vishnu) manifested to counteract Sivajwaram, the fever of destruction unleashed by Lord Siva. This battle is described in the Srimad Bhagavatam, particularly during Krishna's war against Banasura. Vishnujwaram was a cooling, serene force, the complete opposite of the burning intensity of Sivajwaram. Sivajwaram (Siva's fever) – Represents extreme suffering, illness, and intense heat of negative karma. Vishnujwaram (Krishna's fever) – Represents peace, divine grace, and the ability to soothe pain. Victory of Vishnujwaram over Sivajwaram – Symbolizes how divine grace, wisdom, and devotion to God can neutralize suffering and hardships. This episode highlights Krishna's supremacy and the power of divine cooling energy (compassion) against destructive forces (suffering).
As Edited By Vk Madhav Mohan

[236] This phrase captures the very essence of Sanatana Dharma, where Bhagavan (God) is not just a supreme ruler but also the ultimate source of compassion (Karunya). It highlights how divine grace, love, and forgiveness are central to the nature of God in Hindu philosophy. This phrase beautifully describes Bhagavan (God) as the ultimate form of compassion (Karunya). In Hindu philosophy, the supreme deity—whether it is Vishnu, Siva, Krishna, Rama, or Devi—is always depicted as the Karunya Moorthi, the one who showers grace and kindness upon devotees.
Examples of Bhagavan as "Karunya Moorthi" (Embodiment of Compassion)
1.Lord Krishna's Compassion
•Sivajwaram's Surrender: When the fiery Sivajwaram (Siva's fever) was overpowered by Vishnujwaram (Krishna's cooling energy), it fell at Krishna's feet. Instead of destroying it, Krishna granted it liberation, showing his divine compassion.

This time he received the ultimate punishment for his arrogance.

Srikrishna cut off all his hands like the branches of a mighty tree are cut down.

Siva came to the rescue and beseeched Bhagavan, "O SriKrishna, Bana is my devotee. Please protect him. In that way, please bless him and me." SriKrishna replied,

"I will do what pleases you. I have made a promise to Prahlada that I will not kill anyone born in his dynasty. To extinguish

---

•Draupadi's Protection: When Draupadi was humiliated in Duryodhana's court, Krishna, despite being physically distant, protected her by providing an endless saree, proving that his grace transcends space and time.

•Bhagavad Gita: Arjuna was in despair on the battlefield of Kurukshetra. Krishna, instead of forcing him into battle, patiently guided him through wisdom and love, revealing the Gita's teachings.

2.Lord Rama – The Embodiment of Compassion

•Hanuman's Devotion: Rama embraced Hanuman, treating him as a divine son and never forgetting his service.

•Ravana's Death: Despite being an enemy, Rama ensured Ravana received a proper farewell, respecting his wisdom and devotion to Siva.

•Forgiving Kaikeyi: Even after being sent to exile, Rama never showed anger towards Kaikeyi, but rather respected her as his mother.

3.Lord Siva's Infinite Grace

•Giving Moksha to Kannappa Nayanar: A devotee who plucked out his own eyes for Siva was granted immediate liberation.

•Drinking Halahala Poison: During the Samudra Manthan (Churning of the Ocean), Siva selflessly drank the deadly poison to save the universe, showing his boundless compassion.

4.Lord Vishnu's Acts of Mercy

•Vamana's Blessing to Mahabali: Though he defeated him, Vishnu granted King Mahabali a place in the spiritual realm, recognizing his devotion.

•Gajendra Moksha: When the elephant Gajendra cried out for help, Vishnu immediately appeared and rescued him from the clutches of a crocodile, granting him liberation.

Spiritual Significance of Divine Compassion

•Even sinners are forgiven when they surrender with true devotion.

•God does not punish for the sake of punishment but uplifts souls towards liberation.

•Divine grace is unconditional, available to anyone who seeks it with faith. As Edited By Vk Madhav Mohan

Bana's arrogance, I have severed all his hands. However, I have left him with four hands. They will remain with him." Bana folded his four remaining hands in reverence.

He fell at Bhagavan's feet and did Namaskaram.

Then, he went into the palace and returned with Anirudha and Usha. He entrusted the young couple to SriKrishna.

Bhagavan took his grandson and the bride back to Dwaraka.

Now, let me tell you a story of redemption from a curse.

Some sons of SriKrishna went to a garden, some distance away. After a while they felt thirsty and so went in search of water.

They came upon a well. It was a disused well.

They looked down into the well. A very large chameleon was in it.

They tried to lift it out but couldn't.

So, they ran to their Father and told Him about the chameleon. SriKrishna went to the garden.

He approached the well. With His left hand He picked up the chameleon and set it free. Instantly the chameleon assumed a divine form!

He was a King named Nruga.

Why did he become a chameleon?

Only if I tell you the background story will you understand! Nruga was foremost amongst the generous.

His generosity knew no bounds. Once, though, he made a mistake.

The cow he donated to a Brahmin somehow got mixed up with other cows.

Unknowingly he donated the cow to a second Brahmin. The first Brahmin saw him taking the cow away.

"This is my cow," said the first Brahmin.

"How can that be? The King gave it to me," said the second Brahmin. An argument flared up.

The argument continued endlessly. Finally, they went before the King.

"This man has stolen my cow," said the first Brahmin.

"O King, you gave this cow to me, didn't you?" said the second Brahmin. The Maharaja was puzzled.

The argument had to be settled, somehow. He came up with an idea.

"Please give up the cow. In return, I will give you a hundred thousand cows," he told the first Brahmin.

But the man did not agree.

"In that case, can you please give up the cow? I will give you a hundred thousand cows in return," he asked the second Brahmin.

He too did not agree.

The first Brahmin was obstinate.

"No way will I give up my cow," he said. The second Brahmin was equally obstinate.

"I don't want a hundred thousand cows; I only want this cow." The Maharaja was very vexed.

He couldn't find a solution.

Much time passed and he passed away. Kaala asked him, "Bad experiences will follow bad deeds and good experiences will follow good deeds. You will have to experience both. Which do you want first?"

"I choose the bad experiences first," replied Nruga.

Suddenly he changed into a chameleon and fell into the disused well.

When SriKrishna lifted him up all his bad experiences and discomfort vanished forever.

That was Nruga's story.

Many more powerful enemies who hated SriKrishna still remained. One of them was the King of Karusha, Paundraka[237].

Paundraka believed the he, not SriKrishna, was the incarnation of Lord MahaVishnu!

Paundraka sent a message to SriKrishna.

"SriKrishna, I am Vasudeva, the incarnation of Lord MahaVishnu. You are pretending to be Vasudeva. Drop your pretence immediately. Seek forgiveness from me. Else, its war against me."

SriKrishnawasintheroyalassemblywhenthemessengerfrom Paundraka arrived and delivered his message.

Whoever heard the nonsense laughed out loud. SriKrishna was angered.

---

[237] There is some doubt about Paundraka's connection with Karusha. Some texts mention Paundraka as a "Karusha Kshatriya," but it is not clear whether he was a king of Karusha. He may have been born into a Kshatriya lineage that had connections to Karusha but ruled elsewhere. The Paundra Kingdom was separate and located to the east of the Kuru and Magadha territories, as edited by VK Madhav Mohan

He sent an apt reply, "Paundraka, you are strutting about displaying my insignia. Because of your impertinence I am discarding that insignia. You are shortly going to become food for the animals."

The armies of SriKrishna and Paundraka clashed.

On the battlefield SriKrishna observed Paundraka carefully. He had donned deceptive garments and accessories.

The conch, chakra, mace, lotus, yellow silk, and Vanamala[238] are all with him like an actor on stage.

The King of Kashi and his army are on hand to help Paundraka. The armies fought valiantly.

The battlefield was drenched in blood.

Bhagavan decapitated Paundraka first and Kashi Raja next. What transpired in Kashi?

A head had fallen in the doorway of the Gopura.

The local populace saw it. Whose head was it?

---

[238] In Vaishnava tradition, Lord Vishnu and Krishna are often depicted wearing a Vanamala—a garland made of wildflowers, Tulasi leaves, and other sacred plants. According to the Bhagavata Purana, Vishnu's Vanamala represents his connection to nature, his compassion for all beings, and his divine beauty. The Vishnu Sahasranama mentions "Vanamali" as one of Lord Vishnu's names, meaning "the one adorned with a forest garland."
Krishna and His Vanamala
•Krishna, the divine cowherd (Gopala), is often described wearing a Vanamala, signifying his bond with Vrindavan's natural beauty.
•In devotional songs and Bhakti literature, poets describe Krishna's Vanamala swaying as he plays his flute in the forests of Vrindavan.
•The Tulasi plant, considered sacred to Vishnu and Krishna, is often included in his Vanamala. As edited by VK Madhav Mohan

They went to investigate.

Then it became known: this was Kashi Raja's head! SriKrishna had made the Kashi Raja's head fall in Kashi! Sudakshina was the son of Kashi Raja.

He was determined to seek revenge for the killing of his father. He began preparations.

First, he had to perform Tapas and build strength. Only then could he defeat SriKrishna.

Sudakshina focused on Siva during his Tapas. Siva advised him to conduct Agni Yagya[239]. Sudakshina did so.

A fearsome being rose from the sacred fire.

It had long hair, beard and moustache, all red-hot hot copper coloured. Round eyes like fire balls. Naked. Long red tongue snaking out of its mouth. A formidable trident in its hand. Legs like palm trees.

The terrifying creature rushed to Dwaraka. People ran in terror.

---

[239] Agni Yagya (അഗ്നി യാഗം) also spelled Agnihotra or Agnihoma, is an ancient Vedic fire ritual performed to invoke the blessings of Agni, the fire deity, and other divine forces. It is a ceremonial offering of materials such as ghee, grains, herbs, and sacred wood into a consecrated fire while chanting Vedic mantras. Agnihotra is believed to purify the environment, enhance spiritual energy, and promote health and harmony.
Key Elements of Agni Yagya
1.Agni Kundam (Fire Altar) – The sacred fire is lit in a specially prepared altar.
2.Ahuti (Offerings) – Ghee, grains, herbs, and other materials are offered into the fire.
3.Mantras – Vedic chants are recited, invoking various deities, particularly Agni.
4.Sankalpa (Intention) – The purpose or intention behind the Yagya is stated, such as seeking prosperity, health, or spiritual growth.
As Edited By VK Madhav Mohan

SriKrishna was playing a game of dice. He was informed of the matter.

Bhagavan sent the Trichakra.

Trichakra chased the creature which then returned to Kasi and destroyed Sudakshina.

Trichakra set fire to Kasi and came back to Bhagavan's divine Hands. Dvivida was a mighty monkey warrior.

He was also a dear friend of Narakasura.

He was bent upon seeking revenge for the killing of Narakasura. His army was bearing down on Dwaraka.

Dvivida was as strong as ten thousand elephants and a restless, troublemaking disposition suitable for monkeys. He set alight villages and towns. Levelled mountains. He got into the sea and diverted seawater to land. Uprooted fruit bearing trees. Desecrated Homas.

Trapping sanyasis inside their caves. Many such atrocities did he perpetrate. Finally, he reached Raivata Mountain.

There he spotted Balarama.

His friends, the Gopi women, were with him. Balarama was intoxicated with alcohol.

He was frolicking boisterously with everyone.

The monkey warrior climbed a huge tree and bent and shook its branches.

Made a lot of noise and showed funny facial expressions. The Gopi women burst out laughing.

Balarama threw a stone.

The monkey dodged.

He jumped down suddenly and ran off with the pot of alcohol. He threw the pot and broke it.

Balarama grabbed a plough and chased after him.

Dvivida uprooted a large tree and smashed it on Balarama's head. But Balarama blocked the onslaught and struck a retaliatory blow.

Trailing blood, Dvivida dug up many trees and used them as clubs. Balrama ripped every tree to shreds.

Dvivida then started pelting rocks. They too had no effect on Balarama. Dvivida bunched his fists and punched.

Balarama punched him back in the most vulnerable spot. Vomiting blood, Dvivida, fell dead.

The fall blew all the leaves from the trees like a small boat caught in a gale.

The monkey warrior's fall was so very heavy! Saamba was the son of SriKrishna and Jaambavati.

The young man participated in the Swayamvara of Lakshana, daughter of Duryodhana.

He was successful and took her away.

Duryodhana was furious.

He had hated SriKrishna for a very long time.

How could his daughter be taken by SriKrishna's son? He must be captured and tied up!

Let SriKrishna come to retrieve his son.

Let's humiliate him before letting his son free! Duryodhana and his companions pursued Saamba. Saamba turned back and fought them.

He killed many adversaries.

In the meantime, he suffered many injuries.

Despite all that, he fought bravely with determination.

Finally, Duryodhana and his men captured him but with great difficulty. SriKrishna got this information from Narada.

He marched His army to Hastinapura. Balarama accompanied SriKrishna.

However, Balarama was reluctant to fight the Kauravas. He had once taught Duryodhana the art of mace warfare. So, in that respect Duryodhana was his student.

The Yadava army reached the outskirts of Hastinapura and pitched its camp.

Balarama requested Udhava to meet Dhritarashtra. Some Kauravas came to see Balarama.

"You have kept Saamba in captivity. In the name of our relationship, we have not reacted. But what you have done is unjust," said Balarama.

The attitude of the Kauravas was sarcastic and contemptuous. "Great!

The slipper wants to sit atop the head wearing the golden crown! Your desire is akin to that.

The vagaries of time!

How did you receive respect and fame? Only because of your relationship with us and now, you act as though as you are equal to us!" The sarcasm and contempt angered Balarama.

The arrogant Kauravas has to be punishThey should be washed away in the Ganges near Hastinapura.

He took a plough and pressed it down into the earth.

The entire town shook and started sliding towards the Ganges. The Kauravas quickly apologised to Balarama to save themselves. His anger subsided.

Duryodhana freed Saamba.

Srikrishna was seated in the midst of prominent Yadavas like the resplendent full moon in the midst of stars.

A messenger entered and submitted a request.

The messenger had been sent by the Kings imprisoned by Jarasandha. They were pleading with SriKrishna to rescue and save them.

Narada too arrived with a message from Yudhishtira[240].

It had been decided to conduct the Rajasuya Yagya[241].

---

[240] Yudhishthira, the eldest of the Pandavas, is one of the most significant characters in the Mahabharata. He is known as "Dharmaraja", the King of Righteousness, due to his unwavering commitment to truth, justice, and Dharma.
Birth & Lineage: •Yudhishthira was the eldest son of Kunti and the god of Dharma (Yama).•He was born due to a divine boon given to Kunti by Sage Durvasa.•His younger brothers were Bhima, Arjuna, Nakula, and Sahadeva.•He was the rightful heir to the Kuru throne of Hastinapura.
Yudhishthira's Character & Personality•Embodiment of Dharma: He always upheld truth and righteousness, even in difficult situations.•Calm & Patient: Unlike Bhima (who was aggressive) and Arjuna (who was strategic), Yudhishthira was known for his patience and wisdom. •Skilled in Spear Combat: Though not as famous as his brothers in warfare, he was an expert in spear fighting.•Believer in Ahimsa (Non-Violence): He avoided unnecessary conflicts but fought when necessary.
As edited by VK Madhav Mohan
[241] The Rajasuya Yagna is one of the most prestigious and elaborate Vedic rituals performed by a sovereign ruler (Chakravarti) to establish supreme authority over other kings. It is prominently mentioned in the Mahabharata and

The essence of the message was that Srikrishna may kindly accept the Agryapuja[242].

---

various Hindu scriptures as a ritual symbolizing royal consecration, Dharma, and absolute sovereignty.

Meaning of Rajasuya Yagna

•Raja – King or ruler.

•Suya – Sacrifice, offering, or worship.

•Together, Rajasuya means "The Royal Sacrifice," a grand yajna that marks a king's supremacy and legitimacy over all other rulers.

Purpose of the Rajasuya Yagna

1.To establish the performer as a Chakravarti (Universal Emperor).

2.To assert dominance over other kings by making them submit and offer tribute.

3.To strengthen Dharma (righteous rule) and bring prosperity to the kingdom.

4.To seek divine blessings and legitimacy from the gods and sages.

Yudhishthira's Rajasuya Yagna

•In the Mahabharata, the most famous Rajasuya Yagna was performed by Yudhishthira, the eldest of the Pandavas, after they established their rule in Indraprastha.

•Krishna advised Yudhishthira that performing this Yagna would solidify his claim as the supreme ruler.

•As part of the ritual, the Pandavas had to defeat or gain allegiance from all other rulers before the ceremony.

•Bhima, Arjuna, Nakula, and Sahadeva set out on military campaigns across India, forcing kings to accept Yudhishthira's sovereignty.

•The ceremony was attended by great sages, kings, and warriors, including Krishna, Bhishma, and Duryodhana. As edited by VK Madhav Mohan

[242] Agryapuja means "the first and foremost worship" or "honoring someone as the most important participant" in a religious or social gathering. It is performed to recognize the supreme authority or significance of a deity, saint, or distinguished guest. In Hindu scriptures, Agryapuja is given to the most deserving being before any ritual begins

Krishna Receiving Agryapuja in Rajasuya Yaga

•In the Mahabharata, during Yudhishthira's Rajasuya Yaga, a debate arose regarding who should receive the Agryapuja (the first ceremonial honor).•Bhishma declared that Lord Krishna was the most deserving, as he was the Supreme Being (Parabrahman) and had protected Dharma.•Shishupala opposed it, leading to his downfall, as Krishna used his Sudarshana Chakra to slay him.•This incident highlights the importance of Agryapuja in recognizing the greatest personality in a gathering.

Some of the members of the assembly were of the opinion that SriKrishna must kill Jarasandha first before participating in the Raja Suya.

SriKrishna knew what was to be done first but he pretended that he did not.

"Udhava, you are the chief amongst ministers. No one is as knowledgeable as you. What is your opinion?" SriKrishna asked.

Udhava replied,"Bhagavan, you know everything. Even so, let me give you my opinion. Yudhishtira's Raja Suya is appropriate. However, there is an important factor. Only if you have the strength for Digvijaya[243] you conduct Raja Suya.

As Edited By VK Madhav Mohan

[243] Digvijaya means "conquering all directions" or "universal victory." It refers to a king, ruler, or warrior's military campaign across different regions to establish their supremacy and authority over other rulers.Dig = Direction(s) (North, South, East, and West).•Vijaya = Victory or conquest.•Together, Digvijaya means "victory over all directions," signifying a ruler's or warrior's ability to establish dominance over all lands.In Vedic and Puranic texts, Digvijaya was a military expedition undertaken by kings, emperors, and warriors to prove their supremacy. Some key figures who undertook Digvijaya include:

Yudhishthira's Digvijaya (Mahabharata)

•Before the Rajasuya Yagna, Yudhishthira sent his four brothers (Bhima, Arjuna, Nakula, Sahadeva) to conquer different regions of India and establish Pandava dominance.

•Each brother successfully defeated various kings and brought tribute to Yudhishthira, making him the supreme emperor (Chakravarti).

Arjuna's Digvijaya

•Arjuna performed his own Digvijaya during the Mahabharata period, traveling across Bharatavarsha to conquer rival kingdoms and establish Pandava rule.

•His victories included defeating the rulers of Dravida, Kerala, Kalinga, and Anga.

Krishna's Digvijaya

•Lord Krishna undertook a Digvijaya mission to destroy evil rulers like Kamsa, Jarasandha, and Shishupala, ensuring Dharma prevailed in the world.

If you have to achieve Digvijaya you have to conquer Jarasandha. Only Bhima can defeat him.

Jarasandha is one who gives Brahmins whatever they ask.

Bhima must go to Jarasandha in the guise of a Brahmin and ask for combat.

Jarasandha will agree and fight.

He will be killed by Bhima. He has to be killed.

Many Kings are his captives.

Their Queens console their children everyday by telling them: Children, don't cry, SriKrishna will kill Jarasandha and free your father. O' Bhagavan, please save all of them".

Srikrishna respected Udhava's opinion. "Messenger, I will get Jarasandha killed. The Kings need have no fear.Please inform them," said SriKrishna and left for Indraprastha[244] along with His army and some of His wives.

Digvijaya of Historical Kings in India
In Indian history, several powerful emperors performed Digvijaya:
•Chandragupta Maurya – Conquered vast regions from Bengal to Afghanistan.
•Ashoka the Great – Initially undertook a Digvijaya campaign but later embraced Buddhism.
•Samudragupta – His Prayag Prashasti inscription mentions his Digvijaya over North and South India.
•Raja Raja Chola & Rajendra Chola – Undertook naval Digvijayas to conquer Sri Lanka, Indonesia, and Southeast Asia.
As edited by VK Madhav Mohan
[244] Indraprastha was the magnificent capital city of the Pandavas in the Mahabharata. It was originally a barren land but was transformed into a grand and prosperous city by Lord Krishna and Vishwakarma (the celestial architect). It later became the center of political, economic, and military power for the Pandavas.•Indra) – Refers to Lord Indra, the king of the heavens.•Prastha – Means

SriKrishna's arrival!

YudhishtiraembracedHimtightlywithtotalloveandcomplete surrender.

He shed tears of joy.

Not just Yudhishtira but also Bhima, Arjuna, Nakula, Sahadeva, and everyone.

Kunti, Subhadra and Panchali welcomed SriKrishna's wives. To meet each other and live together, so much happiness! Srikrishna set out for Magadha.

He took Bhima and Arjuna with Him.

All three were disguised as Brahmins[245]. Jarasandha possesses one good quality.

____

a settlement or land.•Indraprastha literally means "The City of Indra," signifying its divine and royal nature.

The Birth of Indraprastha

•The land where Indraprastha was built originally belonged to the Khandava Forest.

•Dhritarashtra, the Kuru king, reluctantly gave this land to the Pandavas to avoid conflict with Duryodhana.

•Krishna and Arjuna assisted Agni (the Fire God) in burning the Khandava forest, allowing them to clear the land.

•Maya Danava, a celestial architect, built the magnificent palace and infrastructure of Indraprastha for the Pandavas.

Features & Grandeur of Indraprastha

•Designed by Vishwakarma & Maya Danava – It had floating illusions, crystal palaces, and divine architecture.

•Golden streets, grand temples, and rich markets made it one of the most beautiful cities in the world.

•Surrounded by defensive walls, gardens, and rivers, Indraprastha was both a fortress and a paradise. As Edited By VK Madhav Mohan

[245] This story is detailed in MaliBharatam

What if anyone approaches him with a request? He would never send anyone away empty handed. SriKrishna is aware of this.

"I have a request," said Bhagavan.

"No matter what it is, I will fulfil it," promised Jarasandha. Then SriKrishna revealed their identity.

The request was for combat.

Jarasandha would never break his promise. He entered the arena for combat with Bhima.

They were equal in strength, aggression and skill.

The bout was finely balanced. Combat in daytime, rest at night. Twenty-seven days and nights passed.

Finally, SriKrishna subtly made Bhima understand a tactic.

The two parts of Jarasandha's body had after all been joined by a Pisachi[246] named Jara[247].

---

[246] Pisachi (िपशाची) – The Female Spirit of Darkness. Piśāchī is a female supernatural being in Hindu and Buddhist traditions, often associated with darkness, spirits, and the afterlife. She is considered the female counterpart of Piśācha, a race of flesh-eating spirits.
Characteristics of Piśāchī
•Spirit of the Dead: Piśāchīs are believed to be the spirits of women who died due to unnatural causes (murder, suicide, or accidents).
•Haunts Cremation Grounds: They are believed to be commonly found in smashanas (cremation grounds) and deserted places.
•Shape-Shifting Abilities: As per lore, Piśāchī can change forms and become invisible at will.
•Possesses Humans: They are believed to enter human bodies, causing mental illness or delirium. As Edited By VK Madhav Mohan
[247] No matter how many times Bhima crushed him, Jarasandha would reassemble his body and rise again (because of a boon from a demoness named

Only if the two parts were ripped apart would Jarasandha die. **Bhima understood, followed SriKrishna'sindication** and killed Jarasandha.

The condition of the imprisoned Kings was pitiable. They were starving.

Clothes were torn and filthy. Bodies were caked in dirt.

Faces worn out by fatigue and depression, unbearably sad.

One day the gates of the prison opened. SriKrishna, the Protector, had come to meet them! It was as if their eyes were soaked in Amruta.

They did Namaskaram and worshipped him with sincerity and devotion. Wasn't it, after all, SriKrishna's compassion that had saved them?

Yudhishtira and others were waiting anxiously in Indraprastha. From a distance they could hear the blowing of conches.

The sound of Panchajanya![248]

Jara, who had joined his body at birth).•Seeing Bhima struggle, Krishna picked up a blade of grass, tore it into two halves, and threw them in opposite directions.•Bhima immediately understood Krishna's hint—Jarasandha could be killed only if his body was torn into two and the halves thrown apart so they couldn't join again.•Bhima followed Krishna's cue, tore Jarasandha in half, and threw the two halves in opposite directions, ensuring his death. This episode taught Bhima that brute strength alone is not enough; intelligence and strategy play a vital role in victory. Until he understood Krishna's subtle hint, he was locked in a never-ending fight. This moment is a perfect example of how Krishna, the ultimate strategist, guided Bhima towards success using wisdom rather than mere power.

As Edited By VK Madhav Mohan

[248] Panchajanya is the divine conch (shankha) of Lord Krishna. He had taken it after killing Panchajana and releasing Sandepani's son (as described earlier). Panchajanya was famously blown during the Kurukshetra war to signify the

It was clear to everyone that the menace of Jarasandha had been removed.

In due course, the Raja Suya commenced. Maharshis arrived in large numbers.

Along with many other invitees and the Kauravas too.

During the Agryapuja the most deserving, outstanding and respected person had to be honoured.

Could it be anyone other than SriKrishna in any of the three worlds? Yudhishtira offered Agryapuja to Bhagavan.

Remember Shishupala [249] who had dreamt of marrying Rugmini? He too was present in the assembly.

---

beginning of battle and instill fear in the hearts of his enemies. The sound of Panchajanya symbolized righteousness (Dharma) and the arrival of divine intervention.

Symbol of Divine Authority

•Krishna's blowing of the Panchajanya conch at the beginning of the Kurukshetra war was a declaration of Dharma.•The sound was said to resonate through the three worlds, filling enemies with fear.

In the Bhagavad Gita (Chapter 1, Verse 15), the conch is mentioned:

"Pāñchajanyaṁ hṛṣīkeśo devadattaṁ dhanañjayaḥ..."

("Hrishikesha (Krishna) blew his conch Panchajanya, Arjuna blew his conch Devadatta...") This verse marks the divine moment when Krishna and the Pandavas prepared for battle Symbolism of Panchajanya

•Victory of Dharma over Adharma – Krishna's conch represents the voice of truth and righteousness.

•Fearlessness and Divine Protection – It was believed that hearing the Panchajanya conch gave warriors immense courage.

•Cosmic Sound (AUM) – The deep resonance of the conch symbolizes the universal vibration of creation and destruction. as edited by VK Madhav Mohan
[249]

The disrespectful Shishupala shouted that SriKrishna must not be honoured and he publicly insulted Bhagavan, repeatedly. Members of the assembly cursed Shishupala.

The Pandavas drew their weapons in anger but SriKrishna moved them aside.

With the Trichakra, He severed Shishupala's head.

From his body a Tejas[250] rose and merged in Bhagavan.

---

[250] Tejas (तेजस्) – The Inner Radiance & Divine Energy. Tejas (also spelled as Tejas in some transliterations) is a Sanskrit term that means brilliance, inner radiance, spiritual energy, or divine power. It represents the fiery essence of life, symbolizing both physical vitality and spiritual illumination.
1. Tejas in Hindu Philosophy
•A Manifestation of Energy: Tejas is one of the five great elements (Pancha Mahabhutas), representing fire (Agni tattva).
•Spiritual Aura & Charisma: A person with high Tejas exudes confidence, wisdom, and an inspiring presence.
•Mental & Intellectual Sharpness: Tejas is also linked to keen intelligence, sharp memory, and clarity of thought.
2. Tejas in the Bhagavad Gita & Upanishads
•Krishna's Divine Tejas: In the Bhagavad Gita, Krishna declares:
"I am the brilliance in the sun and moon, the radiance in fire, and the intelligence of the wise."
•Chandogya Upanishad describes Tejas as a divine energy that sustains the universe, present in the sun, fire, and all beings.
3. Tejas in Leadership & Warriors
•Kshatriya Dharma (Warrior's Radiance): Tejas is often associated with the aura of great warriors, like Krishna, Arjuna, Bhishma, and Hanuman.
•Chakra & Kundalini Energy: In yogic traditions, Tejas corresponds to the Manipura (Solar Plexus) Chakra, which governs personal power, confidence, and transformation.
4. Practical Applications of Tejas

Yudhishtira's Raja Suya was concluded successfully and auspiciously. SriKrishna had another mighty foe - Sishupala's powerful friend, Shalva[251].

•In Ayurveda: Tejas is one of the three subtle forces (Ojas, Tejas, and Prana), responsible for metabolism, digestion, and vitality.

•In Meditation & Yoga: Developing Tejas means increasing one's inner fire, discipline, and wisdm.

•In Leadership: A leader with Tejas commands respect without force, leading with vision, clarity, and purpose.

How to Enhance Tejas?

•Discipline & Self-Control – Practicing tapasya (austerity) builds inner Tejas.

•Right Nutrition & Fasting – Eating sattvic (pure) foods enhances Tejas.

•Meditation & Focus – Developing one-pointed concentration (Dhyana) increases mental brilliance.

•Serving Dharma – Following righteous actions increases Tejas naturally.

Final Thought

Tejas is not just physical brightness but an inner fire that fuels greatness. It is the power of wisdom, courage, and spiritual purity. In the Mahabharata, Krishna, Arjuna, and Bhishma radiate Tejas because of their inner strength and commitment to Dharma

[251] Who Was Shalva?

•King of Saubha: Shalva ruled over the kingdom of Saubha and was an ally of many kings who opposed Krishna.

•Friend of Shishupala: He was a close friend of Shishupala, the King of Chedi, who was killed by Krishna during the Rajasuya Yajna.

•Sworn Enemy of Krishna: After Krishna killed Shishupala, Shalva vowed revenge and waged war against Dwaraka.

Shalva's Attack on Dwaraka

1.Acquiring a Flying City (Saubha Vimana)

•After Shishupala's death, Shalva performed severe tapasya (austerities) to please Lord Shiva.

•Shiva, pleased with his penance, granted him a divine aerial vehicle (Saubha Vimana) that could become invisible and move anywhere instantly.•With this flying fortress, Shalva launched a massive attack on Dwaraka.

2.Battle with Krishna's Army

Shalva was with Shishupala during Rugmini's Swayamvara. SriKrishna had defeated them while taking Rugmini away. Shalva had then sworn an oath, "I will destroy the Yadavas." To fulfil the oath did he not need to build strength?

Shalva performed Tapas to Siva.

Siva got Maya[252] to construct an aircraft and presented it to Shalva. The aircraft was extraordinary!

•Shalva's forces, using the mystical powers of the Saubha Vimana, caused immense destruction.
•The people of Dwaraka were confused and terrified as the flying city appeared and disappeared unpredictably.
•Krishna was not in Dwaraka at that time, as he was with the Pandavas at Indraprastha.
3.Shalva's Illusions & Trickery
•Using Maya (illusionary magic), Shalva created a fake image of Vasudeva (Krishna's father).
•The illusion made it seem like Vasudeva had been captured and killed, shocking Krishna's forces. Krishna's Return & Shalva's Defeat
•When Krishna returned to Dwaraka, he immediately engaged in battle.
•Despite Shalva's magical illusions, Krishna's divine vision (Jnana Drishti) allowed him to see through the deception.
•Krishna destroyed the Saubha Vimana with his Sudarshana Chakra.
•Shalva was beheaded by Krishna, ending his reign of terror.
Symbolism & Lessons from Shalva's Story
•Illusions & Deception Cannot Defeat Truth – Shalva relied on Maya (illusion), but Krishna, representing Dharma and clarity, destroyed it effortlessly.
•Revenge Leads to Destruction – Shalva's blind hatred for Krishna led him to seek power, but it ultimately resulted in his downfall.
•Divine Protection of Dharma – No matter how powerful evil appears, Krishna's Sudarshana Chakra represents the ultimate protection of righteousness.
[252] Maya Danava - Maya the Architect – The Master Builder of the Asuras. Maya Danava was a legendary architect and engineer in Hindu mythology, particularly in the Mahabharata and Puranas. He was a Danava (demon race) and an expert in architecture, engineering, and sorcery. His creations were magnificent, advanced, and often magical
1. Who Was Maya Danava?

Sometimes it could multiply into many andsometimes it could disappear!

•He belonged to the race of Danavas, an ancient group of beings often opposed to the Devas (gods).

•He was known for building incredible cities, palaces, and divine weapons.

•Despite being on the side of the Asuras, he sometimes aided great warriors like Arjuna and Krishna.

2. Maya Danava in the Mahabharata

The Construction of the Maya Sabha (Palace of Illusions)

•After the Pandavas established their kingdom in Indraprastha, Krishna spared Maya Danava's life when they defeated the Khandava forest.

•In gratitude, Maya built the most magnificent palace for the Pandavas, known as Maya Sabha.

•The Maya Sabha was filled with illusions, where floors looked like water and water appeared as solid ground.

•This led to Duryodhana's famous humiliation when he fell into an invisible pool, causing Draupadi and others to laugh— fueling his hatred and desire for revenge.

3. Other Marvels Built by Maya Danava

•Tripura (Three Flying Cities) – Maya helped create three floating cities for the Asuras, which were eventually destroyed by Shiva in the Tripura Samhara.

•Sudarshana Chakra (Krishna's Divine Weapon) – Some legends credit Maya Danava with helping in its creation.

•Divine Weapons & Sorcery – He was an expert in crafting powerful weapons, many of which were used by the Kauravas and Asuras.

4. Symbolism of Maya Danava

•Mastery Over Illusion & Engineering – His name "Maya" signifies illusion, showing that the physical world is deceptive.

•Knowledge Without Dharma Leads to Destruction – While he had great wisdom, his association with the Asuras often led to ruin.

•Technology in Ancient India – His stories hint at advanced knowledge of architecture, metallurgy, and illusionary sciences

5. Lessons from Maya Danava's Story

•Illusion (Maya) Can Create Both Beauty & Traps – His palace amazed everyone but also caused Duryodhana's downfall.

•True Knowledge Must Serve Dharma – Unlike Vishwakarma (the divine architect of the Devas), Maya Danava's work often supported chaos rather than order.

•Creativity Can Be Used for Good or Evil – Just like modern technology, his genius could serve either righteousness or destruction.

It could travel not just in the sky but also on land and in the water. Shalva's strength increased manifold, many times over!

When SriKrishna was busy with the Raja Suya, Shalva marched his army towards Dwaraka.

He destroyed Gopuras and forts.

From the aircraft he showered missiles.

Pradyumna, Satyaki [253] and others fought bravely and held Shalva at bay. The battle continued, causing death and destruction on a massive scale. At Indraprastha SriKrishna witnessed ill omens.

Realising that Shalva was attacking Dwaraka, he reached there in an instant.

Shalva was decimating the Yadava army.

Bhagvan rushed in and struck Shalva's aircraft a blow with his mace.

The aircraft shattered into pieces and fell into the sea. Shalva came ashore and charged Bhagavan with his mace.

---

[253] Satyaki – The Loyal Warrior of Krishna and the Pandavas. Satyaki, also known as Yuyudhana, was a valiant Yadava warrior, an ardent devotee of Krishna, and a powerful ally of the Pandavas in the Mahabharata. He played a crucial role in the Kurukshetra war, demonstrating exceptional bravery and loyalty.
Who Was Satyaki?
•A Yadava Prince: Satyaki belonged to the Vrishni clan of the Yadavas, the same clan as Krishna.
•Disciple of Arjuna: He was personally trained in archery and warfare by Arjuna, making him an expert in bowmanship (Dhanurveda).
•Krishna's Close Associate: He was deeply devoted to Krishna and followed his guidance throughout his life.
•Supporter of Dharma: Unlike some Yadavas who remained neutral, Satyaki strongly supported the Pandavas. As Edited By Vk Madhav Mohan

With a barrage of arrows, SriKrishna severed the hand that held the mace.

And with the Trichakra, severed Shalva's head. Amongst the wicked lot Dantavaktra[254] remained.

---

[254] Dantavakra or Dantavaktra – The Fierce Enemy of Krishna. Dantavakra was a powerful king and a sworn enemy of
Krishna. He was one of the last great warriors Krishna had to defeat before completing his earthly mission. His story is deeply connected to Shishupala, Jarasandha, and Krishna's divine play (Leela). Meaning of the Name:•Danta
(दन्त) – "Tooth" or "Tusks"•Vakra (वक्र) – "Bent" or "Twisted".The name Dantavakra roughly translates to "one with
deformed or twisted teeth/tusks," which could symbolize his fierce nature or physical appearance.
1. Who Was Dantavakra?
•King of Karusha: He ruled over the kingdom of Karusha, a small but powerful region.
•Reincarnation of Vijaya: In his previous life, Dantavakra was Vijaya, one of the gatekeepers (Dwara-Palas) of Vaikuntha, the abode of Vishnu.
•Cursed to Be Born as an Enemy of Vishnu: Along with Jaya (his twin), Vijaya was cursed by the Sanat Kumaras to be reborn as Asuras three times and fight Vishnu before returning to Vaikuntha.
• First birth: As Hiranyaksha and Hiranyakashipu (killed by Varaha & Narasimha).
•Second birth: As Ravana and Kumbhakarna (killed by Rama).
•Third birth: As Shishupala and Dantavakra (killed by Krishna).
Dantavakra's Final Battle Against Krishna
•After the Kurukshetra war, Dantavakra marched toward Dwaraka with a massive army to challenge Krishna.
•He was furious and filled with vengeance, knowing that Krishna had already killed most of his allies.
•Instead of fighting with regular weapons, he rushed at Krishna with a massive mace, engaging in a ferocious one- on-one duel.
•Krishna, with his Kaumodaki Gada (mace), struck Dantavakra on the chest, instantly killing him.

His size and strength were such that the earth would tremble when he walked.

"Krishna, I have come to kill you. Did you not kill my friends?For that I will now extract revenge from you," Roared Dantavaktra and swung his mace.

Bhagavan parried the blow and issued one in return. Blood spurted from Dantavaktra, he collapsed dead.

From his body a Tejas issued forth and merged with Bhagavan - like it had happened with Shishupala.

Remember, Jaya and Vijaya, the gatekeepers of Lord MahaVishnu? Shishupala and Dantavaktra were the third incarnations of Jaya-Vijaya. After three births, the curse of the Sanaka Maharshis was lifted.

Both of them returned to their previous abode, Vaikuntha!

• Upon death, his soul merged with Krishna, signifying his return to Vaikuntha and liberation from his curse.
Final Thought
Dantavakra was among Krishna's last great enemies, and his death marked the completion of Krishna's mission to remove Adharma (unrighteousness) from the world. Despite his hatred and rage, he was ultimately freed from his curse, showing that Krishna's actions were not just about destruction but also liberation.
As Edited By Vk Madhav Mohan

Balarama embarked on a pilgrimage, accompanied by many Brahmins. Sudarsana Tirtha[255], Brahma Tirtha[256], Chitra Tirtha[257] - he visited them all, and finally reached Naimisa Aranya[258].

---

[255] Sudarsana Tirtha is a sacred water body linked to Lord Vishnu and his divine weapon, the Sudarshana Chakra. It is considered a holy pilgrimage site in Hindu tradition, and visiting it is believed to grant spiritual purification and protection from evil forces.
Possible Locations of Sudarsana Tirtha
Several places in India are associated with Sudarsana Tirtha:
(a)Sudarsana Tirtha in Puri, Odisha: Located near the famous Jagannath Temple in Puri. Devotees believe that offering prayers here grants divine protection. Since Jagannath is a form of Vishnu/Krishna, his Sudarshana Chakra is also worshipped separately in the temple.
(b)Sudarsana Tirtha in Rameswaram, Tamil Nadu, Rameswaram, one of the Char Dhams, has 64 sacred Tirthas, and one of them is linked to Sudarshana. Pilgrims believe that taking a dip in these holy waters removes past sins.
(c)Sudarsana Tirtha Mentioned in the Mahabharata & Puranas Some texts mention a Sudarsana Tirtha near the Saraswati River, where Rishis meditated. It is also believed that Sudarsana Chakra once descended to this Tirtha to cleanse itself after slaying demons
ChatGPT 4o as edited by VK Madhav Mohan
[256] Brahma Tirtha is a holy pilgrimage site associated with Lord Brahma, the creator of the universe in Hindu tradition. This Tirtha (sacred water body) is believed to grant spiritual purification, wisdom, and blessings of creation. It is mentioned in various scriptures and is linked to divine penance, sacrifices, and cosmic balance.
Significance of Brahma Tirtha
•Associated with Lord Brahma & Creation
•It is believed that Lord Brahma performed yajnas (sacrificial rituals) at this Tirtha to maintain universal harmony.
•Bathing in its waters is said to bestow wisdom, clarity, and divine blessings.
•Spiritual Purification & Liberation
•Many scriptures state that taking a dip in Brahma Tirtha washes away sins.
•It is considered a place for performing ancestral rites (Pitru Tarpana).
Notable Brahma Tirtha Locations
There are multiple places in India associated with Brahma Tirtha, some of which are:
(a)Brahma Tirtha in Pushkar, Rajasthan :Most famous Brahma Tirtha is in Pushkar, where the only known major Brahma temple exists. It is said that Brahma

performed a great yajna here after killing the demon Vajranabha. The Pushkar Lake is considered Brahma Tirtha, and a dip here during Kartik Purnima is believed to be highly auspicious.

(b)Brahma Tirtha in Kurukshetra, Haryana,Kurukshetra: the land of the Bhagavad Gita, has many sacred Tirthas, and Brahma Tirtha is one of them. It is believed that Brahma performed penance here before the great war of Mahabharata. The site is considered highly sacred for ancestral worship and liberation (moksha).

(c)Brahma Tirtha Mentioned in the Puranas: Some texts mention a Brahma Tirtha along the Saraswati River, where rishis performed penance. The Brahmanda Purana and Matsya Purana refer to this as a place where Brahma's energy still resides.

As edited by VK Madhav Mohan

[257] Chitra Tirtha is a holy water body mentioned in Hindu scriptures, known for its spiritual significance, connection to divine beings, and power to cleanse sins. It is often associated with the god of justice, Chitragupta, or other celestial events in Hindu mythology.

Significance of Chitra Tirtha

•Connected to Chitragupta, the Divine Record-Keeper

•Chitragupta, the scribe of Yama (the god of death), who records human deeds, is believed to have meditated or performed penance at Chitra Tirtha.

•Bathing in its waters is said to purify past karmic records and lead to spiritual liberation.

A Holy Spot for Ancestral Worship

•Many people visit Chitra Tirtha for Pitru Tarpana (offering to ancestors) to ensure peace for departed souls.

•The site is believed to reduce the effects of negative karma.

Associated with Celestial Phenomena (Chitra Nakshatra)

•Some traditions link Chitra Tirtha to Chitra Nakshatra, a star ruled by Tvashta (a celestial artisan and creator deity).

•It is considered a place where divine creativity and cosmic energies converge.

Locations of Chitra Tirtha

Several places in India are identified as Chitra Tirtha, each having its own sacred legends:

(a)Chitra Tirtha in Kurukshetra, Haryana

•Located in Kurukshetra, the land where Krishna delivered the Bhagavad Gita.

•The Mahabharata and Puranas mention it as a sacred spot where sages performed penance.

•Pilgrims visit to cleanse sins and gain divine blessings.

Maharshis were conducting a great Yaga, Maha Yaga.

They welcomed Balarama and the Brahmins with warmth and honour. Balarama was always quick to anger and when angry he would be terrible.

A Suta[259] was seated on a raised platform.

(b)Chitra Tirtha in Odisha (Near Puri)
•Some ancient texts mention a Chitra Tirtha near the Jagannath Temple in Puri.
•Devotees believe that bathing here brings divine grace and removes obstacles in life.
(c)Chitra Tirtha in Prayagraj (Allahabad)
•Prayagraj (formerly Allahabad), home to the Triveni Sangam, is believed to have several small Tirthas, and one is referred to as Chitra Tirtha in certain texts.
•It is connected to Yama and Chitragupta, making it a sacred site for prayers to mitigate the effects of bad karma.
[258] Naimiṣāraṇya (नैoमषारण्य) is one of the holiest pilgrimage sites in Hinduism, known for its spiritual wisdom, sacred texts, and deep connection to divine sages and gods. It is often referred to as the "Forest of Enlightenment", where many Hindu scriptures were composed and recited. It is believed that rishis and sages gathered here to perform penance and listen to divine knowledge.Many of the Puranas, the Mahabharata, and the Bhagavata Purana were narrated here by sages like Suta Maharshi. Naimisharanya is considered one of the oldest Tirthas (pilgrimage sites), where time itself is believed to be under divine control. It is said that one moment in Naimisharanya is equivalent to many years in the material world.
Naimisharanya in Hindu Scriptures
(a)The Mahabharata : Many episodes of the Mahabharata, including discussions on Dharma, were narrated here.The entire Mahabharata was recited by Ugrashrava Sauti at this location.
(b)The Bhagavata Purana : The Bhagavata Purana was first narrated in Naimisharanya by Suta Maharishi to Shaunaka and other sages.
(c)The Ramayana Connection : It is believed that Lord Rama visited Naimisharanya after his return to Ayodhya.
[259] Suta (also spelled Sootha or Sutha) refers to a class of narrators in Hindu tradition, particularly those who preserved and recited epic stories, Puranas, and historical events. The most famous Suta is Ugrashrava Suta, who narrated the Mahabharata, Bhagavata Purana, and other scriptures to sages in Naimisharanya.

He was narrating the Puranas to the Maharshis.

He did not greet Balarama and his Brahmin companions with folded hands.

He did not even bother to stand up when they arrived. Balarama lost his temper and killed the Suta.

The Maharshis were shocked and dismayed.

"Suta had been provided with the elevated seat and position by us. What you have committed is Adharma. You will have to seek Prayaschitta[260]." Balarama felt deep remorse.

Who is Sūta?
•A Traditional Storyteller and Historian : The Sūtas were bards and oral historians, preserving the knowledge of Itihasas (epics:), Puranas, and DharmaShastras •They were highly respected in spiritual circles for their deep understanding of scriptures.
•Ugrashrava Sūta – The Greatest Narrator•He was the son of Lomaharshana, a disciple of Maharishi Vyasa.•He played a key role in transmitting the Mahabharata and Bhagavata Purana to later generations.
Symbolism of Sūta :•The Preserver of Dharma – Sūta represents the oral tradition of Hinduism, ensuring that wisdom is passed down.•A Messenger of Truth – His role is similar to a seer or divine messenger, delivering knowledge from sages to humanity.•Guru for Generations – Since he learned directly from Vyasa's disciples, Sūta is seen as a teacher of timeless wisdom.
[260] Prāyaścitta refers to atonement, expiation, or penance in Hinduism. It is a spiritual and moral practice meant to cleanse sins (Pāpa), correct mistakes, and restore Dharma. The concept is found in the Vedas, Smritis, and Dharmashastras and is practiced in various forms across Hindu traditions.
Meaning & Purpose of Prāyaścitta
•Cleansing of Karma – Prāyaścitta helps remove the negative effects of sins (Pāpa) and bad karma.
•Restoration of Dharma – It brings a person back to the path of righteousness (Dharma).
•Self-Discipline & Transformation – It helps in developing self-control, repentance, and inner purification.
Types of Sins (Pāpa) and Their Atonements
(a) Mahāpātakas (Great Sins) & Their Prāyaścitta

"What Prayaschitta should I perform?" he asked.

"You must do the kind of Prayaschitta that does not reflect badly on either you nor us; that is all we can say" replied the Maharshis.

"I agree. May the father live through the son. I hereby bless Suta's son, may he be endowed with strength, long life and competence. I must do the right Praysachitta," said Balarama.

"An Asura named Balvala appears every full moon night. He scatters blood, flesh and other impurities and desecrates our Yagas. You must kill him to protect the Yagas. Further, you must go on pilgrimage for a full year. Then your sin will be cleansed," the Maharshis advised Balarama. Balarama waited for the night of the full moon.

These are the gravest sins in Hindu Dharma, requiring severe atonements:
1.Brahmahatya (Killing a Brahmin or Sage) → Pilgrimage, fasting, reciting scriptures.
2.Surāpāna (Drinking Liquor) → Fasting, meditation, charity.
3.Stealing Gold from a Brahmin → Donating wealth, serving the poor.
4.Gurudāra Gaman (Illicit relations with a Guru's wife) → Severe penance, exile, pilgrimage.
(b) Upapātakas (Lesser Sins) & Their Prāyaścitta
•Speaking lies → Reciting Vedic mantras, feeding Brahmins.
•Neglecting daily rituals → Chanting Gayatri Mantra, performing Yajna.
•Breaking a vow → Observing strict fasting, charity.
3. Methods of Prāyaścitta
Prāyaścitta is performed through various forms of penance, depending on the severity of the sin.
•Tapa (Austerity & Fasting) •Chandrayana Vrata – A gradual fasting ritual linked to the lunar cycle.•Krucchra Vrata – Austerities like living on water or only milk for a certain period.
Bhagavad Gita (9.30-31) – Krishna assures that even the greatest sinner can be purified through devotion..Prāyaścitta is not just about punishment but purification—a way to correct mistakes, restore Dharma, and attain inner peace. It is a path of self-reflection and transformation, as edited by VK Madhav Mohan

On the full moon night, a gale blew strongly, kicking up dust. Blood, flesh, and other impurities fell like rain.

Balvala's frightening form became visible. His body was as big and black as the Anjana Mountain[261]. His hair was the colour of red-hot copper.

Whoever saw him was terrified.

Moustache, beard and long, wicked protruding teeth. Balarama hit him hard with his plough.

The Asura's head was smashed.

Blood poured out, reddening his body. Screaming pitiably, he collapsed and died.

Now that Balarama had removed the obstacle to their Yagas, the Maharshis were pleased and blessed him.

Balarama continued his pilgrimage.

He arrived at the lake from which Sarayu River originated. From there he proceeded to Prayag.

From there, to Pulaha Ashrama.

Further, to the rivers Gomathy, Gandaki, Shona and others. After that to the delta where the Ganga merged with the ocean. Then he travelled south.

He prayed at the important temples in Dravida. Parasurama Temple in Mahendrachalam, Subrahmania Temple in Thiruchendur, Devi Temple in Kanyakumari, Vishnu Temple in Anantapur, and Siva Temple in Gokarna.

---

[261] Anjana Mountain (Anjanadri or Anjanagiri) is believed to be the birthplace of Lord Hanuman, the mighty devotee of Lord Rama. It is named after Anjana Devi, Hanuman's mother, who performed intense penance here to be blessed with a divine child, as edited by VK Madhav Mohan

So the pilgrimage continued.

During that period, SriKrishna was in Dwaraka.

SriKrishna had a very dear friend, a childhood classmate. He was a Brahmin named Kuchela.

Kuchela followed the path of Dharma and was a Bhakta.

However, he was suffering a great sorrow - the sorrow of extreme poverty. He had no means to take care of his wife and children.

Most of the time they were all starving. How long can this situation continue? "Isn't SriKrishna your close friend? Please go to Dwaraka and meet SriKrishna. Bhagavan will protect us. He always helps those who surrender to Him. Surely, he will give us something," the wife said to her husband. At first, Kuchela was not very willing.

How will I be able to tell Bhagavan about my poverty? But that was the only way to alleviate the starvation.

His wife's insistence persisted, he decided to go.

After all, I will have the good fortune to meet Bhagavan! "How do I go empty-handed? I have to, somehow, offer Him something. Please pack up something for me to take" he told his wife. There was nothing in the house!

What is to be done?

The poor lady, she searched and found just four handfuls of beaten rice.

She tied up the beaten rice, Aval, in a worn piece of cloth and handed it over to her husband.

Kuchela walked all the way to Dwaraka.

He entered the grand, palatial house of SriKrishna's beloved wife Rugmini.

SriKrishna was resting on a gemstone bedecked bed in his bedroom. From a distance He saw the Brahmin entering the house.

HerecognisedKuchelaimmediatelyashischildhoodfriendfrom yesteryears.

Leaping up from His luxurious bed SriKrishna ran towards Kuchela. When He reached Kuchela, He embraced him with all His heart.

He took Kuchela to his bedroom and made him sit on the ornate bed. Washed his feet, anointed him with vermillion and sandalwood paste. Made Rugmini fan him.

Sat next to him, holding his hands and then enquired about his situation.

Wealth, good fortune, fame - SriKrishna had every great fortune. While Kuchela had nothing but starvation.

His bones were jutting out.

Wearing worn, torn, clothes stained with age and dirt.

But does Bhagavan see any difference between money and its absence?

Much time had passed since their shared childhood of studying and playing together.

How much fun it was to renew childhood memories! SriKrishna brought up one memory.

"My dearest friend, don't you remember that incident? When we were in Sandeepani Maharshi's Gurukula. Gurupatni, Guru's wife, sent us out to fetch firewood. Together we went into the forest. Heavy rain started to fall, accompanied by strong winds, thunder and lightning. Darkness set in. The forest started flooding. We couldn't make out the difference between mounds and ditches. The children that we were, we were badly frightened. We were lost not knowing the direction, wandering hand in hand. Finally, just around daybreak, our beloved Guru who had been searching for us all night, found us. We had the blessings of our Guru, that is our wealth!"

After exchanging many stories and memories, SriKrishna did some mischief.

"My dear friend, what have you brought for me?" Bhagavan asked innocently.

Kuchela was terribly embarrassed.

SriKrishna was the very King of everything auspicious and elegant. And look at me, emaciated and starving.

What have I brought for him? Just four handfuls of Aval.

The cloth containing it was held tightly under his arm. It's too shameful to even talk about it!

Kuchela was silent. How could he talk?

Bhagavan's eyes could see everything, couldn't they? They spotted the bundle of cloth.

"What's this?" SriKrishna asked while snatching and opening it. He took a handful of Aval and put it into his mouth. Chewed it with relish and ate it.

Then He extended His Hand to take another handful. Rugmini suddenly caught hold of His Hand.

"Eating one handful of Aval is more than enough," she said.

There was a hidden meaning in Rugmini's words. Bhagavan knew. But poor Kuchela could not understand it!

He stayed the night, enjoying comforts that he'd not seen even in his wildest dreams.

In the morning Kuchela bid farewell and left for home. He walked, immersed in thoughts.

Why did I come to Dwaraka?

To meet SriKrishna and to get something from Him. I met Him but He did not give me anything. But that is not His fault.

After all, I did not ask for anything. All that doesn't matter.

Actually, did I not enjoy great good fortune?

Did Bhagavan not embrace me with so much affection? Did He not make me sit on his wonderful, decorated bed? Did He not wash my feet?

Did He not get His wife to fan me?

Even people who have earned great spiritual benefits due to their good deeds cannot attain Bhagavan's feet.

And yet, He held my feet?

There is a good reason why Bhagavan did not give me anything. What if He had given me wealth?

I would then immerse myself in comfort and forget Bhagavan! I must continue to live in poverty.

Only then can Bhakti survive.

Just look at Bhagavan's love for Bhakti! Kuchela was walking, lost in thought.

Eventually, he reached his house.

Strictly speaking, not his house but the location where his house used to be.

The old house was not to be seen. But a big, palatial beautiful house was standing in its place. Surrounded by pretty floral fabrics.

Well-dressed men and women were standing around. Kuchela was looking at everything in amazement.

Coming towards him were some ladies. Every one of them was wearing expensive clothes and ornaments. Amongst them was Kuchela's wife, the centre of attraction.

With great respect they led him inside. Walls made of quartz crystals and emeralds. Cots made of gold. Mattresses soft as butter. Golden chairs. All kinds of wonderful things!

Wealth and abundance were dancing in gay abandon everywhere! What is all this? Magic or illusions?

Kuchela thought deeply, understanding dawned. SriKrishna's compassion!

When Bhagavan presents valuable things? He considers them insignificant.

Not just that, he gives without prior notice too. I offered Him only a handful of Aval. And what did Bhagavan give in return?

Limitless wealth, prosperity, and abundance, material and spiritual.

Kuchela's Krishna Bhakti expanded and knew no bounds.

Once a great solar eclipse was to occur.

The time of the eclipse was known in advance.

A pilgrimage was undertaken to mitigate the ill effects of the eclipse.

Srikrishna, Balarama and many other Yadavas went to a sacred place named Syamantapanchaka[262].

Relatives from Gokula and Indraprastha also come to this place - Vasudeva, Nandagopa, Balarama, SriKrishna, the Pandavas, Kunti, Subhadra, Panchali, the wives of SriKrishna. How happy everyone was!

All aspects of the pilgrimage were observed. Yagas were conducted. Rituals were performed.

It was time for everyone to take leave. But no one had the heart to leave.

They were all bound by the rope of affection. Tightly!

We'll leave today. No, tomorrow. They kept postponing for three months. Now it was no longer possible to put off the departure.

Everyone who was together had to go their separate ways.

One group to Dwaraka; another toGokula and yet another to Indraprastha.

They all departed reluctantly with copious tears in their eyes. Devaki nursed a desire.

Kamsa had killed six of her children.

She wanted to see her dead children alive once more. SriKrishna and Balarama had the ability to make this happen.

---

[262] It refers to a region believed to be the site of the great Kurukshetra War, where immense bloodshed took place. The name "Syamantapanchaka" is derived from five (panchaka) large lakes that were said to have formed due to the blood of warriors slain in battle. Another legend associates Syamantapanchaka with Parashurama, the warrior-sage and an incarnation of Vishnu. After eliminating the Kshatriya clans 21 times to avenge his father's death, Parashurama performed penance at Syamantapanchaka to purify himself of the accumulated sin, as edited by VK Madhav Mohan

Did they not bring back the son of their Guru, the one who had died? Therefore, they could very well bring their elder brothers back to life.

SriKrishna knew the secret of those who had been born as his elder brothers.

They were the children of a Maharshi named Mareechi in their previous birth.

They had once made the mistake of making fun of Brahma.

As punishment they had to be born on earth. They were born as Devaki's children.

Their life as human beings was short-lived - it ended when Kamsa killed them.

From earth they went to Sutala[263]. They were still living in Sutala.

Sutala was under the rule of Mahabali.

SriKrishna and Balarama went there and spoke to Mahabali. Mahabali summoned all six of the brothers.

SriKrishna and Balarama took them and returned to Dwaraka. Devaki's happiness was limitless.

Which mother wouldn't be overcome with joy when her dead children come alive?

---

[263] Sutala is one of the seven Patala Lokas (netherworlds) in Hindu cosmology. It is considered a highly opulent and comfortable realm, often described as being even more splendid than Indra's heaven (Swarga). Sutala is best known as the kingdom granted to Maha-Bali, the benevolent demon king, by Lord Vishnu in his Vamana (dwarf) avatar, as edited by VK Madhav Mohan

The six of them went to Devaloka later.

Hadn't SriKrishna and Balarama fulfilled their mother's desire?

Their love for their mother was infinite[264]. Bringing back the dead from another world! SriKrishna performed another similar miracle.

When a King who is a Dharmistha[265] rules the land, children do not die. Conversely, if children do die, then it means that the King is not a Dharmistha.

The death of a child occurred in Dwaraka. It was the child of a Brahmin. The father's grief was unbearable. Not just grief but anger too.

He took the dead body of his son and entered SriKrishna's palace.

The Brahmin blamed SriKrishna and found fault with him for the tragedy. SriKrishna did not utter a word.

---

[264] Matrusneham (Sanskrit: मातृस्नेहम्) translates to "mother's love" or "maternal affection" in English. It signifies the deep, unconditional, and selfless love that a mother has for her child. In Indian philosophy, literature, and spiritual traditions, Matrusneham is often regarded as one of the purest forms of love, embodying sacrifice, compassion, and boundless care, as edited by VK Madhav Mohan

[265] Dharmishtha (धिमर् ष्) can also be understood as an adjective or title that means "one who is steadfast in Dharma" or "the most righteous". It comes from the Sanskrit root "Dharma" (धमर्), meaning righteousness, duty, or moral order, and "-ishtha" (इष्), which signifies excellence or devotion. In another legend, Dharmishtha (धिमर् ष्rा)

is a character from Hindu mythology, particularly mentioned in the Vishnu Purana and Bhagavata Purana. She is known for her secret marriage with King Yayati, from whom the Kuru dynasty (including the Pandavas and Kauravas) originated, as edited by VK Madhav Mohan

One after the other, eight sons were born to the Brahmin. And one after the other, all sons died soon after birth. The misfortune repeated the ninth time too.

Arjuna was in Dwaraka at the time.

He had empathy for the Brahmin and also concern at SriKrishna's indifference.

"Hey Brahmin, let bygones be bygones. I will protect the son who is born next. If I can't do that I will die by fire," Arjuna took oath.

"Arjuna, you are a fool. How can you do that which even SriKrishna and Balarama cannot?" the Brahmin scoffed

Arjuna's ego sprang to life.

"I am not SriKrishna and neither am I Balarama. I am Arjuna. Do not denigrate me. I will defeat Kaala and retrieve your son. That is a certainty," he said.

Arjuna was brimming with courage and self-confidence.

Hope blossomed in the Brahmin's heart.

"If my son dies, Arjuna will bring him back alive," he thought. A tenth son was about to be born. The time of birth was near. The Brahmin informed Arjuna.

Arjuna was prepared to fulfil his pledge. He bathed and purified himself. Prayed to Ishvara. Strung and cocked his bow. Did Japa[266]

---

[266] Japa: The Power of Mantra Repetition.Japa is a spiritual practice of chanting or repeating a mantra, usually done with a rosary (mala) or in silent meditation. It is an integral part of Hindu, Buddhist, and Jain traditions, helping practitioners cultivate focus, devotion, and inner peace.
Types of Japa

for his arrows. Arranged his divine weapons and readied them for use. Then he stood guard outside.

The tenth baby was born and died soon after birth like the nine before him. But there was a difference.

The bodies of the earlier nine were present when they died. But the body of the tenth was not visible!

How unfortunate!

The Brahmin lost his balance and abused Arjuna, "You're neither a man nor a woman! How foolishly I believed you! What tall talk you indulged in and what false promises you made! Let the entire world discredit you!"

1.Vaikhari Japa – Loud verbal chanting.
2.Upamsu Japa – Whispered or soft chanting.
3.Manasika Japa – Silent mental repetition.
4.Ajapa Japa – Continuous mantra repetition that happens automatically with breath awareness.
Popular Mantras for Japa
•Om Namah Shivaya – Devotion to Lord Shiva.
•Om Mani Padme Hum – Buddhist mantra for compassion.
•Hare Krishna Maha Mantra – Bhakti (devotion) mantra.
•Gayatri Mantra – For wisdom and spiritual awakening.
•Om – The primordial sound of the universe.
Benefits of Japa
•Increases mental clarity and concentration.
•Reduces stress and anxiety.
•Enhances spiritual connection and devotion.
•Strengthens positive thinking and self-discipline.
•Aligns with breath and meditation practices, promoting mindfulness.
How to Practice Japa Effectively
1.Choose a Mantra – Select a mantra that resonates with you spiritually.
2.Set a Fixed Time – Early morning (Brahma Muhurta) or evening is ideal.
3.Use a Mala (Rosary) – A 108-bead mala helps maintain count and focus.
4.Maintain a Steady Posture – Sit comfortably with a straight spine.
5.Focus on the Meaning – Understand and internalize the mantra's essence.
6.Practice Regularly – Consistency builds deeper spiritual benefits. As Edited By VK Madhav Mohan

Arjuna was sad and forlorn. He had pledged to save the tenth child. That was not possible. But he had to try one more time.

He went to Kaalapuri. The child was not seen there. He reached Indrapuri. There too the child wasn't seen.

He searched in the cities of Paasi, Niryati, Agni, Vayu, and Varuna. Nowhere was the child found.

Crestfallen and distressed, Arjuna returned to earth.

Now that he had not been able to save the tenth child, what next? Die by fire, that is the only way left.

Only then could he honour his pledge.

Honouring the pledge was far more important than his life.

Arjuna gathered firewood, set them afire and was about to jump in. Suddenly someone appeared and stopped him.

SriKrishna!

"Arjuna, I will show you the Brahmin's children. Come with me," said SriKrishna.

Bhagavan boarded His divine chariot. He helped Arjuna aboard.

They sped past the seven islands, seven mountains and the seven seas. Beyond was the pitch darkness of space.

The four directions were invisible. Horses could see nothing.

SriKrishna sent Sudarsana Chakra ahead.

The Trichakra streaked forward, piercing the darkness with its light. Bhagavan steered the chariot behind it.

After a long time, the destination was reached. Lord Mahavishnu's world, Vaikuntha!

SriKrishna and Arjuna prostrated and worshipped the Lord.

"Krishna and Arjuna, I had a desire to meet you two together. That is why I brought the Brahmin's children here," Lord MahaVishnu spoke graciously.

Then, He gave handed over the children.

SriKrishna and Arjuna returned to Dwaraka with the children. The Brahmin's happiness was the real happiness!

The wicked have to be punished and the righteous have to be protected. That is why SriKrishna had taken this Avatara.

Bhagavan had destroyed many of them Himself. But countless evil wrongdoers were still alive.

A lot of them were the remnants of Asuras. Every one of them had to be eliminated.

What way did Bhagavan adopt for this? The Kurukshetra War.

Pandavas on one side and Kauravas on the other. Many Kings on either side.

Countless soldiers in each King's army.

It was impossible to count the number of soldiers. Bhagavan too took part in the Bharata War. Not as a warrior but only as a charioteer. Yet, everything transpired exactly according to Bhagavan's wishes. The Bharata War stretched for eighteen long days.

The Pandavas were victorious.

Amongst those who died were not just the Kauravas but also many, many Kings on both sides and an incalculable number of soldiers.

Bhoomi's burden reduced but was not lifted entirely. Many of the wicked and unrighteousness had survived.

Not amongst anyone else but amongst the Yadavas, Bhagavan's Own lineage.

Their proximity to Bhagavan had bestowed great wealth, abundance and comfort on them.

That had made them arrogant.

The result of arrogance is destruction.

Destruction could not happen from outside because of the presence of Bhagavan.

It could only come about from within.

This can be compared to a fire in a bamboo grove.

The fire is sparked by two bamboo sticks rubbing against each other.

That fire gathers strength and burns the two sticks to ash. Then it spreads rapidly and devours the entire grove.

The extinction of the Yadavas must arise from amongst themselves. That was Bhagavan's decision.

How could Bhagavan's decision not be executed? Shortly, an incident occurred.

That was the beginning of the end. A group of Maharshis arrived.

Some youngsters impishly thought of a prank.

They could not imagine that the prank would destroy the entire family, lineage and dynasty.

Saamba, the son of SriKrishna was dressed up as a woman. Then they asked the Maharshis,

"Will this woman give birth to a boy or girl?" "Either a boy or a girl," replied the Maharshis. Both the possibilities were wrong!

Saamba was merely dressed up as a woman and so could not give birth to a child.

Maharshis had to be made to look like fools - that was the intention of the youngsters.

But they had not reckoned with the greatness of the Maharshis. With one look the Maharshis had seen through the game.

They were annoyed, and, inevitably, they issued a curse, "An iron pestle will be born and that iron pestle will destroy your entire lineage."

The curse of the Maharshis would certainly prevail! From Saamba's stomach an iron pestle emerged.

The youngsters panicked. They ran to Ugrasena and told him about what had happened.

Ugrasena ordered the pestle to be ground, powdered and scattered in the sea.

The royal attendants ground and powdered the iron pestle but a tiny fragment was left intact.

The powdered pestle was thrown into the sea. Now, there was no need for fear!

No need for fear?

Just a thought!

How wrong they were!

The iron powder was washed ashore by the waves.

They transformed into Eraka[267] grass and grew on the land. The leftover iron fragment was swallowed by a fish.

Fishermen caught the fish and sliced it open.

They found the iron fragment and gave it to a hunter.

The hunter fashioned the iron fragment into an arrowhead and made an arrow.

The iron powder and fragment had both changed forms. But the intention of both was the same: destroy the Yadavas!

How could Eraka grass and an arrow with an iron arrowhead destroy an entire lineage?

Soon that became evident.

Brahma, Siva, Devendra and other Devas arrived in Dwaraka.

A special reason lay behind their arrival. Srikrishna has completed His divine task.

---

[267] In the Mahabharata's Mausala Parva, the term "eraka grass" refers to a specific type of grass that played a
pivotal role in the demise of the Yadava dynasty. After a curse led to the creation of an iron pestle, it was ground into powder and cast into the sea. This powder washed ashore and transformed into eraka grass. During a subsequent conflict among the Yadavas, they grabbed blades of this grass, which miraculously turned into iron weapons, leading to their mutual destruction. Botanically, Eraka is identified with Typha elephantina, commonly known as elephant grass. This perennial plant grows along riversides, ponds, and wetlands, reaching heights of 6 to 12 feet. It has linear leaves and dense flower spikes. In Ayurveda, various parts of Typha elephantina are utilized for medicinal purposes, including treatments for urinary disorders, inflammation, and bleeding issues. The transformation of the iron powder into Eraka grass in the Mahabharata underscore's themes of fate and the inescapable consequences of one's actions, as edited by VK Madhav Mohan

There was no further need for him to remain on earth. He must return to Vaikuntha.

All of them had come to submit this request to SriKrishna. SriKrishna explained the situation to them.

"It is true that the burden of Bhoomi has been lightened. But the arrogant Yadavas remain. Given an opportunity they will destroy the world. It is only my presence that prevents this. My situation is like the shore that hugs the sea and prevents it from flooding the land. Be that as it may, I will return soon to Vaikuntha."

After bidding farewell to the Devas, SriKrishna said to the chief of the Yadavas,

"All of you must go to the place of pilgrimage named Prabhasa[268]. Take a bath there and perform the ritual donations."

What was SriKrishna preparing to do?

Only the most perfect of the perfect, Udhava, understood.

With a breaking heart the Bhakta spoke to Bhagavan. "O Lord, I know that you are about to leave this earth. I do not have the strength to be away from you for even half an instant. When I walk, recline, sit - why, every moment, I remember and pray to you. When you go, please take me with you," Udhava held Bhagavan's Feet and beseeched.

---

[268] Prabhasa Tirtha: Located on the Western coast of India in the Saurashtra region, Prabhasa Tirtha is a revered pilgrimage site. It's closely associated with the Somnath Temple, one of the twelve Jyotirlingas dedicated to Lord Shiva. This site is historically significant as the place where Lord Krishna is believed to have departed from His earthly incarnation. The Mahabharata references Prabhasa as a sacred tirtha (pilgrimage site) near Dwaraka.
As Edited By Vk Madhav Mohan

Bhagavan informed Udhava, "Dwaraka would be submerged by the sea within seven days. I will leave Bhoomi. The Kali Era will commence." Then Bhagavan spoke at length. He imparted priceless wisdom.

Udhava's heart and mind cleared and were purified. What was Bhagavan's instruction?

Udhava must go to Badari Ashrama[269]. There he must do Tapas on Bhagavan.

He must think about and internalise all the wisdom Bhagavan imparted. When the time is right, he would certainly unite with Bhagavan.

Udhava circumambulated, did Pradakshina around SriKrishna. Prostrated full length, he placed his head on the Divine Feet, washed them with his tears, and left for Badari Ashrama. The Yadavas reached Prabhasa.

Arrogance was already in their blood.

Now, it was compounded by alcohol, they had indulged in the great sin of drinking.

What else was needed for their virtuous intellect to be clouded?

---

[269] Badari Ashrama, also known as Badarikashrama, holds significant importance in Hindu tradition, both as a sacred geographical location and as spiritual centers inspired by its legacy. Located in the Himalayas, Badarikashrama, or Badrinath, is a revered pilgrimage site dedicated to Lord Vishnu. According to Hindu scriptures, it's the place where sages Nara and Narayana performed penance for the welfare of humanity. The area is named after the 'Badari' (jujube) trees that once covered the region. The Badrinath Temple, situated on the banks of the Alaknanda River, is a central attraction for devotees. The temple's significance is highlighted in texts like the Bhagavata Purana, which mentions, "There in Badrikashram, the supreme being (Vishnu), in his incarnation as the sages Nara and Narayana, had been undergoing great penance since time immemorial for the welfare of all living entities, as edited by VK Madhav Mohan

They became cross with each other. Arguments broke out.

Fists were thrown. And then, full scale war broke out among themselves. Anger wiped out affection.

Everyone was bent upon killing everyone else with whatever came to hand.

As a result, large numbers of people died.

Weapons broke with intense use and had to be discarded.

Those remaining used blades of Eraka grass as weapons - the very same Eraka grass that had grown out of the iron pestle powder!

What happened eventually?

The entire Vamsa, the lineage and heritage were wiped out.

Adishesha, who had taken the form of Balarama, decided to depart from Bhoomi.

He went to the seashore and sat in Yogic meditation, gave up his body and returned to Vaikuntha.

SriKrishna sat under a banyan tree[270]. He was adorned with the crown and all His ornaments. Their radiation diffused in all directions. But their glow was dimmed by another aura. The aura of that Divine Body.

Bhagavan was radiating brilliance like the light from a smokeless fire. He had crossed His left foot over the right thigh.

---

[270] Banyan tree (Ficus benghalensis), which holds deep cultural, spiritual, and symbolic significance in Indian traditions. The Banyan tree is often associated with wisdom, longevity, and divine presence. Many sages and rishis in Hindu traditions meditated under its shade.The Bhagavad Gita (Chapter 15) describes the world as an inverted Banyan tree, representing Maya (illusion) and the cycle of life. Krishna's presence under the tree can symbolize transcendence over illusion and the ultimate truth of existence, as edited by VK Madhav Mohan

The divine Feet were the colour of a lotus.

From a distance a hunter spotted saw the beautiful splash of colour.

The same hunter who had fashioned an arrowhead from the fragment of the iron pestle.

Thinking that he had spotted an animal the hunter shot this arrow. The arrow pierced the divine Foot.

The hunter ran up to check on what his arrow had hit.

That's when he saw that the arrow had struck not an animal but Bhagavan Himself!

What a horrendous sin he had committed! The hunter's distress knew no bounds. He fell down and thrashed around crying inconsolably.

He gathered up the bleeding divine Feet and placed them on his head and pleaded to be punished for this, the gravest of sins.

His heartrending screams shredded the silence of the forest. SriKrishna consoled the hunter, "You have not committed any crime or sin. You have merely carried out my wishes."

Bhagavan handed him not punishment but Moksha! An aircraft arrived for the hunter.

He performed Pradakshina around Bhagavan and did Namaskaram. Then he boarded the aircraft and rose into the sky.

Meanwhile, Daruka was driving the chariot in search of Bhagavan. Can any direction be discerned on a dark night if the moon hides? That was the condition of the charioteer without the Master.

Finally, he found the banyan tree under which Bhagavan was seated. It was as if he had found light in darkness, but in the next instant he saw something else.

An arrow had pierced Bhagavan's Foot. Daruka wailed loudly.

An amazing turn of events occurred.

Bhagavan's divine chariot rose into the sky and vanished.

Along with it the divine horses and divine weapons too, disappeared. Srikrishna despatched Daruka to Dwaraka with an instruction.

Arjuna was present in Dwaraka.

He had to be informed about his elder brother's Transcendence. Then, everybody had to evacuate Dwaraka immediately.

For, Dwaraka was about to be submerged into the sea.

Can there be a greater sorrow than separating from the Master? Yet, His orders had to be followed.

Daruka circumambulated Bhagavan. Did namaskaram repeatedly.

Then walked away, his eyes brimming with tears.

Brahma, Siva, Devendra, all the other Devas and the Maharshis arrived.

In their presence, while they watched, Bhagavan gave up His human life and left for Vaikuntha.

Vasudeva and Devaki renounced their bodies, unable to bear the sorrow.

SriKrishna's wives entered the fire of self-immolation and so, a Yuga ended.

A new Yuga began. Dwapara Yuga had ended and Kali Yuga had begun. Dharma is weakening.

Adharma is strengthening.

Righteousness is perishing while unrighteousness is flourishing. Virtue is decreasing while sin is increasing.

It is a time of difficulties, the time of Kali, our time! But, the time of Kali too will end.

Good times will return. Lord MahaVishnu will incarnate as Kalki.

The Avatara will occur in the village of Shambhala. A horse named Devadutta will also arrive.

Kalki will move around, mounted on Devadatta.

He will follow in the footsteps of the previous Avataras. Adharma will be destroyed. Dharma will be protected.

It is said in the Bhagavatam:

The eyes that see the image of Bhagavan are the real eyes,

The ears that hear the stories of Bhagavan are the real ears,

The hands that offer Puja to Bhagavan are the real hands,

The tongue that glorifies Bhagavan is the real tongue,

The mind that always remembers Bhagavan is the real mind,

Therefore, O Eyes, see the image of Bhagavan!

O Ears, hear the stories of Bhagavan!

O Hands, offer Puja to Bhagavan!

O Tongue, glorify Bhagavan!

O Mind, always remember Bhagavan! Not for today.

Not for tomorrow.

Forever and ever!

Hare Krishna Hare Krishna Krishna Krishna Hare Hare Hare Rama Hare Rama Rama Rama Hare Hare

V.Madhavan Nair
"Mali"

V.Madhavan Nair "Mali" wrote 53 books in various genres, mostly in Malayalam. Generations of Malayalees have grown up on his work. His MaliRamayanam, MaliBharatam and MaliBhagavatam have been pub lished in dozens of editions over the last 50 years. These are classics that re-tell the Ramayana, Mahabharata and Srimad Bhagavatam in simple, story form. Mali's entire writing was wholesome and entertain ing while subtly teaching, without being preachy, the timeless values and principles on which the Indian heritage rests.

His is a writing style that is endearingly easy to understand, brilliantly evocative and fast paced. The stories, their contexts, characters and lessons establish themselves in the consciousness of the reader and linger for a lifetime, gently encouraging right thinking and action at all times.

Many consider Mali's magnum opus to be the Kathakali "Karnasapatham" that he authored. It was first staged in 1966 and has gone on to be the most popular Kathakali authored in the last 50 odd years. Even today, it rules, unquestioned, as the most sought after Kathakali. It has been staged thousands upon thousands of times. Some of the reasons for Karna saptham's iconic status is the quality and simplicity of the "padams" which combine lyrical simplicity with ragas carefully selected by Mali to accen tuate the poignancy of the story. The result is a mesmerising portrayal of Karna's noble but tragic persona and his impossible dilemmas on stage.

Mai was undoubtedly a versatile genius who strode like a colossus across genres and fields as diverse as literature, poetry, Kathakali, music, the entire landscape of Sanatana Dharma, sports (tennis in particular, in which he was a legendary champion) and broadcasting, among others. MaliBhagavatam is the story of Krishna, told in a direct and enchanting manner, for all to enjoy and be blessed.

V.K.Madhav Mohan

V.K.Madhav Mohan is the son of V. Madhavan Nair "Mali".
V.K. Madhav Mohan is a renowned Corporate Mentor whose transfor
mative thought leadership has reshaped businesses across India, Sri
Lanka, Qatar, and the USA. As a trusted mentor to CEOs and execu
tives, he has guided organisations through periods of remarkable
growth, including guiding an agro-chemical company from $60 million
to $6.5 billion in global sales and increasing revenues and cash
surpluses multiple times for research and healthcare institutions.

Madhav Mohan's distinguished career includes serving as the youngest
director at one of India's largest banks and as Chief Advisor to the
Governor of West Bengal. His expertise extends to higher education,
where he serves on the boards of several leading universities
across India (including Calcutta University)

A prolific author, his published works include "Lonely at the Top:
Reflections of a Mentor" and over 700 original writings on leadership,
management, economics, and personal development. His popular
Military Leadership Series on YouTube translates military principles into
corporate decision-making practices.

Though a global citizen who has delivered more than 5,000 lectures
worldwide, Madhav Mohan lives in Kochi, Kerala, India, from where he
continues to mentor leaders and shape organisational futures all over
the world, in person and online, through his signature Corporate
Mentorship & Personal
Growth programs, lectures and writings.